Women's Work:
Essays in Cultural Studies

LOCUST HILL LITERARY STUDIES
NO. 15

Locust Hill Literary Studies

1. *Blake and His Bibles.* Edited by David V. Erdman. ISBN 0-933951-29-9. LC 89-14052.

2. *Faulkner, Sut, and Other Southerners.* M. Thomas Inge. ISBN 0-933951-31-0. LC 91-40016.

3. *Essays of a Book Collector: Reminiscences on Some Old Books and Their Authors.* Claude A. Prance. ISBN 0-933951-30-2. LC 89-12734.

4. *Vision and Revisions: Essays on Faulkner.* John E. Bassett. ISBN 0-933951-32-9. LC 89-14046.

5. *A Rose by Another Name: A Survey of Literary Flora from Shakespeare to Eco.* Robert F. Fleissner. ISBN 0-933951-33-7. LC 89-12804.

6. *Byron's Poetic Technique.* David V. Erdman. ISBN 0-933951-39-6.

7. *Blake's Milton Designs: The Dynamics of Meaning.* J.M.Q. Davies. ISBN 0-933951-40-X. LC 92-32678.

8. *The Slaughter-House of Mammon: An Anthology of Victorian Social Protest Literature.* Edited by Sharon A. Winn and Lynn M. Alexander. ISBN 0-933951-41-8. LC 92-7269.

9. *"A Heart of Ideality in My Realism" and Other Essays on Howells and Twain.* John E. Bassett. ISBN 0-933951-36-1. LC 90-46908.

10. *Imagining Romanticism: Essays on English and Australian Romanticisms.* Edited by Deirdre Coleman and Peter Otto. ISBN 0-933951-42-6. LC 91-36509.

11. *Learning the Trade: Essays on W.B. Yeats and Contemporary Poetry.* Edited by Deborah Fleming. ISBN 0-933951-43-4. LC 92-39290.

12. *"All Nature is but Art": The Coincidence of Opposites in English Romantic Literature.* Mark Trevor Smith. ISBN 0-933951-44-2. LC 93-27166.

13. *Essays on Henry David Thoreau: Rhetoric, Style, and Audience.* Richard Dillman. ISBN 0-933951-50-7. LC 92-39960.

14. *Author-ity and Textuality: Current Views of Collaborative Writing.* Edited by James S. Leonard. ISBN 0-933951-57-4. LC 94-15111.

15. *Women's Work: Essays in Cultural Studies.* Shelley Armitage. ISBN 0-933951-58-2.

16. *Perspectives on American Culture: Essays on Humor, Literature, and the Popular Arts.* ISBN 0-933951-59-0. LC 94-14908.

17. *Bridging the Gap: Literary Theory in the Classroom.* Edited by J.M.Q. Davies. ISBN 0-933951-60-4. LC 94-17926.

18. *Juan Benet: A Critical Reappraisal of His Fiction.* Edited by John Baptist Margenot III. ISBN 0-933951-61-2.

19. *The American Trilogy, 1900–1937: Norris, Dreiser, Dos Passos and the History of Mammon.* John C. Waldmeir. ISBN 0-933951-64-7. LC 94-48837.

20. *"The Muses Female Are": Martha Moulsworth and Other Women Writers of the English Renaissance.* Ed. by Robert Evans and Anne C. Little. ISBN 0-933951-63-9.

Women's Work:
Essays in Cultural Studies

by

Shelley Armitage

LOCUST HILL PRESS
West Cornwall, CT
1995

Library of Congress Cataloging-in-Publication Data

Armitage, Shelley, 1947–
    Women's work : essays in cultural studies / by Shelley Armitage.
    312p.   cm. -- (Locust Hill literary studies ; no. 15)
    Includes bibliographical references.
    ISBN 0-933951-58-2 (lib. bdg. : acid-free paper)
    1. Women--United States--History. 2. Women--United States-
-Employment. 3. Women artists--United States. 4. Women authors-
-United States. 5. Women's studies--United States. I. Title.
II. Series.
HQ1410.A76   1995
305.4'0973--dc20   95-6180
                                                                          CIP

Printed on acid-free, 250-year-life paper
Manufactured in the United States of America

Contents

Acknowledgments

Several of these essays have been previously published, although many are revised and newly titled. They are printed here with the permission of the original publishers as follows:

"The Illustrator as Writer: Mary Hallock Foote and the Myth of the West," in *Under the Sun: Myth and Realism in Western American Literature*, ed. Barbara Howard Meldrum (Troy, NY: Whitston Publishing Co., 1985).

"'Negro' Folklore and the South: The Illustrations of Rose O'Neill," in *The United States South: Regionalism and Identity*, ed. Valerie Gerda. Rome: Bulzoni Editore, 1991.

"Pa'i ki'i and Pohaku: Photographic and Indigenous Values as Narratives of Change," in *Ethnicity and Representation*. Conference Proceedings, University Art Gallery, Memphis State University, Memphis, Tennessee, 1994.

"An Interview with Maxine Kumin," *Paintbrush: Journal of Poetry, Translations, Letters* (1980–81): 48–58.

"Red Earth: The Poetry and Prose of Alice Corbin Henderson," *El Palacio* 92 (December 1987): 11–20.

Introduction to *This Dancing Ground of Sky: Selected Poetry of Peggy Pond Church* (Santa Fe: Red Crane Books, 1993).

"Marietta Holley: The Humorist as Propagandist," *Rocky Mountain Review of Language and Literature* 34 (1980): 193–201.

"Comic Columnists Since the Civil War," *Journal of American Studies Association of Texas* (Fall 1992): 15–22.

"Emily Dickinson's Crackerbox Humor," *Thalia* 3 (1980): 11–15.

"Rawhide Heroines: Popular Culture Cowgirls," *Myths, Popular Culture, and the American Ideology: The American Self*, ed. Sam B. Girgus (Albuquerque: University of New Mexico Press, 1980).

"The Lady as Jock," *Popular Culture: Mirror of American Life*, eds. David Manning White and John Pendleton (Del Mar Publishers, Inc., 1977).

"Mary Austin: Writing Nature," *Wind's Trail: The Early Life of Mary Austin*, ed. with an introduction by Shelley Armitage (Santa Fe: Museum of New Mexico Press, 1990).

"The Correspondence of May Sarton and Peggy Pond Church," in *A Celebration for May Sarton* (Orono, ME: Puckerbrush Press, 1994).

The following essays were delivered in slightly different form at these conferences:

"Revisioning Landscape: Southwest Women Photographers," Women Artists and Writers of the Southwest, Museum of Albuquerque, 1980.

"The Eye and the Story: The Photographs of Eudora Welty," Modern Language Association, Chicago, Illinois, 1991.

"The Widow Bedott Meets Samantha Allen," paper delivered for National Endowment for the Humanities Seminar on Mark Twain and American Humor, University of New Mexico, Albuquerque, 1980.

"Violence as Liberation: Belle Starr as Heroine," Meeting of the South Central Modern Language Association, New Orleans, Louisiana, 1977.

Preface

Almost twenty years ago, I began research on the first of these essays for the same abiding reasons I wrote on subsequent subjects very recently: I remain curious about women whose lives and creative work were missing from histories and literature I read as a child. Not only that; I *knew* some of these "missing" women. Growing up in rural northwestern Texas, country known locally as the rolling plains or the high plains and historically even into the 20th century by map-makers as the southern tip of the "Great American Desert," I knew that women participated fully in what needed to be done, often redefining the heroic through vernacular or domestic activities. Farming and ranching seemed not at odds with baton-twirling or, in an earlier era, starring in rodeos. Life in such a small town and a wide-open region even into the 1960s offered oddly a chance to do it all. In my own time girls could be basketball stars and cheerleaders; National Merit Scholars and football queens. Yet I must confess that when I read Dorothy Parker's "The Waltz" in junior high school (one of the few women writers then anthologized), Parker's depiction of the ironic inner dilemma of a female necessarily pleasing a male dance partner ("Yes, you dance beautifully," "ouch") struck a vague chord. Later in college, studying to be a writer, I finally realized there were limits. One could not major in agriculture and English, or play basketball as a career while planning post-baccalaureate work at Duke. Sure, we assume all this has changed with the so-called Second Wave of feminism, but still by the time I was teaching in colleges there were few female writers or women heroines available in print. I remember when I was a junior high athlete I hungered for more models like Babe Zaharias or Wilma Rudolph. When I got to college and finally taught there I found few stories about white women and none about women of color.

One year, while teaching E.B. White's essay "The Ring of Time," I was struck by his observation about seeing a girl in an equestrian act in a circus. Seeing the girl almost magically guide and ride the animal reminded White of his own mission: a writer was a conservator of that momentary sight, that ring of time. I began to take heart about the possibility of a writer and critic interacting with these unseen, buried, ignored, or forgotten lives. My interests almost wholly turned to what had not been studied at that time before: the lives and creative work of women who nontraditionally offered new histories, creative forms, truths in an almost wholly male canonical marketplace. Early pieces on "the lady as jock" and Faulkner's women came about as much from the full sense of my own daily knowledge as the dearth of criticism at that time.

My initial interest broadened through the years to encompass women's photography, popular art (illustration, cartooning), biography, poetry, humor, popular culture, and personal history. In most of the cases of these articles in this collection, I worked in primary materials—often personal and family papers, original art collections, archives, historical societies, forgotten photo files. I began to realize the complex network that existed in women's creative culture and the rich continuum that connects folk and fine arts. In fact, researching women's lives and arts confirmed for me again the intertextuality and cross-disciplinary nature of women's work. Critical categories, theories, and histories seemed inadequate often as contexts or interpretative means.

Though I must admit I share E.B. White's preference for the essay, I have struggled myself to find an appropriate form for the content and suggestiveness of these women's lives. "Methodology"—if we can even continue to think in such terms— necessarily grew, changed, was challenged by the non-categorical nature of these women's creations. Whereas the original "text" was "missing" still in the mid-1970s, today the preponderance of feminist and women's studies' criticism often risks obscuring the very subjects it proposes to illuminate. The "partial truths" James Clifford speaks of, indicating the limits of each discipline's ability to comprehensively explicate its shared subjects, can, I find, be balanced somewhat through inter-textual, interdisciplinary approaches. Thus, this collection represents my own discoveries of more than gender-related issues and subjects. It is also an exploration of the relationships between various creative forms.

In admitting that my own odyssey in the above matters is an ever-changing one, it is my hope that reading these pieces will be informative and lively, never closed, but suggestive. In creating culture through their own subjective production of meanings, the women represented in this collection suggest something further: the on-going process of identity and community as related to expressive culture. It is hoped that these lives add in their apparent uniqueness not a single attitude or method but a study of variety which in itself is a touchstone for larger truths.

Introduction

The critical relationship between gender and creative expression has been advocated and ignored by historians and critics of women's arts.[1] Though scholars generally acknowledge that the expressive culture of American women artists and writers has been regarded by the dominant culture as secondary or inferior, often the notion of history as a cultural construction still may be ignored. In an article in which she addresses the reason for the "dearth of women photographers," Judith Fryer cautions: "It is a cultural blindness. There have been hundreds of professional women photographers, producing hundreds of thousands of prints and negatives.... Women photographers have disappeared from History in the same way as women novelists, though their works were best sellers, have, until recently, disappeared."[2] Fryer goes on to explain the deliberateness of her capital "H": "History is a cultural construction—something like the version Henry Adams constructed in his *Education*." The fact that Adams, at the Paris Exposition of 1900, thought considerably about women (as he stood in front of the Dynamo engine in order to write his chapter about the meaning of history) is all the more ironic when we note that he missed, in that same exhibition, prominent and important works by American women photographers—142 photographs by 28 women including the well-known Frances Benjamin Johnson, Gertrude Kasebier, and others.

Recent debates about multiculturalism also encompass the essential denial of "whose history" and offer analogues for the consideration of issues of authenticity, voice, identity, and representation in terms of creative women. Native identities continue to be influenced by the historic lens of imperialist and colonialist imagery, even in their reactions to such foreign definitions or more recent attempts to ignore them. As in the case of the consequences of commodified images of minority or non-dominant peoples, the debate about self-identity, determination, and the nature of representation of women may be shaped by the perceptions of the relationship between "the one" (the dominating culture) and "the other." To this point, some feminist critics argue that women, as a minority, negotiate the cultural prescriptions of themselves, both as subjects and authors. Representing "the other" when "the other" is oneself may be the essence of any minority culture's creative acts. In a study by Abigail Solomon-Godeau, "Just Like a Woman," in which she analyzes women's photography, she begins with a discussion of Simone de Beauvoir's well-known theory of otherness as a construct within patriarchy. Says de Beauvoir:

> As variable, contingent, and mutable as the concepts of femininity and masculinity may be—a function of discourses and not biology—the former is inevitably positioned as Other, the latter invariably as the One. Thus, whether feminine Otherness is celebrated and valorized or perceived as a structure of oppression and subjugation, its prevalence as an apparently universal social and cultural given has not been disputed.[3]

In the over fifty years since de Beauvoir's observation, the discussion of the stakes and the consequences of women's identity as Other has resulted in a range of critical attitudes. Foremost among these has been the analysis of differences, heightening an awareness of alienation, in language as in all symbolic systems of cultural identity and reality. Whether critical methodologies employ Freudian or post-Freudian psychoanalytic study, structural linguistics and anthropology, semiotics, deconstruction, or poststructuralism, they have ultimately led to the undercutting of the premise of a unified identity. Such studies through their nondeterminacy have redirected the inquiry into articulation of means of expression—focusing instead on the production of subjectivity and the production of meaning. Therefore, the various critiques of the sign, of representation, and of the subject which concern these critical investigations have obvious implications on the examination of cultural constructions through the agency of representation. Along with other minority artists, women have been asking in their work, if the "alien" point of view (and the language and imagery marked by that view) are the accepted, the "One," in what terms can the Other become the One?

Nancy Walker in her study of women's literary humor, *A Very Serious Thing*, identifies similar questions and issues, particularly in her connection of women to minority humor and in her differentiation between male and female humor. As Walker demonstrates, women's humor typically has been perceived as minority; thus what is funny about women is the juxtaposition of such insider humor and the conventionality of the joking relationship. Minority humor exists due to the specter of the other, even as the insider group celebrates differences. The ostracizing of the subdominant group from the mainstream fundamentally defeats the effects of humor as therapy, supposedly one of its benefits. Instead, the minority member's sense of his or her own ironic stature is heightened in regard to the dominant culture. In his book on the humor of blacks, *The Book of Negro Humor*, Langston Hughes explains:

> Humor is looking at what you haven't got when you ought to have it. Of course, you laugh by proxy. You're really laughing at the other guy's lacks, not your own.... Humor is when the joke is on you but hits the other fellow first—before it boomerangs. Humor is what you wish in your own heart were not funny, but it is, and you must laugh. Humor is your own unconscious therapy.[4]

Hughes shows Freud's idea of humor as aggressive to be subversively so for the minority group. It is directed, even in its aggression, toward what one doesn't have access to. This gap—between the promised aggressive power of humor and reality—like the gap between the official promise of equality and the actual experience of subordination, leads to a sharpened awareness of disparity and incongruity. Therefore, the usual lack of balance, wrong proportions, disharmonies, incongruities, which mark humor at its most ironic, for minorities result instead in a world a little apart.

This world a little apart is accentuated for certain women, for, among other reasons, women, as in the case of minorities, have developed in the institutional structures the consciousness of separation. Carolyn Heilbrun has maintained that, unlike minority groups, women are not even expected to have a culture—an identity derived from linguistic patterns or common cultural ties.[5] Therefore, even though they may be members of the dominant culture (if they are white women), they may feel even more marginalized because of this ironic double identity. When women do iden-

tify with what marked the general identification of minorities—
discrimination, subordination, and oppression—Walker argues
this situation enabled them to seize upon the codes of the second-
class citizen, creating and subverting them through humor:

> Women's humor, like minority humor, displays a conscious-
> ness of a group identity, often posing a "we-they" dialectic,
> and both types of humor feature common stereotypes of the
> dominant culture. Women's humor is usually expressed
> within groups, rather than mixed company—orally in
> groups composed of only women, and in print, in public
> only for women.... The humor is frequently a means for deal-
> ing with the frustrations of anger, rather than simply
> celebration or fun.[6]

However, even as Walker identifies some common themes to all
women humorists—the tension between intellect and femininity,
male and female separate spheres, women's subordinate status—
her work points to a larger irony: how women's humor, like
women's history, if probing, questioning, and challenging of dominant values, may be at odds with the very system which allows it.
Walker says: "To be a woman and a humorist is to confront and
subvert the very power that keeps women powerless, and at the
same time to risk alienating those upon whom women are dependent for economic survival."[7]

This double bind of a double standard for women further
clouds the issue of representation when we consider historically
the expressions of women artists whose subordinate, secondary, or
separated status complicates the active role they play in their own
image-making. Especially in the arena of popular culture, the way
in which women practitioners acknowledge and apply their
"world a little apart" is important to the dialogue between the One
and the Other. Although women have always played a central role
in the creation and consumption of popular culture, their most significant role has been the largely passive one of providing popular
culture its major images. That is, the images of women, more than
those of men, pervade the various forms of popular culture
through which we manifest our national identity and signify our
national intentions. As Katherine Fishburn writes in her introduction to *Women in Popular Culture: A Reference Guide*: "Women as a
group—a class, a sex—have been used for over two hundred years

to represent most of the social mythology that is expressed in popular culture."[8]

Fishburn goes on to show how a measure of this social mythology expresses the nation's desires and fears. Therefore, in tracing the even older forms of the image of woman as idealized lady to terrible mother, one must note more profoundly the use of these predominant images of reflecting and projecting various desires and fears through time—and that these desires and fears have often applied to the idea of woman herself within American culture. Given this positive and negative valence, the consideration of sequence, chronology, time periods and the images themselves suggests a range of local, regional, and national issues. These issues may reflect on the corresponding technology of the times—on the very forms that the popular culture may take. As Fishburn argues: "The study of women in popular culture follows two concurrent and dialectical streams that converge only to clash and not to join—with the forces of popular culture taking the reactionary or conservative position and the foes of popular culture, the radical or revolutionary position.[9] However, within this conflict is the effort of individual women themselves to convert the group mentality, through reshaping ideas and technology (forms), therefore freeing their own identities which have been subject to the desires and fears of the collective imagination.

Women's attempts to remake their own mythologies are particularly intriguing when we consider individual artists who, despite their identity with margins or separateness, seize upon aspects of "women's culture" to remake the Other as One. These women must consider the demands and expectations of editors, audiences, and expressions of social formulae historically prescribed. When a woman herself is a product of a period which gave birth to popular images of her gender, she faces not only the covert influences of such images, but the difficulty in forging another set of valences. How can she reinvent herself even as she attempts to work through the prescribed social mythology? Even when women have been touted as what is best about American society, they have been denied equal footing, the opportunities afforded a seriousness which would allow them full participation in the American experience. Because of such limitations, for the most part women artists and their audiences have shared a powerlessness to help people see social myths which control thinking and behavior. Most recently, in the consciousness-raising period of the 1960s and 1970s, contemporary women have been shown how mostly male writers, filmmakers, and advertisers have pictured women, identifying the pervasive mythology as still rooted in the "Cult of True Womanhood." Contemporary artists are reminded that the primacy of this mythology about women is traced to our very origins as a people. Remaking myth, therefore, during any period has been a mighty task, tied as our notions of ourselves are to "fundamental truths" of American culture.

Another reason for the difficulty in recognizing the cultural and historical sources of female (and American) mythology—and remaking it—is the way in which commodification has influenced not merely women as consumers and subjects but the possibility of success for women artists. Success often has come to popular and serious female artists when their subjects, themes, and styles were deemed appropriate. One example of this cycle may be seen in the growth of the profession of illustration for women during the late 19th and early 20th centuries in America, the so-called "Golden Age of Illustration." Scholar Helen Goodman estimates that during the height of American illustration at least 80 women illustrators were active, enjoying adequate salaries. Though they flourished in a time when illustration as an activity for women could contribute, within societal sanctions, as an essential part of a "lady's" character—as in the case of fancywork or mastering a musical instrument—still they could "dabble" in a professional way. To be sure, these women faced the pervasive notion that though art was woman's acknowledged domain, she was not to be taken seriously. Yet, at a time when growing numbers of middle- and upper-class women needed to support themselves, art work, especially when done at home, could be seen as an extension of the domestic role, not encroaching on male-female labor divisions. Some especially enlightened leaders in the art world, such as Howard Pyle, began promoting art education for women who needed vocational training because of the few occupational opportunities available to women. With the corresponding expansion of numbers of publications, the growing markets for illustrators made the career potentially lucrative and dependable—especially for women as illustrators of literature and children. Probably because illustration was viewed as largely inferior to "fine art," it was "appropriate" for women as well. The work was seen as practical and commercial so that "real genius" was not necessary.

But the seriousness with which several male artists formulated their training schools and their own wish to be taken seriously as artists working in commercial fields paralleled some women's interests in their real abilities, needs, and creative futures. Alice Morse's remarks in *Art and Handicraft in the Woman's Building in the Building of the Columbian Exposition* (1893) noted a new independent spirit among women at the turn of the century. A qualified woman, Morse wrote, "working in reproduction, is assured a profitable return for her labor.... Illustration opens so wide and attractive a vista, occupies so high a place in the art of the country, and is withal so remunerative, that women would do well to follow it more largely than they have done heretofore."[10] At the same time, advertisements promised: "Draw for Money," "Illustrators and cartoonists earn $25–$100 a week." Even though a teacher of Pyle's reputation maintained that "the pursuit of art interferes with a girl's social life and destroys her chances of getting married ..." and that "girls are, at best, only qualified for sentimental work," still the women who did not give up their careers for or after a marriage often achieved enviable popularity.[11] However, they were nearly always assigned—still—the subjects of motherhood, childhood, romance, and fantasy. None of these women has been thought to have achieved powerful intellectual, philosophical, or cultural insights. Most art historians persist in describing them as charming, anecdotal, and decorative.

Even in the case of a "serious" artist such as Mary Cassatt, whose artistic accomplishments did garner her aesthetic praise which largely her illustrator-sisters did not receive, her execution of safe and appropriate subjects—mainly mother-and-child imagery—assured her acceptability. The vestiges of Victorian motherhood and the romantic notion of the child were still popular enough in 1910 for a writer in *Good Housekeeping* to comment: "The mother and child in painting is art's supreme subject. It has humanized the world's greatest religion and it has spiritualized the world's greatest art." The writer praises Cassatt for her work with the impressionists, particularly her mentor, Degas, but she hastens to add this comment:

> One must not be frightened away by this talk of impression-
> ism. There are no perversely blue cows, pink sheep, or pur-

ple faces devised for specific contortionists.... Her technique
makes a strong appeal to the layman ... this great artist who
paints with the perfect fidelity that nobility of womanhood
which is the American ideal.

Thus, popular magazines, such as this one, paraded advocacy of
safe and time-honored themes of the mother and child, romance,
and fantasy, as critical opinion. The ideal was synonymous in this
thinking with reality. Such artists as Cassatt were rewarded with
praise and success as long as they seemed to conform to traditional
or appropriate imagery. Therefore, as in the case of her illustrator
sisters, a serious artist like Cassatt also suffered the limits of what
categorized women's art and the woman artist.

In her comparative study of Cassatt and the illustrator of the
same period, Jessie Wilcox Smith, scholar Lucy Rollin demonstrates how even contemporary criticism of these women artists'
work revolves around a psychobiographic analysis which still may
question the content of these women's paintings. Rollin establishes
the historic reasons for the dominance of the idealized image of
children, well-mannered and well-dressed, and of mothers, in-
variably young and beautiful, for both a popular and a fine artist.
Rollin does argue that psychobiography offers a lens through
which to contemplate "the nature and limitation of human choice
and commitment."[12] She also acknowledges that the overall tendency in psychological studies of women artists has been to find
their characteristic rejection of marriage and children pathologic in
some way. She cites, for example, Phyllis Greenacre's work on
women artists (1960) which takes the classic Freudian stance, assuming penis envy, the close connection of women's art to their
biological functions, and the generally troubled lives of women
who do not choose traditional feminine roles.[13] Greenacre does,
however, identify a strong bisexual component in all artists and
comments further that the more complex oedipal situation of girls
leads them to caution a careful balance and diplomacy which re-
stricts the artistic impulse. John Gedo, in his analysis of women
artists, agrees. He acknowledges that though cultural oppression
may be partly responsible for women artists' problems, one may
locate within that oppression the role of the family, especially the
father.[14] Overall, studies such as these suggest that the art of such
women is a flawed substitute for the fulfillment that marriage and
children naturally would have brought them.

As the critical work of Rollin, Gilligan, Chodorow, and others indicates, however, women artists in general have both worked within and through dominant imagery and expectations in order to begin to reconstruct their own identities as women and as artists. Critical studies of women's autobiography, for example, offer a model for understanding the process by which women seized upon their differences, socially coded and privately expressed, not only to find their own voices but to create new artistic forms. When compared to the public spheres of women artists and writers, the creators of private life stories would appear comfortably exempt from either the influence of the marketplace or the social critic. However, as Estelle Jelinek shows in her study of women's autobiography, women historically have learned to deny themselves a voice, believing their lives inconsequential or undynamic when compared to men's adventures, ego-centered endeavors, or success stories.[15] Even though most autobiographies (men's and women's) avoid the deeply personal, women have privately believed in the significance of documents, such as letters, journals, and diaries, while reluctantly taking the next step to fuller life stories. This is understandable, given the general social bias historically against interest in women's lives. The pervasive conventional way in which women's experiences may be described—heartbreak, anger, loneliness, confusion, self-abnegation—is not that of men whose stories tend to heroism and the exceptional. In fact, men's personal histories are nearly always augmented by their place as success stories in the larger political arenas or at least as a part of public history. Women, by contrast, are much more personal, often not as related to career but to people—to the private or interpersonal rather than the public.

Thus, the study of women's autobiography tends to further the scholarship of differences while plotting the process through which individuals work within often dominant or time-honored forms. Even in the case of avoiding deeply personal issues of self or emotional revelations, women and men detach themselves from such inner stories differently. Women tend toward varieties of understatement. In a straightforward, more objective rather than glowing narrative, they nevertheless write obliquely, elliptically, camouflaging their feelings. Often their style may be abstract or intellectual, ironic or mocking. This penchant is enhanced by the way in which lives are organized in the retelling. The issue of how organization defines true autobiography has been wed to the view of the coherent whole, a linear narrative, as mainly men's lives of accomplishment and success are connected to a traditional view of history. Such unity speaks to a belief in control and the primacy of a theme, a characteristic or personality, or a concentration on a period of time during which these men lived.

Public and private differences in how men and women are perceived and perceive themselves result in a non-linear style by women which admits to irregularity rather than order. Portraits of women are more disconnected, fragmentary, organized in self-sustaining unities rather than chapters. Therefore, style matches social and psychological influences, so that multidimensionality marks the pattern of diffusion and diversity in women's autobiographical writing which has typically been devalued, even in the so-called subforms of memoir and reminiscence. New forms which seem to corroborate old instances of separateness and subordination result when women writers work through the sanctioned yet masculine forms of men as women seek to redefine themselves and the form. Carolyn Heilbrun observes in her *Writing a Woman's Life*: "The woman's life must pass through the veil of predetermined ideas about the patterns of men's lives and often even if addressed autobiographically, the subject must struggle behind the masks she adopts in response to conventional expectation or for the purpose of telling some truth safely."[16]

The significance of such ongoing creative struggle is borne out in the comments of women artists themselves as they comment on the creative act and how it is influenced by issues of gender, nature, and culture. Adrienne Rich argues that there is an essential conflict between the ego necessary for creativity and traditional expectations of womanhood:

> For a poem to coalesce, for a character or action to take shape, there has to be an imaginative transformation of reality which is in no way passive. And a certain freedom of the mind is needed.... Moreover, if the imagination is to transcend and transform experience it has to question, to challenge, to conceive of alternatives, perhaps to the very life you are living at the moment. So often to fulfill being a female by trying to fulfill traditional female functions in a traditional way is in direct conflict with the subversive function of the imagination.[17]

Rich's analysis of active transformation may ironically take place in the very laboratory of safety Heilbrun describes. In fact, the subversive function of the imagination which she advocates may thrive on the tension between the conventional masks of behavior and attitudes of inner reality. Those masks, in the form of sanctioned social imagery, idealized art, or gentle humor, may indeed enable a deeper, more radical and transforming imagery which passes itself off as acceptable even as it subversively or subconsciously effects change.

In certain reverberating ways, the arguments that shape our understanding of women's natures, Nature, and culture also make note of how unconscious creative responses reveal women's attitudes about dominant imagery and thought. Sherry Ortner submits that the act of defining and bounding is defined by men. Consequently, Ortner asks an essential question: "Is Female to Male as Nature is to Culture?" Even as this may be so, Ortner concludes that women are essentially the "mediators" of culture—"Members of the human community but less responsible for the creations of culture than men."[18] Annette Kolodny in her *The Land Before Her* notes that women do define themselves according to geography, but that they create a "languagescape" through which they change the male mode of dominance. According to Kolodny, this languagescape for pioneer western women was primarily a metaphor for the internalized home, however, not for wildness with which some historians identified women's "nature." Internalizing the domestic, said Kolodny, meant turning inward, even backward so that women still were guided by men's own ideals of them as well as their own.[19] Another scholar of western women and nature, Vera Norwood, has reasoned that there are regional differences which alter or refocus Kolodny's thesis. Norwood believes the Southwest to be exceptional and women's reactions to it different because it was an area which "resisted" culture, remaining for a longer time wild.[20] General scholarship on women and the West submits that the frontier years tended to free women in certain ways from conventional social expectations due to the independence and self-reliance often required by living conditions in the West.

If women could be thoroughly defined neither consistently nor comfortably with Nature or culture, what then? Folklorist, creative writer, nature essayist, feminist Mary Austin, who made her life in the Midwest, East, West, and Southwest, set out to alter the stereotypes of women's nature by redefining the conceptualization of Nature itself. Using the repeated example of Native cultures as they related to the Southwest landscape as well as the cultural lives of non-white women, Austin attempted to reconstruct the domestic metaphor. She anticipated later feminist critics when she celebrated the meaning of matrilineal creativity in women's lives—for example, the oral storytelling and creation of material culture. She also worked to revive an understanding of devalued creative forms associated with "women's work"—basketmaking, food preparation, rug weaving, the like. Ultimately, she argued that through such symbolic structures in the West and Southwest, the muted culture of women defined that world. By implication, she sought to demonstrate how women's vernacular traditions, while appearing to fulfill expected elements of so-called domestic culture, were diverse, multicultural, and artistically inspiring.

As these and other critics have shown, as women writers, artists, and critics have responded diversely to the meaning of metaphor and myths of the dominant group, they have simultaneously been prompted to creative expression by their land and region. An interesting discovery deriving from the study of regional women and creativity has been the way in which white women have attempted to locate their own creative voices in world views corresponding to those of Chicanas and Native American women. While "otherness" is complexly realized, especially when we talk about white women and women of color, scholars of the Southwest region in particular have argued that white women have sought creative expression about land and life because they feel estranged from their own culture. Some theorists suggest that women alienated from their culture seek renewal in landscape and landscape arts. Their work, recalling the process of women's biography, may be a search for reciprocity rather than transcendence, based on personal vulnerability rather than heroism. Certainly women artists whose expressions turn on place, region, and landscape counter the prevailing argument that the historic dearth of scholarship on women means that there were no women artists. On the contrary, as they are the creators of their own metaphors of renewal, they are transformed and transforming of conventional forms of creativity, often traditionally overlooked because they are humble rather than egocentric in their relationship to Nature.

Transference and transformation, reciprocity and reification ideologically mark the scholarship of feminist studies of women's creative identities. Carolyn Gilligan's book, *In a Different Voice*, advocates that women identify through association rather than individuation—that connections rather than separateness comprise their special kind of individualism so different from men's. Likewise, recent scholarship on creative women, initiated by a group of scholars at Stone Center in Wellesley, Massachusetts, posits an objects relations psychobiographical principle which, when connected to Gilligan's thesis, argues the significance of relationship to the mother in the conceptualization of the self. Against the social fabric of men's creative forms and critical standards, these scholars offer new models for women's development, noting the "centrality and continuity of relationships throughout women's lives."[21] According to this model, the close relationship of mother and daughter provides a matrix of emotional connectedness that empowers them both and leads to the development of "self-in-relation" as opposed to the more male-conceived idea of the autonomous self that gained currency as a cultural norm in the 20th century. Rather than individuation, these critics argue the importance of differentiation, a process by which we distinguish ourselves from one another while remaining related. Reconsideration of women's identities in this light provides a way for appreciating further the creativity of women. Gilligan's metaphor of the "web" which she uses to imagine women's relationship development is also a suitable image for women's creative work. It suggests a positive and different way in which women identify, relate, and hence *create*.

Notes

1. For the purposes of this collection of essays, the term "arts" is given its broadest reading to include the many forms of expressive culture.

2. Judith Fryer, "Women's Camera Work," *Prospects*, Vol. 14 (1993), p. 212.

3. Quoted in Abigail Solomon-Godeau, "Just Like a Woman," in *Photography at the Dock* (Minneapolis: University of Minnesota Press, 1993), p. 69.

4. Langston Hughes, *The Book of Negro Humor* (New York: Dodd, Mead, 1966), p. 23.

5. Quoted in Nancy Walker, *A Very Serious Thing* (Minneapolis: University of Minnesota Press, 1988), p. 34.

6. Walker, p. 52.

7. Walker, p. 54.

8. See Katherine Fishburn, *Women in Popular Culture: A Reference Guide* (Westport, CT: Greenwood Press, 1982).

9. Fishburn, p. 93.

10. Goodman, *The Art of Rose O'Neill* (Chadds Ford, PA: The Brandywine River Museum, 1989), p. 22.

11. Quoted in Michelle Bogart, "Artistic Ideals and Commercial Practices: The Problems of Status for American Illustrators," *Prospects*, Vol. 15 (1990), p. 227.

12. Lucy Rollin, "Haunted by the Vision of Two Faces: Images of Mother and Child in the Work of Mary Cassatt and Jesse Wilcox Smith," unpublished paper, p. 13.

13. See Phyllis Greenacre, "Woman as Artist," in *Emotional Growth: Psychoanalytic Studies of the Gifted*, Vol. 2 (New York: International Universities Press, 1971), p. 580.

14. See John Gedo, *Portrait of the Artist: Psychoanalysis of Creativity and Its Vicissitudes* (New York: Guilford, 1983).

15. Estelle Jelinek, *Women's Autobiography* (Bloomington: Indiana University Press, 1980), p. 5.

16. Carolyn Heilbrun, *Writing a Woman's Life* (New York: W.W. Norton and Co., 1988).

17. Adrienne Rich, *Adrienne Rich's Poetry*, ed. by Barbara Gelpi and Albert Gelpi (New York: Norton, 1975), p. ix.

18. Sherry Ortner, "Is Female to Male as Nature Is to Culture?" in *Woman, Culture, and Society*, ed. by Michele Zimbalest Rosaldo and Louise Lamphere (Palo Alto, CA: Stanford University Press, 1974).

19. See Annette Kolodny, *The Land Before Her: Fantasy and Experience of the American Frontiers, 1630–1860* (Chapel Hill: University of North Carolina Press, 1975).

20. See Vera Norwood, "Woman's Place: Continuity and Change in Response to Western Landscape," in *Western Women, Their Lands, Their Lives*, ed. by Lillian Schlissel, Vicki L. Ruiz, and Janice Monk (Tucson: University of Arizona Press, 1987).

21. Carolyn Gilligan, *In a Different Voice: Psychological Theory and Women's Development* (Cambridge: Harvard University Press, 1982).

ART
Illustration, Comic Art

Mary Hallock Foote:
Angle of Repose

In *Regeneration Through Violence: The Mythology of the American Frontier, 1600–1860,* Richard Slotkin reasserts the idea that the genesis of myth is essentially "low-brow," that is, it originates in shared, popular experience:

> True myths are generated on a subliterary level by the historical experience of a people and thus constitute part of that inner reality which the work of the artist draws on, illuminates, and explains. In American mythogenesis, the founding fathers were not these eighteenth-century gentlemen who composed a nation in Philadelphia. Rather, they were those who ... tore violently a nation from the implacable and opulent wilderness—the rogues, traders, missionaries, explorers, and hunters who killed and were killed until they had mastered the wilderness; the settlers who came after, suffering hardships and Indian warfare for the sake of a sacred mission or a simple desire for the land.... Their concerns, their hopes, their terrors, their violence, and their justifications of themselves, as expressed in literature, are the foundation stones of the mythology that informs our history.[1]

Slotkin mentions neither mining engineers nor women in his lusty pantheon, and for good reason. Eastern-educated engineers and "protected" women typically suggest those eighteenth-century gentlemen theorizers rather than the grassroots progenitors Slotkin writes of. Yet both these groups played an important, if minor, role in western mythogenesis, for they wrested a living from the land *and* were educated to write about it. Mary Hallock Foote, a Quaker-born and eastern-reared woman who came west with her mining engineer husband in 1876, is a classic example. For over sixty years the Footes lived in the West, Arthur advancing cement,

mining, and irrigation schemes, and "Molly" recreating these and
other events in woodblock illustrations, short stories, and novels.
Mrs. Foote was accomplished in each of these genres, but her original training as an illustrator best accommodated these new environments and people. The techniques required of the illustrator
allowed Mrs. Foote to participate in the "subliterary level" of
myth-making—that is, to conceptualize the West, not in terms of a
sublime eastern style of art or literature, but in reportorial fashion.
Certainly she did not live the lives of the rogues, traders, explorers,
or hunters, but she etched real life into the block. The result is a
vernacular style in her illustrations which, in turn, influenced her
attitudes about the West and her consequent writing style.

Before Mrs. Foote went west, her artistic talents flowered in
two particularly idealistic settings which conditioned a sensitivity
for nature and the social environment. The first was her home in
Milton, New York—a farm in the picturesque Hudson River Valley
where physical and human surroundings encouraged an optimistic
if diligent spirit. The Hallocks were avid readers and thinkers.
Their library provided the family English classics along with
current periodicals such as the New York *Tribune* and its
Congressional Debates which Mr. Hallock delighted in discussing.
Intellectual curiosity was a tradition in the family (grandfather
Hallock especially loved history), and the Hallocks entertained
such astute guests as Susan B. Anthony and other abolitionists.
When there was a rift with local "Friends," they became even more
resourceful and family-directed, relying on their intellectual interests for entertainment. As a child Mary Hallock showed artistic
ability, using walls and furniture for drawing surfaces. Later, as a
teenager, the family arranged for her to stay with relatives in New
York so that she could attend the Cooper Institute School of Design
for Women. This second environment continued to encourage her
rosy spirit. Here she studied with such luminaries of woodblock illustration and drawing as Dr. Rimmer and W.J. Linton, and at this
time, during the popularity of the Hudson River School painters,
she began to illustrate gift books in a romantic style. New York life
and art offered her the opportunities of a new, sophisticated, and
exciting world, and through her friendship with classmate Helena
de Kay, a well-traveled young woman of a prominent New York
family, she was ushered into the local high society. Years later,
when Mrs. Foote was known as "the dean of women illustrators"[2]

and the "best of our designers on the wood,"[3] critic Regina Armstrong detailed the characteristics of the "woman illustrator":

> The personal point of view is peculiarly feminine ... so it naturally follows that in the interpretation of character, the woman illustrator finds a field especially fitted to her temperamental equipment. The genre attracts her, the conventional is understood by her, and in turn the poetic, the homely, and the picturesque.... Owing to her environment and to the customs that surround her, life in its concrete forms lies near to the woman's hand, and in her interpretation of its typical phases she brings a subtle and sympathetic appreciation that goes to the heart of the subject. In matters of caste and circumstance, also, there is no delusion about her classification, although she may display a certain enthusiasm in some lines of portrayal, for she is usually an idealist.[4]

By the time Mrs. Foote completed her training at the Cooper Institute School of Design, these characteristics had emerged from her personal and professional background. Familiar with the personal, the conventional, and the concrete of domestic rural and urban New York, she illustrated for *Hearth and Home* and Longfellow's *Hanging of the Crane* (1874; Plate I) in a style true to genteel subjects.[5]

Thus, when she married and prepared to go west to California, Mrs. Foote outfitted herself according to her cultural baggage and her career. On that first trip west, she took a girl to function as maid and model, woodblocks to be done in illustration of *The Scarlet Letter*, and a philosophy that said "No girl ever wanted less to 'go West' with any man, or paid a man a greater compliment by doing so."[6] Yet the very art form that reinforced her idealistic and genteel personal background also equipped her to observe the subtleties of a new environment; for if, as Regina Armstrong noted, women illustrators naturally observed and recorded "life in its concrete forms" (the interpretation of character, the personal, and the conventional), then such an artist's eye could particularize new people and settings. The resulting picture, moreover, need not idealize the subject, particularly if the new subject were part of the actual environment rather than a formally posed model. Due to the artist's attention to concrete details, the rendering could be realistic instead. Other factors could effect a realistic portrayal as well. For

Plate I. Illustration by Mary Hallock Foote for
"The Hanging of the Crane" (1874),
in *The Complete Poetical Works of Henry Wadsworth Longfellow*
(Boston: Houghton, Mifflin and Co., 1902), p. 397.

instance, Mrs. Foote, like many illustrators, drew directly onto the woodblock, making immediate the artist's response to the spontaneous subject. Furthermore, the newness of western subjects required other than the genteel style suited to eastern characters and scenes. If the artist had no first-hand observation to draw upon, the work of other artists who had utilized their western experience became a source for the appropriate style. As an example, Mrs. Foote's only illustration of a western subject before she went west was a Catlin-like depiction of Flathead Indians for A.D. Richardson's *Beyond the Mississippi* (1867), done during the same period as her romantic gift-book illustrations. This illustration served its purpose by achieving a fidelity or an affinity for the subject. Unlike the more formal arts, the art of illustration had in its technique and purpose the means for recording new experiences. It had, in its "vocabulary," more flexibility than painting and sculpture. As Joshua C. Taylor notes in *America as Art*, this adaptability made the art of illustration well suited as a cultural mirror:

> The share that the pictorial arts had in creating the image of America may seem quite subordinate to that borne by literature and the theater, and in a strict sense it was. The style of discourse and the character description were vivid beyond the accustomed scope of most American painters and sculptors. Brought up on a heady idealism of academic theory and taught to draw people by studying casts of antique statuary, they were ill-equipped to catch the flavor of the vernacular style. The visual impact was made less through the elevated arts of painting and sculpture than through illustrations and prints. These formed the real pictorial galleries for most Americans.... The expansion of book illustration and issuance of popularly priced lithographs and engravings coincided with the growth of the self-consciously American image.[7]

Consequently, Mrs. Foote was able to use her skill as an illustrator to capture the essence of the West and thus participate in what Slotkin calls "historical experience" at the subliterary level of myth, creating from this experience an image of the American West which evolves in her letters, reminiscences, and fiction into a mythology expressive of her real experience.

I emphasize the role the West played in leveling Mrs. Foote's personal and professional idealism because her confrontation with

Plate II. "The Water-Carrier of the Mexican Camp," illustration
by Mary Hallock Foote for her sketch
"A California Mining Camp,"
Scribner's Monthly, 15 (February 1878), 491.

hard reality was the first step in her eventual use of art to mediate between the poles of the real and the ideal of what is and what should be. Because of her fascinating accounts of New Almaden, California, in her early letters to friend Helena de Kay Gilder, Richard Gilder as editor of *Scribner's Magazine* (later *Century Magazine*) requested her first written sketch accompanied by illustrations.[8] Done as a young bride, these first illustrations of the West are sublime rather than documentary, but this style disappears in subsequent illustrations. By the time we reach Mrs. Foote's best art work—"Pictures of the Far West" which appeared in *Century Magazine* in 1888–1889—she has achieved an authentic and realistic style. A number of related personal and professional experiences influenced this outcome. Though Arthur Foote tried to shelter her from the rawness of the West, chronologically Mrs. Foote moved from the rather cultivated environment of eastern friends in San Francisco (close to the Foote's first home in New Almaden) to Leadville, Colorado, where she covered the walls of their one-room cabin with geological maps, and finally to the Idaho desert where the couple initially lived in a tent. Psychologically, these subsequent "homes" were increasingly taxing. In New Almaden Arthur quit his job, unable to work for men he did not respect; in Leadville he was faced with the violence of a miners' strike and the problem of absentee eastern investors; in Idaho he attempted to realize the then-impossible dream of irrigating up to 600,000 acres of desert. Besides other personal factors, such as Arthur's drinking due to worry over his projects and Mrs. Foote's miscarriage, conditions altered her career. She was forced to give up the gift-book market while in Leadville, noting in her reminiscences that she couldn't get models for her work. Gradually, she adapted her formal training to spontaneous life of the mining camps. Working from actual subjects in New Almaden, she sketched a Mexican water-carrier and the Mexican camp where the miners lived (Plate II). Leadville experiences gave her a host of actual scenes which later appeared in the illustration of her Colorado trilogy, *The Led-Horse Claim* (1882), *John Bodewin's Testimony* (1886), and *The Last Assembly Ball* (1889). When the Footes went by horseback from Morelia, Mexico, to Vera Cruz, she sketched the entire distance—over 200 miles—on horseback. She made other drawings of the villages they passed through. Certainly Idaho, with its "miles and miles of pallid sagebrush," was the ultimate lesson in realism.[9] Neither pic-

turesque nor romantic, it fostered an attention to isolated details—
the birds, the rocks, the river. Indeed, each of her western homes
challenged in some manner the concept of nature the farm home of
her childhood had fostered. Stark scenes, strange ethnic groups
and characters, and an absence of the social manners she was accustomed to—all, when recorded on the woodblock, constituted a
very different view of life.

A brief review of her treatment of this life in "Pictures of the
Far West" will confirm her understanding of it. Included with the
serialized essays which she wrote were these pictures: "Looking
for Camp," "The Coming of Winter," "The Sheriff's Posse," "The
Orchard Wind-Break," "The Choice of Reuben and Gad,"
"Cinching Up," "The Irrigating Ditch," "The Last Trip In,"
"Afternoon at a Ranch," "A Pretty Girl in the West," and "The
Winter's-Camp—A Day's Ride from the Mail" (Plate III). Robert
M. Taft praises these pieces for their excellence and authenticity:

> These illustrations were beautifully engraved woodcuts, for
> this period marks the golden age of American woodcut illus-
> tration; a period which produced magazine illustrations
> which have never been excelled, and *The Century* was the
> leader in its field.... Mrs. Foote is the only woman who can
> claim company among the men in the field of the Western
> picture.[10]

As an example, "The Coming of Winter" shows in detail a typical
situation for a homesteader family (Plate IV). The man, gun in
hand, stands outside the sod cabin while the wife, holding their
baby, looks on. The authenticity of the clothing, the preciseness of
the fence, the details of the house—the rub-board, pan, and mop
hung on the outside wall—assure the accuracy of the scene. In
"Looking for Camp," a lone hunter, his dog and horse, travel
down a hill, the moon in the background (Plate V). In particular,
the horse (as is characteristic of Mrs. Foote's horses) is masterfully
done with careful attention to the mane and saddle trappings.
"Cinching Up" depicts a couple out on a ride. The man is adjusting
the lady's saddle while she sits on the horse in front of a rugged
background. Critical to the fidelity of each of these illustrations in
"Pictures of the Far West" is not only the affinity for detail, scene,
and character, but a sense of captured motion. Like the photographers of the same period, Mrs. Foote not only documents but

Plate III. "The Winter's Camp—A Day's Ride from the Mail,"
from Pictures of the Far West series,
Century, 39 (November 1889), 57.

Plate IV. "The Coming of Winter,"
from Pictures of the Far West series,
Century, 37 (December 1888), 162.

Plate V. "Looking for Camp,"
from Pictures of the Far West series,
Century, 37 (November 1888), 108.

implies an intimacy with the scene which allows her to arrest these scenes.

This brings us to another dimension of her illustrations—one that allowed her to suggest in these real scenes an interpretation of her western life. Mrs. Foote was recognized for this quality from the beginning of her career. The first review of her early New York work noted: "It is in the conception as well as the execution of her work that Miss Hallock will delight the appreciative reader.... These ideas central to the poem Miss Hallock has realized with a delicacy and perfection worthy of the poem, into which she has entered not only with intelligence but with divination."[11] Regina Armstrong observed this same talent when she discussed Mrs. Foote's work later in her career:

> Mrs. Foote's talent has been more individual [than other women illustrators]; she has occupied a field to herself, per-haps because of the distinct types which interpret her own text, depicting a remote environment.... She links the poetic and the actual in a manner which makes them inseparable. This indefinable quality is peculiarly hers, and is admired as much by artists as by laymen.[12]

This quality can best be examined and explained by looking at a series of illustrations that date throughout Mrs. Foote's career. These pictures are of women, probably the earliest subjects Mrs. Foote mastered in a studio setting. All of these illustrations exem-plify the "poetic" and the "actual" quality Regina Armstrong notes as inseparable in Mrs. Foote's works. That is, the pictures are con-vincing in their use of setting and character, but there also is an at-titude in the characters which makes the illustrations "speak." Generally, this attitude may be described as "wistful," for the women, whether sad or serene, seem to long for something. Yet there is a marked difference between Mrs. Foote's eastern and western women. For instance, consider two illustrations of women in eastern settings done during the Footes' tenure in Idaho. "The Hermit-Thrush" (1893), drawn for the *Century's* American Artist series, portrays a lone young woman in the woods, mournfully looking up from the solitary road (Plate VI). In an almost identical pose, "The Mourning Dove" (1893) carries a similar message: against the backdrop of a lonely road and wood, the woman looks sad and heartbroken (Plate VII). The poetic quality of both is a sen-timentality in the tradition of Mrs. Foote's early romantic style. The

Plate VI. "The Hermit-Thrush,"
from American Artists of the American Scene series,
Century, 46 (June 1893), 236.

Plate VII. Illustration by Mary Hallock Foote for
"The Mourning Dove,"
Century, 45 (February 1893), 545.

latter drawing illustrates a poem by Edith M. Thomas which explains this essence:

> It is the wild dove's vanishing note I hear;
> She sits her nest, and darkness and sun, and dew
> Touch her soft throat, but never to utterance clear—
> "Who, who, who?"
> Only this, but I catch at the slender clew,
> And follow it back till I reach the heart of a wrong—
> "Who, who, who delays thee so long?"[13]

However, in the drawings of women in the West during this same period the poetic quality is not romantic yearning, but a sense of expectation. These women may be posed similarly to the eastern pictures—that is, in an illustration for *The Led-Horse Claim* and for the much later short story, "On a Side Track" (1894), the women look away from the center of the picture—but their expressions suggest strength, patience, and resoluteness. One of the best examples of this attitude is from *The Led-Horse Claim*, a scene in which the young woman, trapped in a dark mining shaft, with only a candle for light, looks expectantly and determinedly into the dark (Plate VIII). One might argue, of course, that this quality is due to the content of the article or fiction the illustration accompanies. Yet an important part of Mrs. Foote's artistic theory was that the illustration should not repeat the "personal situations of the story already described in words," but enlarge upon the subject.[14] Mrs. Foote saw the illustrations as extensions of the text; moreover, because they did "speak," she attempted to use the illustrations to tell a story, or part of a story. In the case of women, clearly these two environments—the East and the West—made very different requirements of them. The story Mrs. Foote was trying to relate in her western illustrations had at its heart a tension between the ideal and the real: the hopeful spirit of her eastern girlhood and the hard realities that she had to cope with in the West. As she says in her reminiscences about life in Idaho:

> I hardly know how to keep a true balance between the two sides of that Cañon existence—the life of dreams it fed in the beauty around us, and the grimy attention it demanded every hour of the day to insistent realities. The children were never really safe without a grown-up eye on them.... There were the high places on all their walks; there were rattlesnakes lurking in holes in the rocks; there was the wire

Plate VIII. Mary Hallock Foote, *The Led-Horse Claim*
(Boston: James R. Osgood and Co., 1882), frontispiece.

bridge, a nightmare to mothers—there was always the river. (p. 290)

Mrs. Foote's illustrations expressed this tension and constituted the subliterary level of myth-making that Slotkin notes in *Regeneration Through Violence*. The West acquainted Mrs. Foote with a new way of seeing; she first articulated this view by reporting it visually for an audience of eastern magazine readers. Working from the direct observation and experience that informed her illustrations, she next moved to the literary arena to fully explain the meaning of these powerful images. Her writing, she said, had "grown from my aborted art, as I found the West and its absorbing material too much for my pencil."[15] The result is a body of writing, including short stories, novels, and reminiscences, in which Mrs. Foote attempts to duplicate the actual poetic quality in her picture in order to dramatize the tension between the ideal and the real. Though her fiction is uneven, no doubt her training on the woodblock with actual subjects enabled her to gradually master particularized settings and carefully drawn characters. Her best works, such as *The Chosen Valley* (1892) and "How the Pump Stopped at the Morning Watch" (1899), are pictorial and imagistic, suggesting the best qualities of her illustrations. Her writings, taken together with the reminiscences, pit tenderfoot against westerner, East against West, the individual against a loose and unpredictable society, and constitute a personal version of the western myth which had its genesis in Mrs. Foote's experiences as a western illustrator.[16]

The most interesting place to trace the elements and development of Mrs. Foote's version of the West is in the reminiscences, *A Victorian Gentlewoman in the Far West*. One obvious mode of development is to juxtapose eastern and western values and experiences, romanticism and realism against one another. Beginning in the early sections of the reminiscences, Mrs. Foote details her Quaker upbringing and life in New Almaden and Leadville by pitting her early career and its romantic subjects against Arthur's determination to go west. For instance, when she meets Arthur in the Emma Beach home in New York, she says she was working on commissioned sketches for *Hearth and Home* and describes Arthur as having "the blood of farmers and homemakers in him, and the brains of a constructor" (p. 80). When he returns from California in

1876 to marry her and take her west, she says she was illustrating a Longfellow book and remarks on the intrusion of his West into her East: "He unpacked his leathery luggage in ... grandmother's room, and laid his pipe and pistol on the bureau where her chaste neckerchiefs had been wont to lie" (p. 104). This method of playing the values of the past against new experiences continues in the Leadville section where she translates the difference between the past and present into the difference between romance and realism. For instance, when she and Arthur are traveling to Leadville by buggy over a dangerous pass, a stage almost sideswipes them, forcing Arthur to whip his team up the embankment to avoid disaster. As a result of this strain, one horse dies, and another, hired the next day, dies of lung fever when they finally reach camp. Mrs. Foote writes: "A. paid for both—and how much more the trip cost him I never knew, but that is the price of Romance; to have allowed his wife to come in by stage in company of drunkenness and vice, or anything else that might happen, would have been realism" (p. 172). Regrettably, Mrs. Foote was always too modest about her own knowledge of the West and thus would be blind to the irony implicit in her description. She did, after all, travel by buggy exposed to the weather and dangers she describes. Once in Leadville, where her home was the meeting place for men such as Clarence King and James Hague, she learned much about the management, operations, and hazards of the mines. Again, she writes of the tension implicit in the actions of Arthur and his assistants, well-bred and educated men who had to act differently in the West: "This was the absurd side of life in Leadville which made them all seem boys together, that the methods of schoolboys and savages should be the ones these grown men were obliged to use, who were not savages nor excited nor warlike nor angry with anyone" (p. 195).

A second method Mrs. Foote used in the reminiscences relies on imagery, metaphor, and motif to reveal her ideas. If we remember the decidedly sentimental handling of the pictures, "The Hermit Thrush" and "The Mourning Dove," we can more fully appreciate the meaning of Mrs. Foote's turning images which are conventionally romantic into haunting motifs. When she recounts her first arrival in "darkest Idaho," she writes:

> But what a morning! Meadowlarks were springing up all
> about us—it was April and we knew there were nests and

wild flowers hid in the sage beneath those jets of song....
Their note was a brief song, sad and sweet, that rained down
to us from the sky. It haunted us, that song, every spring of
all our years in Idaho, as it welcomed up that April morning.
The birds and the wind filled the vast, brooding silence—the
desert wind that talks, that whispers, that brings messages
from the infinite filled with whatever each human soul that
listens can put into it. (p. 275)

Later, after discussing the "nest-building" she and Arthur attempted in the Cañon, Mrs. Foote remembers, with poignancy, the
dove's call:

And every day and all day the wood doves up the gulch
were calling, calling, hid in the willow thickets.... And we
knew that Harriet Hawley was dead, and Spencer Foote and
his wife were dead, and their little Margaret.... The air was
heavenly soft and sweet, wild roses scented every breath of
wind from up the gulch and all day the patient, maddening
doves kept saying something we could not get out of our
heads and could not understand. (p. 299)

This last passage, perhaps the most stylistically beautiful in all of
Mrs. Foote's writing in its almost Faulknerian imagery and pace,
exemplifies how she was able to move from the concrete to the poetic. Moreover, the conventions she uses are not artificial, but expressions of very real conflicts and ironies; yet in using them, Mrs.
Foote creates another level of reality symbolically. She is, in fact,
the tenderfoot of her own reminiscences and, like her own fictional
characters, suffers the tragic consequences. In the following example from the Idaho years, note how she begins the passage with
concrete experience and ends with an almost surreal, and certainly
nightmarish, image. At first, she remembers the particular irony of
giving birth to a girl just before joining Arthur in Idaho:

And a girl baby! Boys for the frontier, but with the arrival of
this little downy head next to my heart, that foolish part of
me turned back to the East of my own girlhood. This meant
farewell music, art, gossip of the workshop, schools that we
knew about, new friends just made who would forget us, old
friends better loved than ever and harder to part from—all
the old backgrounds receding hopelessly and forever. Mexico had not been farther to the imagination that this—and
what compensations! You reached it by the gulfs enchanted,
by moonlight nights in old Spanish-American cities, by

strange, medieval roads. But—darkest Idaho! Thousands of
acres of desert empty of history. The Snake River had an evil
name—the Boise, the source of our great scheme, emptied
into and was lost in it.... I felt adrift, as it were, cast off on a
raft with my babies, swept past these wild shores uninhab-
ited for us. My husband steering with a surveyor's rod or
some such futile thing.   (pp. 265-66)

Such imagery in these selected passages, as well as those that
establish the thematic poles of East/West, romantic/realistic, and
tenderfoot/westerner, expresses a concept of the West quite antithetical to that recognized by Frederick Jackson Turner and other
proponents of the frontier thesis. What Mrs. Foote writes in her fiction and her reminiscences constitutes her version of the western
myth which she builds from her conceptions as an illustrator.
Turner saw the frontier as a molder of character and as an impetus
for individualism, a unifier of the nation that melded various
stocks and regions and nurtured democratic forms. For Mrs. Foote,
however, excessive individualism resulted in anarchy; unity was
impossible because of the diversity of special interests, and democratic forms—especially as manifested in law and order—were often limited because of the newness of the country and a consequent lack of manners governing behavior. Hence, her inverted
use of imagery—images typically suggestive of dreams and ideals,
such as the bird's call, the nest-building, the surveyor's rod—allows her to construct a myth counter to Turner's thesis. She explains the heart of this myth in this expository passage from *The
Chosen Valley*:

The ideal scheme is ever beckoning from the West, but the
scheme with an ideal record is yet to find—the scheme that
shall breed no murmurers, and see no recreants; that shall
avoid envy, hatred, malice, and all uncharitableness; that
shall fulfill its promises and pay its debts, and remember its
friends, and keep itself unspotted from the world. Over the
graves of the dead, and over the hearts of the living, presses
the cruel expansion of our country's material progress; the
prophets are confounded, the promise withdrawn, the people imagine a vain thing. Men shall go down, the deed arrives; not impeachable, as the first proud word went forth,
but mishandled, shorn, stained with obloquy, and dragged
through crushing strains. And those that are with it in its lat-

ter days are not those who set out in the beginning. And victory, if it come, shall border hard upon defeat.[17]

This passage clearly relates to Mrs. Foote's repeated references to
her husband as a dreamer throughout the reminiscences. As she
says of Arthur's stubborn faith in his Idaho irrigation scheme:

> The author of this scheme was thirty-three years old. He had
> lost two years of his technical training which never could be
> made up quite to his own satisfaction, though he was always
> at school, the school of self-training. What he wanted was
> opportunity, like the days of the early discoverers, or the rise
> of the American merchant marine, or the Civil War which
> had taken his older brothers and tested them and wrung
> them out. And if a man desires to be wrung out to the last
> dregs and take the risk of failure and years of work with no
> return, a better job than this could not be found.   (p. 270)

Thus, rather than deal with the West in ideal or opportunistic
terms, Mrs. Foote's fiction and reminiscences tell a story of constant tension between dreams and reality—a tension which is most
often resolved in disappointment. This narrative, as we may call
the body of Mrs. Foote's work when we acknowledge the pervasiveness of the repeated tension between the real and the ideal, is a
story whose meaning is best explained by Lyman Ward's comment
about his grandmother (who is based on Mary Hallock Foote) in
Wallace Stegner's novel, *Angle of Repose*:

> When frontier historians theorize about the uprooted, the
> lawless, the purseless, and the socially cut-off who settled
> the West, they are not talking about people like my grand-
> mother. So much that was cherished and loved, women like
> her had to give up; and the more they gave it up, the more
> they carried it helplessly with them. It was a process like ion-
> ization: what was subtracted from one pole was added to the
> other. For that sort of pioneer, the West was not a new coun-
> try being created, but an old one being reproduced; in that
> sense our pioneer women were always more realistic than
> our pioneer men.[18]

Despite Mrs. Foote's reputation as a local color writer and,
sometimes, a sentimentalist, Stegner's definition of realism fits her
well. In both her reminiscences and her letters to editor Richard
Gilder, it is evident that she changed both endings and story content to please the editor whose readership preferred a happy end-

ing. The heart of her writings remains, nevertheless, firmly grounded in the perception of the artist's eye. The resulting conception is an effort to dramatize the tension between the poetic and the actual. Mrs. Foote's ability to externalize the subliterary experiences of the West hinged on her sensitivity and technique as an illustrator. The result is an authenticity in her fiction generated by the perception and depiction of a mythical West other than that popularized by mainstream western critics and authors—an inner reality with all its attendant ambiguities.

Notes

1. Richard Slotkin, *Regeneration Through Violence: The Mythology of the American Frontier, 1600–1860* (Middletown, CT: Wesleyan University Press, 1973), p. 4.

2. Regina Armstrong, "Representative American Women Illustrators: The Character Workers—II," *Critic*, 37 (August 1900), 131.

3. W.J. Linton quoted in *American Art and American Art Collections*, ed. Walter Montgomery (Boston: E.W. Walker, 1889), I, 1449.

4. Armstrong, "Representative American Women Illustrators: The Character Workers—1," *Critic*, 36 (July 1900), 43.

5. The first review of Mrs. Foote's work appeared in *Atlantic Monthly* (December 1874) and praised her work in Longfellow's *The Hanging of the Crane*. Longfellow himself was pleased with her work.

6. Mary Hallock Foote, *A Victorian Gentlewoman in the Far West: The Reminiscences of Mary Hallock Foote*, ed. Rodman W. Paul (San Marino, CA: Huntington Library, 1972), p. 114. Mrs. Foote wrote her reminiscences in the early 1920s. Subsequent page references to this work are included in the text.

7. Joshua C. Taylor, *America as Art* (New York: Harper and Row, 1976), pp. 93–94.

8. Mrs. Foote eventually contributed a variety of writing to the *Century* beginning with sketches of life in New Almaden and then short stories and serialized novels.

9. The Idaho years, 1883–1893, marked the Footes' most difficult period in the West. Arthur not only abandoned the area in which he had trained for the new field of irrigation but, as the reminiscences show, Mrs.

Foote finally admitted that the West was to be their home, despite earlier hopes that they would make their "fortune" and return to the East.

10. Robert M. Taft, *Artists and Illustrators of the Old West* (New York: Charles Scribner's Sons, 1953), p. 174.

11. "Recent Literature," *Atlantic Monthly*, 34 (December 1874), 745-46.

12. Armstrong, "Illustrators—II," p. 132.

13. Edith M. Thomas, "The Mourning Dove," *Century Magazine*, 45 (February 1893), 545.

14. Letter from Mary Hallock Foote to Richard Gilder, June 1, 1891, The Mesa, Boise, Idaho, the Huntington Collection.

15. See Armstrong, "Illustrators—II," p. 135.

16. The full genesis of this myth may be traced through the novels, though I do not discuss them fully here. As an example, *The Led-Horse Claim* (1882) explores the running of mines by uninformed and unrealistic eastern interests; *John Bodewin's Testimony* (1886) dramatizes Arthur's own court testimony against a claimjumper (a case that paid him the same amount as that earned by the dishwasher for a night at the Clarendon Hotel); *The Last Assembly Ball* (1889) explores the difficulty of "manner" and the social differences between western and eastern society. These novels make use of a "new" hero, the "professional-exile," as Mrs. Foote called him, who was a tenderfoot easterner—often a mining engineer—who had come west. Though the works are marred by the intrusion of audience-appeal and the requirements of her editors, Mrs. Foote attempted to portray the West's corruptibility, rather than its conventional garden image.

17. Mary Hollock Foote, *The Chosen Valley* (Boston and New York: Houghton Mifflin, 1892), pp. 313–14.

18. Wallace Stegner, *Angle of Repose* (Garden City, NY: Doubleday, 1971), p. 277.

Black Folklore and Subversive Imagery: The Comic Illustrations of Rose O'Neill

Rose Cecil O'Neill (1874–1944), cartoonist, painter, sculptor, poet, and novelist, is remembered primarily for her kewpies—impish and sometimes waggish, cupid-like creatures that populated her magazine pages for *Puck, Life, Cosmopolitan,* and other magazines from the 1890s to the 1930s, making their most lasting impressions as dolls, still copied and produced today. O'Neill, divorced by her second husband, Harry Leon Wilson, for, among other things, "talking baby-talk," had a rich childhood history and "child-mind" which encouraged her early accomplishments as a visual artist—for example, the first place she earned for her drawing in an adult art contest in the Omaha *World Herald* in 1887 at age thirteen. Born on June 25, 1874, in Wilkes Barre, Pennsylvania, she moved as a child with her family to Battle Creek, Nebraska, and later to Omaha, attending the Sacred Heart convent school. Later, after two tours with theatrical companies and a precocious artistic beginning with a weekly cartoon series for the Omaha *World Herald* and the *Great Divide* magazine in Denver, Colorado, she went to New York City in 1893 at age 19 to find markets for her art. There she stayed at the convent of the Sisters of Saint Regis, making rounds to offices to sell her cartoons. By age 22, after her marriage to Virginian Gray Latham, she moved to Bonniebrook, a 300-acre Ozark homestead in the mountains of Southern Missouri where she continued her work for *Puck* and *Life* magazines. Bonniebrook remained her home throughout her life, despite fame and financial success which enabled her to own residences in Washington Square, the art community of Westport, Connecticut, and a villa on the island of Capri. She made more than a million dollars by 1913 on the kewpie dolls, personally overseeing the firing of the bisque

faces in Germany where she—at a crucial point—stopped production to appeal to the workers on behalf of the children of the world
for a more careful design. With the royalties from her kewpies—both illustrations and
cartoon work and the dolls—she supported her fine art as well. A
well-established illustrator by 1910, she illustrated two of Harry
Leon Wilson's books, wrote four novels, a collection of poetry, and
children's books, including *Kewpies and Dotty Darling*, and, as late
as 1928, *The Kewpies and the Runaway Baby*. But from her childhood
drawings of titan-like "sweet monsters," begun at age thirteen, to
her one-woman show in 1922 in Paris and at the Wilderstein Galleries in New York City featuring her paintings, drawings, and
sculpture, she remained dedicated to a serious and successful
strain of art that reflected an imagination fueled by European folklore and classical and romantic traditions. Rose O'Neill once described the "coming of the kewpies" as an experience in a dream
she had in a hammock one day on her Bonniebrook porch. The little creatures sprang full-blown from the artist's head in an experience reminiscent of O'Neill's fusing of folklore, vernacular elements and classical references in this Zeus-like, yet Missouri experience. Until her death in Springfield, Missouri, after living in New
York City, France, England, Germany, and Capri, she returned
regularly to Bonniebrook and the "folk"-rich Ozarks.[1]

Thus, much more than a simple retreat, these Southern mountains formed a psychic homeplace for O'Neill's imagination, and
they became her workplace. Bonniebrook housed not only her family (her mother, two sisters, a brother largely supported through
the years by O'Neill, especially when her antiquarian-bookdealer
father periodically took to his own cabin in the woods) but also her
father's classical book collection, and was home and haven for
numerous local and far-flung artistic friends who gravitated to the
O'Neill's for rounds of story-telling, performances, readings, and
the like. Her father and mother both were collectors and avid en-
thusiasts of their own Scotch-Irish background and folklore materials, as well as interested in local characters, customs, and ethnic
expressions. O'Neill's peregrinations, therefore, between the
Northern magazine markets and the steady supply of creative resources from the South, express certain aspects of personality and
taste and the ability to blend artistically these two worlds. It is
hardly surprising that one of her last guests before her death—and

one whom she sketched while he was there—was her friend, Vance Randolph, the most famous of the Ozark folklore collectors. As a result of her cultural awareness and diversity, there is a creative tension in her use of black Southern folklore materials. Though she worked within the prevalent conventions of magazine humor, she managed to reflect the roots of black folk culture, and in-group humor, while alluding to the phenomenon of the immigration of the Southern black to the city.

One of the most crucial and formative periods for O'Neill's black magazine art was spent in the Ozarks, when Southern folklore collecting along with study of black culture stimulated great curiosity for white audiences. The homogeneity of the white plantations and pockets of black occupation in the slave states distinguished the Southern black from the Northern freedman and the blacks of Surinam, Brazil, or the West Indies. While popular detailed books of travellers historically ignored folklore as an element, they nevertheless recorded all of it in detail: a revivalist religion with exhorting preachers, poetic and scriptural languages of congregations, shout-jumping in the praise houses, singing and dancing in slave cabins, occasions of personal possession of the devil, tales, witch and ghost stories, accounts of life among various animals, the events of satirizing old "marster," patting, handclaps, jingles, and refrains. At least some survey of folk forms in daily Negro life in Rose O'Neill's South had been treated in *Slave Songs of the U.S.* and popularized in *Uncle Remus: His Songs and Sayings* by Joel Chandler Harris.

Yet at the same time this rich vein of Southern black lore was beginning to be recorded and interpreted either in creative literature or in scholarly studies and collections, a number of distortions also were perpetuated. In the 1830s and 1840s the blackface minstrel show, comic Sambo stage plays, jokebooks and newspapers depicted Sambo and Rastus, along with the Downeast peddlar, French exquisite, and Irish drunkard. The Daddy Rice and Jim Crow dance, modeled on the limping slave's shuffle, came to the New York stage in 1832, initiating a series of vogues for pseudo-Negró and Negro-derived song, dance, and humor. The Virginia Minstrels performed in 1843 for New York and Boston audiences, ushering in a half-century of popularity for ministrelsy. This form, not surprisingly, grew into ridiculous caricatures of the darky; a travesty on, rather than a simulacrum of, his folklore. Nevertheless, after the Civil War, with the criss-crossing and interrelating of folk and mass culture, according to Richard Dorson several hallmarks of black folklore could be identified: (a) the emergence of a personality rather than a type; (b) the fluidity between forms, such as tales, songs, folk phrases, notions, verses, and incidents; (c) the primacy of the folk rhyme as the centerpiece of music, games, stories, and sayings into which they were compressed; and (d) a fluidity between secular and religious elements, so that talking songs, rhythmical phrasing, spirituals, biblical metaphors, popular sayings, wise-saws, fictional tales and true experiences were prevalent in both realms.[2]

At first glance it may appear that O'Neill was unaware of these elements of black folklore and that, working with the stock cartoon conventions of *Life* and *Puck*, she conformed to the general popular topics of these magazines as well as the sources and standards of their humor. Domestic exchanges, upper-class social conventions, leisure activities are treated through the usual "he-she" jokes or the stock statement or question and humorous reply. A magazine audience's interest in the comedy of manners confronting social conventions is satisfied by O'Neill as her family scenes, chic and debonair ladies and gentlemen, golf players, and others, replicate a safe, parlor-brand of humor that often alludes to but cloaks more vital Victorian themes of sexuality, family relationships, and gender roles. But along with this expectation of a calm comedy of manners is that of the role of other classes—the urban immigrant, the black—both urban and rural—and the child, within the context of the family and his or her own gang or group. While the preponderance of magazine humor at the turn of the century either perpetuated the stereotypes of these groups or largely ignored them, favoring the genteel humour of upper-class couples, O'Neill centers on the shifting role of women, ethnic groups, and children, often using a member of one of these groups to subvert the pretentiousness of the polished and urban upper class or treating humorously the exchanges within each of these groups as a kind of in-group humor rather than the typical "put-down" of the lower-class character. Her children, for example, often are savvy, Dickens-like characters, street-wise resourceful, to whom the adult world represents a sort of superficiality and sentimental, unrealistic existence. The Irish, also typified in these cartoons, speak in a brogue or dialect, but do so illustrating their wit and survival skills through the story-telling and life-enhancing qualities of language—not as an indication of their lack of education, undesirability, or foibles. Class distinctions and the implied value judgments hence are inverted for an audience whose expectations are quite the opposite—in fact, familiar with the external "topic" of the cartoon so as to be drawn into it. The subtlety of execution of these cartoons lies in the seemingly conventional depiction of dialect, dress, character, and setting, often made even more convincing by the detailed and illustrative quality of the drawings, and simultaneously by the removal of the lens of superiority that made these subjects typically the quaint object of the viewer.

This leveling effect is perhaps best exhibited in the black cartoons where the realistic and illustrative style, yet stereotypic subject, demonstrates Dorson's hallmarks of black folklore while directly involving the largely white middle- and upper-class audience with the commonalities it may share with people usually assumed to be different. Of the almost seven hundred cartoons published between 1897 and 1908 for *Puck*, forty-nine treated black subjects. Topics ranged from issues of gender, class, and manners to those of literature and education, any particularized Southern setting identified by region or state. Typically, common sense or experiential wisdom triumphs over genteel or sentimental attitudes; dialectic, rhythmical language characterizes the witty exchange—indeed sometimes the joke turns on the language itself; characters are personalized in behavior or attitudes, though they may appear predictable.

To examine one cartoon as an example of these aspects of O'Neill's black cartoon work, the piece "Quieted Him" employs the standard he-she joke line and gives insight into the expected domestic repartee of husband and wife. On this level, the cartoon subscribes to the usual Victorian conventions of magazine humor. Further, it depicts a black family in their kitchen, suggesting the rural stereotype of the poor black and inviting common cultural assumptions about black men, women, and children, the family, and their environment. In an approximation of black dialect, Mr. Jackson says: "Huh! Dat new-fangled coffee-mill yo' bought doan grind at all," to which Mrs. Jackson retorts: "Yeas; it's lak some husbands. Expensive, goes aroun' a lot, en doan do no wuk." The wife turns the husband's typical complaint about a wife wasting his money on useless things for the kitchen to the uselessness of

QUIETED HIM.

MR. JACKSON.—Huh! Dat new-fangled coffee-mill yo' bought doan grind at all.
MRS. JACKSON.—Yeas: it 's lak some husbands.   Expensive, goes aroun' a lot, en doan do no wuk.

idle husbands, a verbal twist particularly ironic, given the demands of a small child at her feet and the orderliness of her kitchen and her own erect stoutness or strength played off against her husband's lounging attitude in his cane rocker with his eyes relaxed and closed. Since the title of the cartoon is "Quieted Him," we may assume the wife has the final word; yet there is irony even in the title, for his quietness suggests his proclivity to remain relaxed—not to be bothered by the badinage of his wife. Though the cartoon evokes the usual male/female-wife/husband joking relationship and assumption one about the other, O'Neill's clever attention to details of Southern black life particularizes the meaning. Rather than function as a joke about the poor, lazy black husband whose verbal acuity frees him from responsibility, the larger theme of the cartoon is that of "new-fangledness."

The propensity of the cartoon reader to assume the drawing is a caricature of black life is undercut by the almost documentary quality of the work. Pots and pans, caneback rocker, gingham dresses—even facial expressions—are almost realistically wrought.

Recording as she does this actual experience, O'Neill dramatizes through this and the other levels of the cartoon its greatest irony: the husband's cravat, likely a hint at the actual urban setting or at least his worldliness, is juxtaposed against the wife's purchase of a new-fangled coffee mill. The message of the cartoon is that though some things never change (the "extravagance" of husband and wife in each other's eyes), dialect, basic dress, and attitudes admit to new influences—and change—in an urban setting. In this O'Neill cartoon as in most of the others of what appear to be typical Southern blacks, there is an awareness of the transporting of Southern folklore to the city—and the consequent changes urban influences will make on this folk group. O'Neill manages to illustrate as well the other phenomenon Dorson argues: that in the interrelationship of mass culture and Negro folklore, the hallmarks of Negro folklore itself admitted to fluidity of forms—in the case of "Quieted Him" and other O'Neill black cartoon work the detailing of language, personality, and cultural experience, in the face of intransigent Victorian stereotypes of behavior.

Though O'Neill continued to treat the generalized assumptions of black life—as a popular song of the 1890s described these simplistic racist emblems, "The Coon's Trademark: A Watermelon, Razor, Chicken and a Coon"—she did so to question the pervasiveness of these attitudes and their source. E.W. Kemble's illustrations of a Negro dialect story for *Life* in 1883, his illustrations for *Huckleberry Finn* in 1884, and his so-called comic images for A *Coon Alphabet* in 1898 helped establish the convention continued during O'Neill's tenure at *Puck*. As critic Elvin Holt writes:

> Underlying the broad appeal of the coon image in American humor was a racist stereotype which most whites, many of whom had little or no meaningful contact with blacks, accepted as reality. A Northern white man living in Virginia in 1916 ... declares: "The negro is lighthearted, irresponsible, careless; he lives in the present like a child or a beast; he does not aim high or persist; he is fond of big words and gay colors; he wants to strut, to display himself, rather than to be; and therefore seen against the background ... of a civilization which he apes with fantastic imitation, he is a subject for comedy, not tragedy."[3]

Kemble's sketches confirmed this perception of blacks by creating dialogue which was a parody of black dialect rather than authentic, by using blacks for comic relief, and by creating characters who were often involved in pathetic self-mockery. Overall, these characters included Zip Coon, the Uncle Remus, and the pickaninny; the coon character unreliable, lazy, often subhuman; the Uncle Remus, a harmless, happy, naive and quaint darky; and the pickaninny, a lovable black child, with bulging eyes, numerous bright pigtails, and amusing antics.

These images may appear mild—or at least harmless in the context of a world of entertainment in forms of mass culture. Yet within them—as actually harmful and self-fulfilling as they were— is a more disturbing side. According to Holt in his research on Kemble in *The Coon Alphabet*, aspects of public humiliation, physical pain, and violence abound, particularly in the ways the pickanninny is depicted for the laughter of white children. As an excuse to amuse young readers, black children are shown to be mindless, subhuman grotesques, subjected to acts of violence. Violence against children, then, is a prominent theme throughout; the humor of these illustrations involving children is callous and cruel. Dehumanized so that often animals are more "human" than blacks, the overall perception of blacks by Kemble, as the most popular and influential imagist of blacks in his time, is that "black is ugly ... and blacks would really like to be white."[4] Because *The*

Coon Alphabet is a children's book, it is even more disturbing as it suggests what the adult white establishment wishes white children to know about black people. Further, it teaches children to regard the race as not worthy of trust or empathy, only ridicule.

Though not as popular individually as Kemble, O'Neill's fellow cartoonists for *Puck* perpetuated Kemble's principles, in their conception of blacks through image and language. Two examples will illustrate what was without exception the image of the black in magazines in the early part of the century. One Nankiwell cartoon shows an all-black host of faces, white eyes and mouths only glowing in crescent smiles. The caption reads: "Annual moonlight excursion of the watermelon association." Another cartoon in a *Puck* issue in 1901 depicts a black family with broad caricatured faces gathered around a modest dining table, one boy with his back to the viewer, perched on a soap box for a chair. Called "Secured in the Night," it reads: "Parson Jackson (dining with member of the congregation)—'Dis am a fine tuhkey, indeed, Mistah Johnsing! What did it cost you?' Mr. Johnsing (absently)—'About two houahs of sleep!'" Though the first cartoon makes objects of the crowd, establishing the outsider's "superior" point of view; the second condemns from the "inside" by suggesting blacks steal without compunction. Yet another cartoon by Dalrymple demonstrates how little even successful blacks have come to think of themselves and how they have learned to conceive of themselves in the negative perceptions of whites. Two elegantly dressed black men are introduced at a party, one as Doctor Jimpweed. To this the other black man responds, while extending his hand: "Umph! Happy to meet yo', Doctah! Horse or hoodoo?"

O'Neill's cartoons of blacks, on the other hand, use the stereotypes in order to deflate or question them. Almost without exception, most black cartoons in *Puck* operate comically at the expense of the blacks involved. But O'Neill often utilizes the "frames" of experience—the popular images of fellow cartoonists appearing alongside her cartoon work—with a slight ironic twist, sometimes having blacks speak for themselves or reversing the expectations of the audience in some way. For example, when she draws children, they may at first appear to "be" pickaninnies as in this cartoon: "Friend: 'Dat am a happy little chile of yourn.' Mrs. Black: 'Happy? She am jes' as happy as a pickaninny in a coon song!'" But the cartoon is entitled "Ne Plus Ultra," and the child depicted is beautiful with a mournful expression. Sometimes O'Neill shows that blacks realize clearly their victim status, so that in the smallest daily dealing, larger philosophical truths are evident. In "A Cloudy Attribute," Miss Johnson comments on a "diamond sunburst" a Mrs. Jefferson has given her on her birthday. To this her friend replies: "Am you shuah it ain't intended fo' a 'cloudburst?' I see it's got a quicksilver lining!" She even shows that blacks are aware they aren't trusted, but in their awareness are not the ones duped. In "A Clever Professor," after a satisfactory visit to a phrenologist, a black woman is told by her husband: "Yes, and den he bit de silvah dollah yo' gib him to see it if was a good one!" The irony occurs in the doctor's telling the woman the bump on her head signified honesty. In cartoons where blacks may not know terminology, such as political terms, they sense their exclusion from equality, even when they misapply the term. Trying to explain to his wife what the term "Open Door Policy" means, a black man says: "It's jest dis—when yo' wants to play policy now, yo' has to do it on de quiet; sneak up a back ally or t'rough a back gate. Well, dis' 'Open Door' policy means dat de game is to be played wide open; dat's what it means." Given how the open door policy was in itself a "numbers" game, and that blacks at home often had fewer rights than immigrating people, the joke, though it seems to turn on the characters' ignorance, attempts to expose how that ignorance is maintained. In "His Excuse," the pun turns also on gender difference. Even more directly, the O'Neill cartoon called "Local Color" focuses on feelings within the black community. A visitor has arrived at a house where the mother is laboring over a washtub, her two children near her. The visitor tells the children not to be afraid, "I ain't de bogey man." One of the children replies: "We know you ain't. De bogey man am a white man." In yet another cartoon she entitles "In Georgia," the attitude of blacks from their point of view clearly is given. Pete asks, "Am dis much bettah dan de ole slav'ry days, Uncle Tom?" to which Uncle Tom replies: "I dunno, zac'ly. In dem times we wuz too valu'ble to be lynched!" As these examples show, the Uncle Tom, Pickaninny, Mr. and Mrs. Jackson names are used to seemingly establish the expected text. The same is true of the dialect, or approximation thereof. But within the text or established formula of the cartoon is the subverting image and message. The cartoons are drawn with care, expressing individualized characters, settings, and cultural concerns, so that the humor is directed outward toward the viewer, subverting through re-directed comedy the erroneous and bigoted stereotypic concepts. Sometimes her humor is effective as it cleverly offsets the companion pieces in the magazine, playing off the visual stereotype itself, holding "reality" up to it. Seen from our contemporary perspective, O'Neill's subtlety and irony stands out when considered from within the pervasive visual depictions of minorities in the humor magazines of the period. It is impossible to know if readers fully realized the joke she attempted to play on her fellow comic artists, even as she attempted to revise the bigoted attitudes toward blacks. Yet the genius of her sensitive and subversive work now can be appreciated.

One may claim that O'Neill's best cartoon work at the turn of the century may be appreciated along with the best of the local color writers. Aware of a usable past and the richness, abundance, and variety of the American scene, theirs was an overall democratic orientation deeply devoted to the common man and a fundamentally realistic analysis of homespun characters. At their best, these writers corrected such stereotypes as the shrewd Yankee character, the shiftless mountaineer, the plantation darky, by making them highly individualized. O'Neill contributed to the fund of images of blacks, altering the familiar caricatured version in popular culture largely due to her fidelity to folk elements. Perhaps most interestingly the humor is largely directed outward toward an audience whose own stereotypical assumptions are spoofed as too simplistic. Her work thus preserves a crucial period in American history and culture when manners, customs, styles, attitudes, and prejudices—along with the cultural landscape—were undergoing change.

Notes

1. For more information on the life and works of Rose O'Neill see Alan McCanse, *Titans and Kewpies, the Life and Art of Rose O'Neill* (New York: Vintage Press, 1968); "The Art of Rose O'Neill," Catalogue at the Brandywine River Museum, Chadds Ford, Pennsylvania; Louis Holliday Holman, *Rose O'Neill, Kewpies and Other Works* (1983; rev. ed. 1989); Trina

Robbins and Catherine Yronwide, *Women and Comics* (Forestville, CA: Eclipse Books, 1985).

2. General but helpful information on Ozark folklore is available in Richard M. Dorson, *American Folklore* (Chicago, IL: University of Chicago Press, 1961). See also Vance Randolph, *Ozark Magic and Folklore* (New York: Dover, 1947) and Vance Randolph, *Pissing in the Snow and Other Ozark Folktales* (Urbana, IL: University of Illinois Press, 1976).

3. Elvin Holt, "A Coon Alphabet and the Comic Mask of Racial Prejudice," *Studies in American Humor* (Winter 1986–87), 310.

4. Holt, 316.

PHOTOGRAPHY
Art, Ethnography, Ethnicity

The Eye and the Story:
The Photographs of Eudora Welty

There has been a considerable amount of insightful criticism of
Eudora Welty's photographic work and books based on her junior
member status as photographer for the Works Progress Administration in the 1930s. Her most recent book, *Photographs*, published
by University Press of Mississippi—a selection of these original
prints from the 1200 photos and negatives collected in the Mississippi Department of Archives and History in Jackson—attests to
this continued interest, for it includes Miss Welty's own appraisal
of her youthful work as an impetus for her writing. But these photographs and the accompanying text signify more than just a
bridge between the eye and the story. Miss Welty's re-visioning of
the initial photographic experience both in the process of printing
from the original negatives and her reorganizing of this material
into two subsequent photo books links the pictures to what she
calls her "visual mind"—experience translated into art over time as
Miss Welty developed a pervasive way of seeing. Most critics attempt to connect the photos and fictional texts through direct
transference—identifying settings and characters in the stories
from the photographs—or by juxtaposing certain critical aspects of
photographic and narrative art. Miss Welty remains her own best
critic, however, as she argues that these photographs are *snapshots*.
This tradition provides the key to understanding not simply the
verisimilitude of one art and another, but how she used the camera, a vehicle of popular culture, to significantly witness the everyday lives that would be the prevalent subject and setting for her
fiction. Her manner of seeing initiated in her photographic experience constitutes a curiosity of kinship, an attitude which allows for
the continued discovery of expansive, universal truths, rather than

the reductive or stereotypic often associated with popular culture, in the details of vernacular life.

Due to the nature of her assignment, which was to record the poverty-stricken daily lives primarily of blacks in rural Mississippi counties, we assume the term "documentary" may best describe Miss Welty's approach to her subjects. But as William Stott shows in *Documentary Expression and Thirties America*, this is a very complex term, allowing for more than the official, social and reportorial approach. It may also be thoroughly personal, when human. Thus documentary treatment of people may carry and communicate feeling, even drama, providing information, but also a glimpse into an inner existence, a private self. It is important to note that social documentary often is value-ridden, corrective, or propagandistic since it shows people at grips with conditions of time and place, neither permanent nor necessary, such as racial discrimination or police brutality. Social documentary deals with everyday life at grips with the man-made, both in its subject matter and in the photographer's attitude toward the event. Human documents, on the other hand, show people undergoing the perennial and unpreventable in experience, what happens to us all everywhere—death, work, chance, rapture, hurricanes, maddened dogs. We may say that the human document deals with the everyday life as it exists with natural phenomena. But even in the recording of human documents there is the temptation to sentimentalize. Though Miss Welty's photographs contain elements of both these aspects of documentary, in their attitude and tone they imply quite a different message from that of other professional documentaries of her day. Many photographers working contemporaneously chose the visibility of "simple" people to either expose social problems or to make observations about the "good and great things, the stupid and sentimental things," to quote Edward Steichen on his pictures, *The Family of Man*, a sentimental lot. In her recounting photographically of daily associations, jobs, friendships, roles, ceremonies, customs, and entertainment, all articulated in the connectedness of the Southern landscape, Miss Welty—rather than show how simple the poor are, how feeble, how limited—reveals their lives as complex, strong, pervasive. She uses their poverty to show how much they possess. Whereas the prosperous attenuate their selfhood through many possessions and roles, the poor condense theirs into a few. Their world, and everything in it, bespeaks them, symbol-

izes them. It is entirely a work of art. Thus, her pictures as documents establish an aesthetic of seeing concerned at once with the
private selves of these people as publicly expressed. It is an aesthetic dedicated to their art of living.

Miss Welty's realization of her subjects in this way is partly
due to her own innocence, both as a Southern white woman and as
a photographer. She remarked to Jean Todd Freeman in an interview in 1984 about her documentary assignment:

> It took me all over Mississippi, which is the most important
> thing to me, because I had never seen it—except Jackson and
> Columbus, never.... That experience, I think, was the real
> germ of my wanting to become a real writer, a true writer. It
> caused me to seriously attempt it. It made me see, for the
> first time, what life was really like in this state. It was a reve-
> lation.

Her own term for this experience—revelation—is extremely important, for Miss Welty also used this term to describe the photographic experience as a rank amateur, untrained either in the expectations of documentary photography or studio work. Thus, as
she was curious of this Southern life unfamiliar to her, she was
doubly innocent. The result is a total involvement with the subjects, a guiding desire for them to reveal themselves. "I learned
about people, you know, in the street," she says. "The value lies in
the subjects.... I have no position I was trying to justify. No thought
I wanted to illustrate. They were pictures because I would see
something I thought explanatory of the life I saw." What she saw
as an innocent outside is the kind of tragic beauty because the
subjects themselves do not see it. She describes this quality of
tragic beauty as "joy the same as courage," which comes from the
inherent dignity of her subjects. In her pictures of mother and
children, children with pets, a lone black woman at work over tubs
of dirty laundry, groups of friends at a circus, a congregation
caught in the throes of religious revivalism, and other distinguish-
ing details of black rural life, Miss Welty does not attempt to transform the actual but rather perceives in the actual a permanent revelation of the spirit. Through time, Miss Welty cultivated this perception and revelation in the photographs because she initially
learned from them. "I learned from my own pictures, one by one,
and had to, for I think we are the breakers of our own hearts," she
says. Thus, her innocence translated itself into an openness and a

growing understanding, what Henry Adams once remarked of art: "Understanding is a feeling not a fact. Learning to feel intelligently is authentic education." Miss Welty said it more succinctly: "Every feeling waits upon its gesture."

If Miss Welty was a foreigner to the rural black lives before her, she did, in her ignorance of photography, fall back upon what little she know about photography—taking snapshots. And if her outsider status afforded an innocent and fresh view, she also had a measure of familiarity to experience these lives by. Unlike most other documentarians, she was a native, a Southerner, and she recognized the relationships between people within families and in regard to place. Many critics, when describing the essence of the snapshot, say it comes closest in photography to the truth of the spiritual moment which cannot be willed, desired, or achieved. As one critic notes: "Some people may never take a snapshot in their lives, though they take many pictures." Innocence is the quintessence of the snapshot. It is not a performance. It is something that happens to the taker rather than his performing or orchestrating it. In taking snapshots, Miss Welty matched the unpretentious with the elemental, resulting in an enormous vitality and expression of these lives. Furthermore, Miss Welty relied as an amateur on what she knew of family photography and the snapshot as an element of the family album. The eye which creates the family album is the heart's eye, without polemic or pity, and its innocence comes from a kind of love blindness that conditions the making of such pictures. The prevalent attitude one comes away with from these pictures is that due to the unselfconsciousness of the taker the subjects are seen as they want to be. Even the apparent disorder and imperfection of some of her shots, therefore, enable the reality of these daily lives. In one shot of a pentecostal group, the camera's off-centered framing, the out-of-focus figures, seem to indicate that the taker is a participant rather than a cold observer. Such photography allows for a radiation of kinship, energy, harmony with one's surroundings. Thus, the snapshot creates a bond between subject and photographer and ultimately the viewer of these pictures. Reynolds Price has written in the introduction to *Photographs* about Miss Welty's gift of revelation, her ability as a single beholder, a watchful child. She has said that she moved to writing stories because she was so moved by the realization through her photographs that the thing to wait for was when people reveal themselves. This impetus in photography called for further narration. But it also set her attitude and objective as a fiction writer to "part a curtain." "Not to point the finger in judgment, but to part a curtain, that invisible shadow that falls between people, the veil of indifference to each other's presence, each other's wonder, each other's human plight."

What also happened to this taker of snapshots occurred in her contemplation of the pictures themselves. Feeling for facts—the details of these Southern lives—often comes through popular culture, those versions of reality either familiar or vernacular, beginning in the simpler lessons of media rather than the equivocal versions of reality given in the greatest art. As Miss Welty worked from the original shots to the final prints, cropping, dodging, recomposing, she realized through the photos themselves that the exalted things of the spirit often come through the mundane. The details sought through documentary are thus not realistic or minutiae but symbolic. In viewing her own pictures, Miss Welty experienced again the power of the snapshot to revolutionize what we see and to reshape our conceptions of what is real and what is important.

Nowhere is this attitude so evident as in Miss Welty's critical vocabulary for her fiction and purpose as a writer, which is full of photographic terms and associations, clarifying further the connection she senses between her photography and writing. In the limited space of this essay, so far I have tried to at least suggest that photography influenced Miss Welty's experience with people and places that would inform her fiction and, most of all, allowed for an attitude toward this subject matter, a tone, a purpose, appropriate to the vernacular world. Photography also has influenced the way Miss Welty thinks of her own work, her aesthetics. As she learned to write so realistically about the Southern landscape and its significance in Southern daily life, she also chose to characterize this realization in the writer as the power of focus—how the meaning of place and one's attitude toward it (point of view) come about through focus. She says:

> It may be that place can focus the gigantic voracious eye of genius and bring its gaze to point. Focus then means awareness, discernment, order, clarity, insight—they are the attitude of love. The art of focusing itself has beauty and meaning; it is the art that continued in, turns art into meditation,

into poetry. The question of place resolves itself into point of
view.

As in the case of this observation, Miss Welty characteristically
uses photographic terminology to describe the process and philosophy of her writing in transformational terms, rather than realistic
ones. Some of her comments about photography would seem to
indicate she finds it an incomplete form for her purpose. "With the
story-writer's truth, real insight doesn't happen with the click of
the moment, but comes in its own time, and more slowly from
within." Yet even in her most imaginative descriptions, she speaks
photographically about the inward eye, the story-writer's truth as
opposed to the assumptions of the world. "The writer always sees
double," she says, "two pictures at once in the frame, his and the
world's. The writer makes the reader see only one of the pictures,
the author's—under the pleasing allusion it is the world's." The
great gift Miss Welty possesses as a writer is locating immanence
in the ordinary. It would seem that she discovered in the so-called
surfaces of photography a light that shapes gesture, a study of a
deeper relief than surfaces, than the shape and skin of things. In
the story "At the Landing," she describes this quality, again in
photographic or visual terms, as she does in other commentary
and stories. Her visual details of person and place are thus clearly
presented yet mysterious. In this story, the amber beads provide a
substance that reflects and changes light as the character, Jenny, attempts to look through the outer surface to the core. "Nobody
could ever know about the difference between the radiance that
was the surface and the radiance that was inside. There were the
two worlds. There was no way at all to put a finger on the center of
light." In this story, as in many others, the downward thrust of realistic detail, linking the story with earth and river, and the up-
ward thrust of light and vision, pushing the story toward mystery,
create a remarkable tension—dream is confronted by reality, innocence by experience, the spirit by the flesh.

Finally, the aesthetic and transformational quality of Miss
Welty's fiction seems to owe something to her initial snapshots because both are about time. Part of the transformational quality of
the eye and the story is a lessening of time's anonymity. So often,
popular culture is thought to be topical, minor, disposable—not
lasting or universal. But from the first snapshot through the revelatory moments accumulated in her family album-photo books, Miss

Welty used the photographs "to see the larger private triumphs of people—moment by moment, winning their lives against time." If the vision of a photograph or of the writer's art is timeless, what it sees is not. Indeed, sometimes its stability and imitations of eternity only further emphasize how instable, how rotted with time, its subjects are. The torn posters, the hand-printed signs, swept kitchens, Model-A Fords, eloquent people and enigmatic events will not endure. The actual subject, then, of this focused, obnivorous eye of genius, is time as seen in the beauties of the fallen world. It insists on doing what we ourselves rarely dare: it takes us, our lives, the things we use and are used by, our civilization, with ultimate seriousness. It stares at our customary locales, advertisements, slums, street corners, relatives, and passersby, cemeteries, as though they had eternal significance.

Revisioning Landscape:
Southwest Women Photographers

In the recent popular film "The Grey Fox," a refreshing character appears—an aging stagecoach robber, just freed from San Quentin—a sensitive, kind, independent man who painfully finds that the new technology of the "iron horse" not only foils his former success as a slick, professional bandit, but signals the end of the Old West as well. Modernity, symbolized by the railroad and all the changes it portends, further is typified by another technological advance—the photograph—which "captures" the ex-con for all to see.

Susan Sontag, among others, has written widely on the photograph as victimizer, the photographer as hunter, and indeed the dangerous, ubiquitous nature of such an ambiguous tool. It's hardly surprising that a filmmaker would seize upon photography as a subtle vehicle for influencing and recording change in the West (and the idea of the Western). Most interesting, however, is that the photographer in the film is a woman, a feisty redhead, a "liberated" woman, whose travelling studio records the social ills experienced by immigrant groups in the Far West. For her, photography is the means to her "modernization": she owns her own business, is able to travel, is free to choose the excitement of her career over the usual need for husband and family typical of her era; and—most importantly—though she cannot vote or hold most offices or publish her writing freely, she can make a statement through her photography.

Photographic "statement," however, as most art historians and historians alike would concur, is a slippery term. The photograph's inherent ambiguity—whether it is factual or art, whether it reflects the maker's intentionality or discovery—makes the interpretation

49

of its use by women to picture "reality" particularly thorny. Baudelaire recognized ambiguity as essential to the discovery of a subject's meaning—of what is real. He called ambiguity that "suggestive magic" which includes "at the same time object and subject, the world outside the artist and the artist himself."[1]

Photographs fix such ambiguity—give it a permanent form— not only by stopping an instant in the flux of time but by freezing images within these instants. Critics of fiction recognize that such contrary relationships can be both concrete and evocative, that ambiguity generates multi-level meaning; yet despite being inherent in the nature of the photograph, ambiguity is the source of its fiercest criticism. Though literary critics such as Northrop Frye see the ironic mode (the realm of ambiguity) as "modern" and sophisticated in its ability to unite periods, to "begin in realism and dispassionate observation and move steadily toward myth,"[2] photo critics view it negatively: "Is photography truth or does the camera lie after it assures us it won't?" asks Peter Plagens in a recent review of this criticism.[3] Clement Greenberg has identified the literary qualities in the photograph,[4] but critics say such characteristics violate the supposed fidelity and intentionality of the medium. Moreover, critics A.D. Coleman and Susan Sontag argue that the nature of the photograph—the frozen instant—is ambiguously related to the real world and that such fragments of time are unreal, "deflected truths."[5] So prevailing is the notion that the photograph's integrity depends on its faithfulness to reality that other critics who attempt to discover meaning via perceptual studies or semiotics quarrel with the medium's obliqueness. Writing "On the Invention of Photographic Meaning," Allen Sekula notes that the interpretation of photographic communication issues from a kind of "binary folklore":

> The misleading but popular form of this supposition is "art photography" vs. "documentary photography." Every photograph tends, at any given moment of reading in any given context toward one of these two poles of meaning. The opposites between these two poles are as follows: photographer as seer vs. photographer as witness, photography as expression vs. photography as reportage, theories of imagination (and inner truth) vs. theories of empirical truth, affective value vs. informative value, and finally, metaphoric signification vs. metonymic signification.[6]

Debate among critics of photography over such critical issues makes it difficult to look backward at historical photographs as well as to interpret the contemporary work of women photographers. Most of these women have written little about their photographic work, and of course there exists no history of women's photography, though a number of books, photo-texts, and exhibitions attest to the subject's importance. The most recent photo-texts on the subject are Anne Tucker's *The Woman's Eye* (1976) and Margaretta K. Mitchell's *Recollections: Ten Women of Photography* (1983), both of which raise the issue of a "woman's photography." Both women cite the difficulty of being an artist and a woman, the major difference in men's and women's photography being, according to Tucker, "the extent to which a woman uses her art to confront her existence as a woman."[7] Mitchell adds another differentiating element: the "coldness" she found typical of what she calls men's photography. She undertook the compilation of *Recollections*, a celebration of older women photographers, because:

> We cannot know ourselves unless we revisit the past, return to the source, reconnect with our cultural tradition through the survivors—in this case, the older women.... It is a challenge to our iconographic memory to summon up images of great older women, to discover a positive, powerful image from our Western culture: a vision of the older woman whose strength of character, intellectual energy, and artistic (or other) achievements in the world give white hair and wrinkles an unambiguous beauty.[8]

Mitchell goes on to argue that powerful older women are perceived as negative, or at least unfeminine, especially if they reach for their own greatness. "Their power appears masculine because achievement is still associated with acting as men do. There seems to be no image at the source of our cultural memory that is not based on biology.[9]

Yet, as pertinent as these arguments appear, in their recent show, "Women of Photography: An Historical Survey," curators Anne Noggle and Marjorie Mann denied the existence of the "fictitious female eye." The only possible distinction between men's and women's photography, according to Mann, was that women appear to photograph people more, a conviction Tucker holds:

Considering the emphasis placed on women's intuitive ability with people, it is hardly surprising that some women
artists have utilized skills of perception and empathy in their
art. In 20th Century America, 90 percent of the women photographers have been portraitists, journalists, and documentarians, whose primary concern has been cultural landscape.[10]

Noggle and Mann are concerned that attempts to discover the
"female eye" deny the ambiguity to women's photography—the
constant tension between viewer and view which so concerns the
critics—in assuming that women are driven to enshroud the outside world within their "feminine" imagination.

It is, however, precisely because of the photograph's inherent
ambiguity that it is an important vehicle for women's expression.
Further, while Mann sees women's tendency to photograph the
cultural landscape as trivial to understanding their work, I argue a
focus on the peopled environment is revelatory of the ways
women have used photography as an ambiguous medium—one
constantly challenging the viewer to question interrelationships between self and other and culture and nature. Just as Annette
Kolodny has noted of women's diaries, letters, journals, and fiction, the photograph contains the metaphors women apply to various landscapes in the act of possessing them. That is, as in the case
of female local color writers at the turn of the century, photography is a way of discovering the reality of place, one's perception of
that reality, and the condition of women in American society.
Women's reality embodies the "sensed forms, images, and symbols" which reflect this reciprocity. As Gyorgy Kepes observed:

> It is not with tools that we domesticate our world. Sensed
> forms, images and symbols are as essential to us as palpable
> reality in the exploring of nature for human ends. Distilled
> from our experience and made our permanent possessions,
> they provide a nexus between man and nature. We make a
> map of our experience patterns an inner model of the outer
> world, and we use this to organize our lives. Our natural
> "environment"—whatever impinges upon us from the out-
> side—becomes our human landscape, a segment of nature
> fathomed by us and made our homes. [11]

As we shall see as we trace women's landscape photography
from the 1800s to the present, women often perceived landscape in

ways both very different from men and from the stereotypic ways
we have been told they related to Western or Southwestern landscapes. Photography of the region offers not only a different vision
of the Southwest landscape, but also, over the 100-year period
studied, provides a history of women's move from the private
domestic sphere into the public world of fine art production (cf.
Figure 4, p. 72).

I. Altered Landscapes: Alternative Visions

In 1890 Margaret Bisland wrote an article for *Outing* magazine,
"Women and Their Cameras." In it she remarked: "Our greatest
painters have been men: have we not a right to expect that our
most famous photographers will be women?" Other articles of this
nature followed, promoting women and photography. Clarence
Bloomfield Moore published "Women Experts in Photography" in
Cosmopolitan in 1893; Marion Foster Washburne wrote for *Godey's*
magazine in 1897 "A New Profession for Women," which she sub-
titled "Photography and the Success Which Follows Earnest and
Diligent Work." That year Frances Benjamin Johnston contributed
"What a Woman Can Do with a Camera" to *Ladies Home Journal*.
Richard Hines, Jr., addressed the Mobile (Alabama) Art League on
the topic "Women and Photography," outlining the careers of several women photographers. In 1899, he rewrote the piece of *American Amateur Photographer* and published yet another version of the
article in *Photo-Era* in 1906. Some twelve years after Bisland's claim
about famous women photographers, Helen L. Davie added in
Camera Craft (1902): "Women, the conservative, the copyist, has in
this instance been the pioneer, leading the way in a pictorial portrait Photography, a way which her brothers have found pleasant
and are making haste to follow.... Mr. Juan Able says that the art-
science of Photography has captured both men and women, but
the number of men who have achieved distinction is out of all proportion to the number who practice it seriously. On the other hand,
a very large percentage of the women who have taken it up are
famous."

The argument, no doubt, will rage on, for there is no conclu-
sive evidence about men's and women's perception. Yet, examina-

tion of the ostensible equality of the sexes in photography and the thesis of a true female sensibility are different matters; one purports to deal with historical and social fact, the other is esthetic conjecture. The origin, technical advancements, and various aesthetic considerations of photography parallel the liberation of women in the 19th century. The emerging women's movement in the mid-19th century released some women from the home into a world that had been exclusively men's. Women, used to roles as mother and homemaker, extended their "natural" talents to social work and teaching, places where they could function in the new industrial capitalistic societies of England and the United States. These women also took to photography, a relatively easy, yet socially and morally useful, medium, to record their new-found freedom in the world, as well as to record their view of social injustices. Women were not "by nature" more sympathetic to the poverty and injustice they encountered, but their social roles led them to seek out occupations and images that would be sensitive to issues of welfare and also be morally satisfying. The instructive value of photography conformed to both the teaching roles and moral commitment.

More importantly, perhaps, photography in the 19th century became a sanctioned activity for women within the home. For women who continued to occupy the "private sphere," photography was considered both respectable and fashionable. Amy S. Doherty in "Women in Focus: Early American Women Photographers" provides a number of examples of socially sanctioned photographic activities for women—among them family photography, using photographs to illustrate letters amusingly, and, as one woman termed it, "my fancy work" (using photography as handiwork). Writing about photography as it was practiced by upper-class Eastern women, Doherty argues: "Most women who went into photography as professionals came from upper-class families and had background in art."[12]

But what about western women, or women who photographed on the successive frontiers of the West and Southwest? Percentages indicate a numerical corollary between the prominence of women photographers in the East by 1900 and those thus far discovered in western surveys of censuses and newspapers. Statistically, women made up approximately twenty percent of the members of the Photo-Secession and by 1902 about three percent of the membership of the Linked Ring. The U.S. Census of 1900 indicated that 3,580 women listed photographer as their profession. On the Southwestern frontiers, Richard Rudisell in New Mexico Territory, David Haynes in Texas, and Jim Blanch in Colorado indicate women made up ten percent of all commercial photographers.[13] More importantly, photography as a suitable occupation for women allowed them to build a bridge between the private and public spheres—women's and men's worlds. As we know, in the West and Southwest, necessity often required that women support themselves. As single women or widows, they could make a living through studio photography. Several instances exist of women who were either retouchers or photographers and married men with whom they continued a joint business.

But the measure of independence that women photographers accomplished in the Southwest goes beyond mere business acumen in studio photography. Particularly suited to that occupation through experience within the private, family sphere, women studio photographers often served a documentary purpose in the villages and towns that sprang up from 1840 to the 1880s in the Southwest. In this way, they recorded and reflected upon the meaning of landscape in their daily lives.

Two examples will illustrate. Mrs. Ola Garrison of Grand Junction, Colorado, travelled as a single woman in the 1880s from her home in Iowa to San Francisco twice working in galleries to pay her way. Experienced as a retoucher and photographer, she worked in San Francisco for Liskey and Bushnell, photographing prizefighters and actors. While visiting her mother in Grand Junction, she decided to build a studio. Her portraits in Grand Junction are startlingly spontaneous and free of the conventions that governed much traditional studio work of the time. Local costume and behavior are important to these photographs; she explains her method in making probably the best of her studio work, a "realistic" photograph of several pioneer women of the town:

> At this time there were four old pioneer ladies who enjoyed good times together, Mrs. White, Mrs. Moore, Mrs. Gronsel, and Mrs. Barr.... I tried to get the four together for a picture but only succeeded in persuading Mrs. Moore, Mrs. Gronsel, and Mrs. Barr. I seated the three in rocking chairs and focused on them. There they sat stiff and proper and solemn. I'd seen them talking animatedly before. I asked Irish Mrs.

> Gronsel to tell a tale. She could tell a wonderful story, even if
> she did suffer from palsy. So I watched my chance and
> caught her head in a moment of rest.[14]

The result is a revealing photograph of regional women's lives.
The photographer appears to be absent.

This is the attitude, too, in which Garrison photographed a
brief oil boom in the area for interested stockholders. Commissioned to capture the oil strike and even rousted out of bed to catch
the oil wells as they blazed in an accidental fire, Garrison attends
to the artifacts at hand: oil workers stand in front of their rigs; necessary equipment towers nearby in the most random way. The
photograph is straight and factual. Significantly, it possesses the
same anonymous view as Garrison's studio work. In other photographs of the activities and occupations around her Colorado
town, Garrison captured the interaction or interdependence of individuals and their landscapes. One in particular—entitled
"Butchershop"—details the inventory, human and animal, of the
local meat shop.

Another Colorado photographer, Julia Skolas, like Garrison,
documented successive railroad and mining ventures in Southwestern Colorado. Skolas, who never married, was a partner to
two men in a studio in Leadville. The work that survives, however,
is a series of landscapes depicting the relationship of miners to
their work or man-made landscapes to natural ones. Her style is
reminiscent of Garrison's: there is no drama in these photographs,
and they are virtually unposed or calculated in technique. Despite
the dazzling landscapes available to her, Skolas persists in a human scale. In "Noon Hour at Golden Cycle" (Plate 1), for example,
the workings of the mine are de-emphasized in the picture in favor
of capturing some detail on the workers' faces. The logs in the fore-
ground upon which some of the men sit integrate them into their
daily setting. In "Altman, Colorado," Skolas juxtaposes the man-
made landscape of the mine against the beauty of the mountains
behind. Other women photographers of the same time period and
whose work appears in the same collection with Skolas (The Mazzulla Collection, Amon Carter Museum, 1870–1890) photograph
similarly.[15] These were studio photographers who convincingly
captured the major events of western expansion—mining, railroads, growth of towns, occupations—in accordance with the people who initiated and participated in them.

Figure 1
Julia Skolas, "Noon Hour at Golden Cycle"
Courtesy Amon Carter Museum, Fort Worth, Texas

At first glance, there may appear to be nothing surprising in these photographs. Yet they differ significantly from the tradition of landscape photography popularized by male photographers working either independently (selling stereographs) or on the geological surveys at about the same period. Seeking to "document" approximately the same activities of the frontier West and Southwest, as John Cawelti, Joel Snyder, and other critics have noted, the expeditionary and stereograph traditions often depicted inanimate landscapes rendered in a sublime way so as to reflect deep strains of artistic, moral, and religious feeling. Nature was seen as a model of grand order and serenity, redemptive and divine.[16] With few exceptions, these landscapes were awesome and unpeopled, the angle of vision and manipulations (by some of the photographers) a grand comment on the fruits of Manifest Destiny—a wilderness, raw and unsettled, awaiting man's domestication. The ironic message of these early landscapes is historically expressed in the fact that William Henry Jackson's work served both to convince Congress to set aside wilderness for the first national park and also to entertain an urban, eastern audience hungry for new visual experiences.

There was then, by 1900, a vernacular tradition of landscape photography by women on the receding frontiers of the West and Southwest. In its view of daily life in these areas, photographed in a straightforward manner without visual pretenses, it constitutes an anti-myth to the role the landscape played in the American Dream of the 19th century. In the eyes of these women, landscape is rarely pure, virginal, or unchanged. Rather, it is constantly and perhaps carelessly and unwittingly altered. Panorama or picturesqueness existing in these photographs is concurrently and ironically disturbed by hordes of people, burgeoning families, social and architectural changes that appear chaotic and haphazard when contrasted to the surrounding landscape. These photographs demonstrate that women's and men's conception of the American Dream differed. For men, the dream involved independence and accomplishment in the outside world; for women, the dream hinged on marriage and the identity and security it assured. As Lillian Schlissel illustrates in her study of frontier women's journals, marriage and family in the West and Southwest meant greater hardships, threats, and insecurity than the Dream had promised.[17]

Women photographers, already exceptional because they oftentimes depended on the profession of photography, not marriage, to sustain them, predictably illustrated women's chagrin well. Moreover, because photography allowed women to move from the private to the public sphere, these women through their work could further contradict another aspect of the American Dream as it applied to western landscapes. Denied what Dawn Lander had called the "female wanderlust," the social sanction to experience nature and the wilderness, these women travelled by virtue of where photography took them.[18] Because photography until the turn of the century was thought to be the pencil of nature—technically true—photography was more liberating than narrative was for women during the same period. What these early landscapes by women reveal, therefore, is not a belief in national character which ignored women's values and contributions, but a detailed and specific record of regionalism. Regional photography, or photography of specific region-oriented landscapes, has the same importance as local color writing did for women at the same time: discovery of place and "realism" was important, but more important was the fact that it gave women the opportunity to render the condition of women in American society and to explore women's perception of reality.

II. Three Styles of Encounter and Reflection

Once women moved out of the exclusively private sphere into the public one, photography became a means of redefining the meaning of formerly experienced landscapes. Unlike the frontier era of amateur and studio photographers, professional women photographers were more aware of the conventions and artistic trends in photography. As aesthetic distance was gained from the immediate frontier experience, aspects of that life were scrutinized by the camera as a new way to encounter the landscape and reflect its significance. The experience of taking the photograph itself constituted an important encounter with aspects of landscape; the photograph as a document or published piece allowed for a period of reflection on the landscape. Three photographers, working in the period from the 1870s to the 1920s, exemplify this vision by women and their consequent distinct treatment of subject and style.

Beginning in 1879, another woman amassed a collection of photographs which signify an understanding and appreciation of the Southwest region. Matilda Coxe Stevenson, an anthropologist, took many of the photographs documenting her research on material cultures of the Zia and Zuni in the late 19th century. Both the 11th and the 23rd Annual Reports of the Bureau of American Ethnology contain the bulk of her research and photographs.[19] Widow of James Stevenson, the anthropologist, and trained herself as a scientist, Stevenson took documentary photographs of artifacts, architecture, the Zias and Zunis, and the surrounding landscapes. This large body of work is antithetical to the major attitudes about Native Americans in the 19th century—that they were either noble or ignoble savages. In addition, Stevenson's work affords a look at the interrelationship of culture and environment without any of the subjectivism of the posed studio photographs of John Hillers or Ben Wittick of the same period. Though Stevenson's photographs are a tool of her trade, they also indicate an appreciation of and desire to understand indigenous regional peoples. As in the case of photography, anthropology attracted several women to its ranks; perhaps women's interest in people made them particularly suited to handle both.

Cultural myth is surprisingly absent from another body of Indian studies of a later period. Gertrude Kasebier, on the eve of her tremendous career as a pictorial portraitist, did a number of very haunting photographs—formal settings—of members of Buffalo Bill's Wild West Show in 1898. The show was in New York, and Kasebier asked if some of the Indians would come to her studio to be photographed. After rounds of tea and hot dogs the next morning, Kasebier launched into a three-hour session during which she photographed nine braves—all Sioux. The results fit into none of the standard categories of Indian portraits of real people, that is, *individuals* the camera woman seeks out (Plate 2). Samuel Lone Bear sits in partial profile, his eyes cocked knowingly at the camera. White War Bonnet crosses his hands casually as he looks straight into the camera. In one portrait (untitled), a brave sits as naturally as by a fire, revealing on his back expert beadwork.

Figure 2
Gertrude Kasebier, "Has-No-Horses," 1898
Courtesy Amon Carter Museum, Fort Worth, Texas

At one point during the sitting, Kasebier exclaimed: "I want a real *raw* Indian for a change. The kind I used to see when I was a child."[20] The reason for her interest in these Indians was the impression she still retained of the Leadville, Colorado, area where she lived as a child. Kasebier's mother recalled hovering over her child during an attack by Indians and declared she could not understand why Gertrude was so fond of the red men. Kasebier, however, remembered the Indians with the fearless fascination of a child, seeing in them rare character and humanity. They were part of the visual experience—"the heartiness of the prairie and the fearless independence of the frontier," Joseph Kelley wrote in 1904—of her formative years.[21] Kasebier readily identified with the qualities she admired in the Native Americans:

> A mother and grandmother ... I do not recall that I have ever ignored the greatest demand on time and patience ... but from the first day of dawning individuality, I have longed unceasingly to make pictures of people ... to bring out in each photograph the essential personality that is variously called temperament, soul, humanity.... You cannot read faces, the joy and sorrow in them, unless you have suffered and enjoyed; we do not see far enough beyond our own development and my development came slowly through much suffering, much disappointment, and much renunciation. I have learned to know the world because of what the world exacted of me.[22]

Kasebier encountered the Native Americans in a situation even more unusual (and perhaps more telling) than the celebrated trips to Washington or the stagnant late forms of reservation life. Yet, even out of native context, Kasebier recognized the art of their lives. Far from making artistic photographs, the prerogative of pictorialism, she helped the subjects speak for themselves. Once, after photographing Rodin, she answered someone who said he'd never seen the tenderness and gentility of the portrait in the man: "That is Rodin in the presence of a woman," she said.[23]

By the 1900s, photography had obviously been a vehicle for women's travel from the traditional private sphere to the public and to this point women had discovered and reflected their regional experiences personally, quite contrary to the more celebrated and popularized images we have of frontier experience. By 1920, after the advent of pictorial, subjective style in photography, an Easterner, Clara Sipprell, noted in Buffalo, New York, for her outstanding soft-focus treatments of still lifes, cityscapes, and people, became one of the first women photographers to travel widely because of her profession. Karen Brady wrote in 1975, after a brief rediscovery of Sipprell's work: "I can tell you firsthand that she was—and may always be—one of the least publicized but most extraordinary women of her time, your time, my time. For more than seventy years, she was not only a photographer, but a woman who, unabashedly, didn't do what most women did.... Instead she went places and met people. 'Kings and queens,' she told me, 'and people like that.'"[24] During her lifetime, Sipprell photographed the greats: Albert Einstein, Robert Frost, Albert Schweitzer, Grandma Moses, the King and Queen of Sweden, and others. Her pictorialist work of New York City, "New York, Old and New," has been compared to Berenice Abbot's work of the same period (1930s) with an important qualifier: she showed an interest in more than the subject.

Sipprell's soft, evocative style discovers in New Mexico in 1920 in a series of photographs of Taos Pueblo an essence that goes beyond Abbot's treatment of New York City. These shots are frontal, but ironically so, for though they're architectural, it's the play of light on the adobe, the angles of wall echoing in shadowed shapes, and the three-dimensional depth of the platinum print that Sipprell is after. Using only available light and an 8 x 10 view camera, she never retouched prints. She used simple, old-fashioned equipment, preferring not even to use a light meter because she wished, as she says, "to be the one who judges who feels, who experiences exactly how much of this or that is included in my work."[25] She used platinum prints because of the range and tone and preferred a soft-focus lens because of the illusion of depth throughout several successive spatial plans which it provided. Taos Pueblo in these shots is appreciated for its subtle details, not its overall design. Light in corners is captured. The whole scene of door or wall or ladder is imbued with light (Plate 3). Sipprell was one of the earliest photographers to celebrate the spirit of place in New Mexico, where the natural beauty of its native architecture suggests the harmonious fit of humans and their landscapes to the land.

Figure 3
Clara Sipprell, "Adobe Walls, Taos, New Mexico," 1920
Courtesy Amon Carter Museum, Fort Worth, Texas

III. Regionalism and the Southwest as a Photographic Place

As Van Deren Coke and other observers have noted, New Mexico developed as a photographic place simultaneously with the discovery of its regionalism. As much as the transformation of the West and Southwest through Anglo-colonization and fascination with Native Americans brought photographers to the region, the physical excellencies of light and exoticism signalled the further photographic exploration from the early 20th century through the 1940s. Much research on the phenomenon of regionalism that swept the country in the 1920s was hotly debated in the 1930s, and waned in the 1940s with national concerns and, perhaps, the inevitable turn of literary, artistic, and critical fashion, concentrates only on the more obvious reasons for the interest in the Southwest. Mary Austin saw the area as the place for "the rise, within appreciable time, of the next great and fructifying world culture."[26] Charles Lummis rhapsodized about New Mexico's timelessness and mystery:

> Sun, silence, adobe—that is New Mexico in three words.... It is the Great American Mystery—the National Rip Van Winkle—the United States which is *not* United States. Here is the land of poco tiempo—the home of Pretty Soon. Why hurry with the hurrying world? The Pretty Soon of New Spain is better than the "Now! Now!" of the haggard States. The opiate sun soothes to rest, the adobe is made to lean against, the hush of day—long noon would not be broken. Let us not hasten—mañana will do. Better still, pasado mañana.[27]

Harriet Monroe, one of many such artists and writers to move to New Mexico as a revolt against standardization and commercialization in early 20th-century America, identified the source of creativity to spring from regional roots: "Why go to Greece or China?" she asked. "This Southwest, which is but one chapter of our rich tradition, is our own authentic wonderland—a treasure-trove of romantic myth—profoundly beautiful and significant, guarded by ancient races practicing their ancient rites, in a region of incredible color and startling natural grandeur."[28] As late as

1977 in his *Eskimos, Chicanos, and Indians,* Robert Coles echoed, with a somewhat more scientific explanation, this response:

> At this altitude the air has lost one-fourth its weight compared to coastal flatlands, is low in carbon dioxide and oxygen, and has therefore also lost its capacity to refract or diffuse light. The hazy somewhat softened, even blurred vision of the coastal plains or the prairie gives way to a clear, bright, almost harsh, sometimes blinding field of view. Air that an outsider has come to regard as transparent suddenly becomes translucent—so sharp, so clean, so light that one feels in a new world or possessed of new eyes.[29]

Indeed, for the Anglo (often well-educated and urban) emigrés of the 1920s and 1930s, exotic, light-charged New Mexico was a spiritual place of new vision. Embracing this place and its tri-culture as their lost roots in a depersonalized America, they proclaimed New Mexico (particularly Santa Fe and Taos) an American Place.

These new settlers held in common some of the issues that had made their fellow writers and artists expatriates in Paris, for at bottom, this response to the Southwest was anti-modern and anti-progressive, a reaction to the American myth of progress as it was manifested in urbanization and commercialism. However, the resulting literature and art carried with it none of the angst and alienation attendant to the works of Pound or even Hemingway or Fitzgerald because these artists and writers were not anti-American or members of the Lost Generation: they had discovered not only another America which still possessed values that were anti-modern, but an older America rich in history, cultures, and myths.

The criticism levied at much of this literature and art, however, is that even as a reaction to the failure of the myth of progress the tone of this work is euphoric or romantic—that these newly possessed eyes tended to champion the same sublime relationships of people and nature typical to explorers, writers and artists in the 19th-century West. Mary Austin alluded to the problem when she wrote in the *English Journal* in 1932 of the ignorance of the American reading public and European critics to the true meaning of regionalism:

> Babbitt is an American type, the generalized "footless" type which has arisen out of a rather widespread resistance to regional interests and influences, out of a determined fixation on the most widely shared, instead of the deepest

rooted, types of American activity.... That Babbitt is exactly that sort of person and that he is unhappy in being it, is exactly what Mr. Lewis meant to show.... Probably the American reading public never has understood that its insistence on fiction shallow enough to be common to all regions, so that no special knowledge of other environments than one's own is necessary to appreciate it, has pulled down the whole level of American fiction.[30]

Moreover, by 1935 Dudley Wynn argued in the *New Mexico Quarterly* that even regionalism had failed in this educative goal because it ignored the very task it introduced: "Wherever the Anglo goes he takes his machines and his standardization with him; and he is everywhere abundantly, overwhelmingly triumphant. No beauty, no picturesqueness, and no other way of life today seem able to stand against this triumphant levelling."[31] What the regionalist ignored, claimed Wynn, was how unchanged Anglos were after their interaction with other cultures:

Southwestern Regionalism is not I believe, assuming this task of interpretation. Perhaps the first step in the task will have to be finding some hole in the Anglo armor where a concept of non-utilitarian values can get in. But Southwest Regionalists seem hardly to be aware yet of the Anglo's way, of the tremendous gap, between Spanish and Indian handcraftiness and the American contempt for such slowness and precision. In short, Southwestern Regionalism has no social program, and this means that it has no program for maintaining or preserving the values it professes to admire.[32]

Erna Fergusson said it yet another way: "The problem is to reconcile 'the ways of the ancients' with the concepts and needs of today: rain dances with farm machinery, inoculations with curing societies, old moralities with modern taboos—or old taboos with modern moralities."[33] Though Wynn's observation seems in part accurate and justified when one considers that the Santa Fe and Taos art colonies foundered as a result of the constricted demand for art caused by the Great Depression and the renewed interest in urban and technological themes in modern art, he ignores the long-term anti-modern or even reconciliatory themes inspired by a contact with Southwest regions.

While virtually every major photographic talent in America has made the creative pilgrimage to the Southwest primarily due to its alchemal light, one gifted woman photographically encountered for over fifty-five years the images and issues raised by regionalists and their critics. Perhaps the Southwest's only full-fledged landscape photographer, Laura Gilpin spent most of her career documenting the lives of Navajo and Pueblo peoples and the psychic wholeness their landscapes signify despite change. Gilpin's work is particularly interesting because it represents an Anglo woman's photographic journey—her education in and interpretation of the Southwest region. This journey chronicles Gilpin's growing knowledge of the Southwest region as a discreet and regenerative landscape and the recognition of region as central to the quality of life in general.

Gilpin first saw New Mexico in the winter of 1920. Driving with her father through Colorado, the two detoured into New Mexico because of the snowpacked mountain passes. "That was my first glimpse of this part of the world, and I fell for it of course. We came to Santa Fe, then all the way down to Belen, over to Laguna and Gallup, and then north to Durango. I remember the great impression Shiprock made on me then."[34] Earlier Gilpin had been impressed by scenes of the Southwest and Indian life. One of Edward Curtis' Canyon de Chelly photographs hung over the Gilpin family mantel in her Colorado home. Too, Gilpin was a born westerner. She lived a ranch life and was a lover of the outdoors. She kept a hand-colored photograph of her father at age 19, a cowboy and champion roper in Colorado. The picture was taken by her father's cousin, William Henry Jackson, renowned landscape photographer and occasional visitor at the ranch. So she came by photography and a love for the landscape naturally; photography was the perfect handmaiden for Gilpin's growing interest in regional land and life.

Several other experiences figure into Gilpin's development of a vision of the Southwest as well. Trained at the Clarence White School of Photography in New York, she developed an early pictorialist style and a preference for the beauty and subtle magnitude of tone of the platinum printing process. Her first exhibition print, "The Prelude," features this style. New York provided invaluable training, a life-long friendship with Gertrude Kasebier, and confidence and knowledge gained from new experiences and travel: "My mother always felt that I should be independent. She was a remarkable woman and she was all for my doing what I wanted to do." Laura attended a lecture of Teotihuacan during this time, and was inspired to apply her photography: "His lecture was so interesting and his slides were so—poor—that I thought, 'Why in the world can't archaeologists and a photographer get together?' So I couldn't go to Mexico, but I could get to Mesa Verde."[35]

The result was Gilpin's first body of photography of the Southwest. Published in 1927, *Mesa Verde* demonstrates Gilpin's familiarity and love for landscape, an attitude rendered in the choice of pictorial, soft-focus style. Photographs of the Native Americans, on the other hand, illustrate her documentary interest in their lives, and these photographs and texts reveal an effort to combine the interests of amateur archaeologist and photographer. In this early book, it would be easy to say Gilpin did not discover much about the Native American. Her photos of them are rigid and posed, reminiscent of the older nostalgic photographs of Indian life. Yet what moved her about landscape, probably inspiring her pictorialist view, was the mystic union of pure physicality and the harmonizing designs of light and shadow on the land. In a few shots, a formalist view almost emerges: the artist perceived the mimetic power of the forms of land, architecture, and humans.

In her next book, *The Pueblos* (1941), Gilpin further explored this mediating vision, through which her eye for visual harmony recognized its display as history, continuity, and peacefulness. These photographs emphasize the interrelationship of people, their built landscapes, and the natural environment activities and architecture derive from and give to nature. Adaptability is the visual theme counterpointed in the text by acknowledgment of change: the rising infant mortality rate, poor health conditions, and the threat of Anglo influence. Gilpin is no longer the tourist or interloper in this book. Understanding the pueblos first as an artistic conservator—wishing, in fact, to preserve through photography a life outside of modernity—Gilpin nevertheless takes another step. The pueblos' history of adaptability may offer a design for their future—one which Gilpin has been forced to admit must face modern problems.

Gilpin's next book, *Rio Grande* (1949), takes her on another journey resulting in further understanding of the changing designs signifying relationships between land and human culture. Forsaking the former romantic visions of pictorialism, Gilpin chronicles the route of the Rio Grande, the consequent changes in geography, flora, and fauna, and the varieties of human life thriving along the river. Because the attitude of the photographs appears to be documentary, contrasting views of peaceful pueblo life and the long and visually unstirring views of cities such as Albuquerque and El Paso speak for themselves. The photographer seems to be saying that one viewpoint, duplicated to see two sites, reveals the subject's own truth. The visual harmony of design that characterized Native American life is absent in the sprawling and seemingly random cities. Yet, as the subtitle of the book indicates, the Rio Grande is the *River of Destiny*, a sobriquet not lost on the photographer or viewers of the book.

By the time of her last completed work, *The Enduring Navaho* (1968), Gilpin had come to resolve the tensions between pictorial and documentary styles. Fifteen years in the making, and representative of Gilpin's life, really, among the Navaho, the book holistically treats the issues of the former studies. Whereas photographically Gilpin had treated landscape and Native American life as a conservator, reserving harder fact for the text, here text and photographs examine the many aspects of Navaho life. The organizational scheme appears anthropological, but is balanced by aesthetic and documentary treatments of native life and landscape and how these figure into the Navaho's experiences in the 1960s. A heartiness characterizes this book; the former attitudes of fear of a loss of this culture are replaced by willing juxtapositions of the old ways and the new. Navahos are pictured adapting to the new man-made landscapes of cities (county fairs, ceremonials, jobs as clerks and policemen) and the country (oil rigs and uranium mines) as well as in their age-old landscapes. Much of the early part of the book is a celebration of the old people. Women are particularly interesting in the way Gilpin sees them. Unlike the earlier Indian odalesques, the romantic renderings of Indian "maidens" that reflect the predominant attitude of male photographers (and a cultural attitude) about Native American women, Gilpin's women are real. They are active, shown as weavers, basketmakers, mothers, grandmothers, wives; many of them are old, bearing the enduring marks of their life in the landscape. These are faces we learn from.

The other lasting idea that comes from these photographs parallels Gilpin's final life's work, her soaring rediscoveries of Canyon de Chelly, a project she was still at work on when she died. Gilpin notes the reasons she loved aerial photography:

Perhaps it is my love for landscape and geography that makes me want to fly. From the air one can see so clearly the great structure of the earth's surface, the different kinds of mountains, the sweep of contours, the age-old erosion. In the air one becomes detached and the mind goes deep into the past, thinking of time in depth.[36]

The recurring, yet unique, views of Canyon de Chelly in *The Enduring Navaho* demonstrate how an understanding of region allowed Gilpin the larger, cosmic view. It is an image of mystic wholeness she is after. Like another woman photographer of an earlier time (Louise Deshong Woodbridge in 1912—Plate 4) who peered at such an angle into the chasm of Yellowstone River that the viewer is plunged into the harmonious tensions of the river's and canyon's designs, Gilpin finds the Southwest's ultimate spirituality reborn again and again in these bird's-eye views. The artist's eye finds the secret of beauty in the harmonious forms of the landscape and what this signifies about the lives that inhabit it. When compared to Alvin Langburn Coburn's view from the heights of the urban world of the first part of the century, they are a testimony to Gilpin's knowledge of what regional forms mean.

If Gilpin's inspiration from and interpretation of Southwest landscapes allowed for the heroic element, both in pictorial and documentary work, Dorothea Lange's work testifies to a similar view of Anglo women whose lives were dependent on the land. Gilpin's persistence in regional traditions far beyond their fashionableness suggests the preeminence of the subject in her life. Hers is an essentially anti-modern view which ignored art movements and traditions. Her photographs of American Indian women, for example, are foils for the emerging modern American women— young, poised, professional, upwardly mobile; the image one might see during the same time period on the cover of *Glamour* or *Vogue*. Lange, too, celebrated women whose lives were counter to the popularized version of American womankind, and the heroic (if documentary) images that came out of the Farm Security Administration photographs made across the Southwest from 1935 to 1942 appear easily interpretable. After all, the Great Depression was a tragedy in American history analogous to the ravages of the Civil War. But Lange's photographs introduce another theme. "If you see mainly massed human suffering in my photographs and decry the selection of so much suffering," she says, "I have failed

Figure 4
Louise Deshong Woodbridge, "Yellowstone National Park," 1912
Courtesy Amon Carter Museum, Fort Worth, Texas

to show the multiform pattern of which it is a reflection. For the havoc before your eyes is the result of both natural and social forces. These are my times, and they, too, are my theme."[37] The familiar photographs, such as "Tractored Out, Texas," reveal not nature at its worst, but yet another interpretation of the failed American Dream. Abused farmland is a symbol for the failed myth of progress. And "The American Country Woman" touts the anti-modern aspects of women's relationship to the land and the larger culture. Lange would have been likely to have said that she was after an objective vision of truths that cannot be discovered by scientific observation. There is no doubt that Lange understood part of her job in the 1930s, when she worked for the Farm Security Administration with her economist husband, Paul Taylor, to be the recording of a specific historical crisis. There is, however, also no question that her ultimate goal was art, specifics made universal. She shied away from the word "art" because the term is in part evaluative, but in 1939 she fought Roy Stryker, the head of the ISA, for the right to have her pictures hung at the Museum of Modern Art. "A documentary photograph is not a factual photograph per se," she observed. "It is a photograph which carries the full meaning of the episode."

As an artist, her prime subjects were two—the beauty of the world, and the courage it takes to survive in it. Of the first she was an advocate from her earliest days as a portraitist, and she evolved into a loving observer of human stance, of the architecture of the body at work and rest. She was also an exceptional landscapist; though she almost never photographed wilderness, she evidenced an enjoyment of natural light and geographic scale, as part of her pictures, that was no less intense than that of her friend Ansel Adams.

Lange's sensitivity to natural light registered, of course, something beyond loveliness; James Agee referred to the quality as "the cruel radiance of what is," and it forms a part of the context for Lange's other subject, fortitude. "I many times encountered courage," she said; "I have learned to recognize it when I see it." The bravery she was concerned to picture was usually set against the most common ordeal—tiredness, having to land. It is perhaps an especially American subject, endurance being one of the few glories open to many in a country where freedom is more valued than justice.

These pictures suggest ways and reasons Lange succeeds as an artist. Visually, for instance, we note that a majority of her best pictures do not stress the so-called photographic vision, that is, composition relying on abruptly cropped borders with important subjects at the edge, divided in two; instead her finest pictures seem usually to be of whole things (and thus seductively to approximate to normal vision). It is as if Lange's gift was to discover artifacts and people that were already perfectly revelatory, rather than to create them by special framing. The beauty of her subjects seems to come from within them, and we are moved by her readiness to be anonymous before them.

Lange was particularly equipped to capture the "decisive moment," a talent which Beaumont Newhall has attributed to her "questing—one who has that drive for defining in pictures the truth."[38] For Newhall, one of Lange's favorite quotations bespeaks her photographic acumen: "Each traveller should know what he has to see, and what properly belongs to him, on a journey."[39] A measure of Lange's "knowing" came as a result of her trip to the Southwest in 1920 where she first contemplated landscapes: "I worked a lot closer, then, to the subject, than I do now. Everything is shot out of my prints by the head—there is no background, no sense of time and place."[40] Trained as a portrait photographer (having studied with Arnold Genthe and Clarence White), Lange's early treatment of subject is understandable. But after her visit to the Southwest with Maynard Dixon, the painter, who was then her husband, she began treating the interrelationship of the individual and environment. That Lange was open to such discovery is clear in the comment on her philosophy. According to Willard Van Dyke, "For her, making a shot is an adventure that begins with no planned itinerary. She feels that setting out with a preconceived idea of what she wants to photograph actually minimizes her chance for success. Her method is to eradicate from her mind before she starts, all ideas which she might hold regarding the situation—her mind is like an unexposed film."[41]

What Lange found in the Southwest was dignity, strength of character, and triumph over suffering that Gilpin had seen in the Navahos. Unlike her early photographs where she says she "used to try to talk people into having their pictures taken in their old, simple clothes, thinking the images would be timeless and undated," the photographs in *The American Country Woman* are specifically topical. Women are identified in the text according to specific place (Texas Panhandle, for instance), occupation, activities, and possibly history. Examples: "She picks in these broad fields of cotton (seen across the road) and lives in one of these cabins ... Arizona, 1941." "Mary Ann Savage was a faithful Mormon all her life. She was a plural wife. She was a pioneer. She crossed the plains in 1856 with her family when she was six years old. Her mother pushed her little children across plain and desert in a hand-cart. A sister died along the way. 'My mother wrapped her in a blanket and put her to one side.'"[42] The photographs are artifactual and attitudinal. Unlike Gilpin, however, Lange was not depicting an exotic part of American life. Mysterious dances, evocative costumes, and awesome vistas were not the subjects of her photographs. Her manner, therefore, is deceptively simple. Documentary as these photographs are, they are, too, an example of the photographer knowing what to see on the journey. The photograph "Migrant Mother" (1936) is a result of at least five pictures Lange shot before she got the image she wanted. She apparently understood the principle of what Joel Snyder has called the photographer as mediator: she mediated between the *image* and the *imaged* by manipulating photographic elements. Because Lange understood her audience to be desensitized to the reality of landscape and country people in a world primarily non-rural, she had to work on her photographs to get the worked-on look out of them. She explains her purpose in the introduction to *The American Country Woman*:

> These are women of the American soil. They are a hardy stock. They are of the roots of our country. They inhabit our plains, our prairies, our deserts, our mountains, our valleys, and our country towns.
>
> They are not our well-advertised women of beauty and fashion, nor are they a part of the well-advertised American style of living. These women represent a different mode of life. They are *of themselves* a very great American style. They live with courage and purpose, a part of our tradition.[43]

It is significant that Lange's stylistic and thematic concern with these pictures began in 1948, when Nancy Newhall wrote asking her to contribute to a proposed International Exhibition in Paris, the theme of which was "the cry for peace and struggle of women in all countries for democracy." Lange responded: "I tried assembling a group of faces of American women, all kinds, from all walks of life, but couldn't make it hang together."[44] The result was that Lange continued to work on the project through the years, finalizing *The American Country Woman* only months before her death. So integral did she feel the photographs to be to one another that she stipulated: "This collection consists of fifteen personages, and all but two are accompanied by a photograph of the place where she lives. In some cases it is the exact house, in others it is the environment. The photographs are carefully captioned.... The edition, I hope, will be regarded as a unit and not be dismembered."[45] Lange saw the congruity of women and their landscapes as inseparable.

IV. The Luminists and the
Sacrality of the Southwestern Landscape

One of the major stumbling blocks in photographic critics acknowledging a "female sensibility" is the prevalence of art historical notions which analyze photographs' formal qualities and consider "emotional" elements to be inherent in the content. That is, this opinion holds that the formal qualities are what transform raw emotion into "art". However, for women photographers interested in cultural landscape and, hence, social content, such interpretation disallows any social meaning and because there is no social context or shared social similarities acknowledged (only vague biological ones), a female sensibility does not emerge. Modern photography by women indeed has made much strictly art historical interpretation necessary. Jeff Perrone observes:

> Much of the new women's work relies on Surrealist techniques and images. These present the action of the artist, but do not ask for an equally energized audience. Being inner-directed and self-reflexive, it does not refer to anything outside its maker or the institution it is shown in. By offering a mild type of social engagement, Mann and Noggle's selections envision a renewal in women, probing women's humanness. Only by delving into herself can she begin to take on the outside world. The circle closes. From domestic role-playing

to mobile professionalism out in the world, women photographers today use images to closet themselves in a dream house of their own. Identity, personal themes, and preoccupations, and images are expressed in conventional surreal, dreamlike or collage forms, freely associating the work with a time when (men) painters were re-evaluating imagery and finding primordial psychic roots using surreal techniques.[46]

But as Perrone suggests of the work displayed at the *Women of Photography* show, an examination of self—of what makes one human, and uniquely so—is itself a social concern. Therefore, rather than search for a "female sensibility" in women's photography, one is struck by the power of women to create intelligent, abstract and formal art, *rigorously* sensitive.

Women depicting cultural landscapes in the Southwest face additional issues that may confound and confuse their audience. Landscape photography is a loaded "genre" in that most audiences expect the stereotypic purposes of 19th-century romantic landscapes of the West. Even more confusing is that a new group of (primarily) male photographers—the New Topographics—have rejuvenated landscape photography to assess the meaning of the man-made or inhabited landscape. If the artist once stood outside of nature as recorder, viewer, and even re-viewer (in the 19th-century sense), these photographers recognize that by the late 1960s the landscape photographer is the domesticator of the land itself; depiction of nature emanates from visual language wherein form is a referent so that the meaning of the photograph exists in ideographic terms. That is, the landscape comes to represent ideas not objects. They begin within the realm of style in order to move to real subject. We may assume that it is the photograph, then, not the real world, that is the artist's and the viewer's referent. We may hold the real world up to the photograph.

Therefore, the recent study of landscape can best be described as the landscape of the photograph. Photographers attend to the photograph as subject: pictures appear with sprockets from the negatives in the print, for example. Consequently, the role of the maker has changed, as evidenced by this comment by William Gass on the reciprocity between the actual and fictional worlds:

> ... aren't we right to seek in language the imprint of reality? Doesn't it shape the syntax of our sentences? Surely the way we speak about the world is a response to it just as thor-

oughly as the world is a reflection of the way we speak?...
But if we were making a world rather than trying to render
one, wouldn't all our questions be answered? *Kennst du das
Land* where all such tricks are fair? where the very sense of
transcendence which is made possible by ontological projection and equivocation and type-token confusion and reification and hidden contradiction and rhetorical sleight-of-hand,
is appropriate and functional ... where the ancient dream of
the rationalist—that somewhere in language there is a blue-
print or a map of reality (where Eeyore's meadow's marked,
and Piglet's tree, as well as where the Woozle wasn't)—that
dream remains a dream because now language is the land—
in fiction—where every fact has to have the structure of the
sentence which states it, value too, and quality, and apprehension, since there is no out-of-doors in the world where
language is the land.[47]

When photography pushes to this point in order to avoid exhaustion and imitation (and to discover new possibilities for the
medium), a curiosity results. How does one counter the culture's
suspicion of photography as, if not an outright lie, a willful distor-
tion of the world?

Wright Morris has said that a distinct characteristic of modern
fiction is that the "maker" writes not from experience but from fictional worlds:

In the craft of image-making there is much to be said for the
slow-grower. The less culture-shaped child, accumulating
experience before he does art, when stimulated by the images of art will have recourse to his own unique resources.
From Twain through Faulkner this has been a characteristic
American experience. Those favored by a more cultivated
background (like Henry James, or Edith Wharton) are felt to
be less American. This is a narrow but telling distinction. The
mind of James was shaped by the images of culture, rather
than the rawer materials of experience. It is the purpose of
culture to produce such minds, but a democratic culture has
not evolved an appropriate place or use for them. Within the
scope of a century, since Whitman, native raw materials
have lost their rawness, and most writers of fiction have
their beginnings as readers of fiction. It is the written image
that now shapes the writer in his effort to become his own
image-maker.[48]

What a regenerative landscape form might mean in regard to our understanding of the real landscape is recalled in D.H. Lawrence's claim in 1923 in his *Studies in Classic American Literature* that our national literature from its beginning has been characterized by brilliant, isolated evasions, escapes from confronting the "reality" of America. Lawrence means that no American literary artist has successfully confronted the spirit of America because the white man has never been at one with the landscape. America, he asserts, is not a real homeland, only an ideal one, and it will remain so until we learn how to come to terms with "The Spirits of Place." Furthermore, as Wright Morris suggests, the truths of vernacular experience can only be reclaimed by grappling with what Gass called the land as language. "The furnishing of the mind with artifacts and symbols that began with Walt Whitman is increasingly a manner of salvage.... For the American writer, repossession may be an act of re-creation."[49] Contemporary women landscapists, after all, deal with the ordinary, the vernacular, rather than the ideal landscape. Such photographs should go a long way in realigning the experienced landscape—the real homeland—with the ideal or sublime one.

Modern art has lost contact with and a capacity to reflect upon the real world. First came what Ortega y Gasset called dehumanization in which the arts purged themselves of human content or lived reality. This resulted in a variety of formalism. Art ceased to serve as a criticism for life; it turned its back on the world and refused to hold a mirror up to nature. However, if not for a practical reason, ideological or spiritual necessity demanded that art reestablish relations with the world and reclaim for itself those aspects of human experience excised in the name of modernist purity. Some of the various activities loosely referred to as conceptual art provide a case in point. Here, the quest for self-purification led art to divest itself of its very objecthood. Significantly, the only factor lending many such experiences a semblance of materiality was photographic documentation. Often, the photograph not only lent a touch of permanence to an otherwise ephemeral event, but it served to situate the event in the larger context of the world.

Photography, at approximately the same time, began to achieve widespread acceptance as an art in its own right. It's probably not a coincidence that the only other art form to flourish visibly at the same time (late 1960s, early 1970s) was dance. Both photography and dance restore to us what John Crowe Ransom called "the world's body" (precisely the aspect of life which modernism sacrificed). Ransom explained that science had robbed the world of its body by concerning itself only with the abstract principles which underlie experience rather than with the concrete immediacy of experience itself.

We can appreciate this dilemma if we consider Malraux's contention that the modern artist's supreme aim is to subdue all things to his style. Imagination freed totally from the world allows for no objective criterion. In this kind of domination, equilibrium is lost between the inner self and the outer world. To a large extent, we dominate in the 20th century and are rarely dominated by our environment. Nature is on the defensive. As Paul Valery noted of this turn of events: "The modern world is being remade in the image of man's mind."

Photography, as an art form, can bring about "a redemption of physicality," and contemporary women landscape photographers anticipated the current "return to the land" phenomenon of artists, like the New Topographics, who find modernism exhausted. Rather than remaking the world, these women have returned, too, to the essentials of the photographic medium, exercising its power to intercept images rather than, in the case of the paintbrush, reconstruct them. This attitude follows the earliest beliefs about photography—that, according to Henry Fox Talbot, in *The Pencil of Nature*, "the operator himself discovers on examination, perhaps long afterwards, that he has depicted many things he had no notion of at the time." André Gide maintains that creative work of the highest order always contains a dimension which the artist himself is unaware of—what he calls "God's share," the artist's acceptance of the intrusion of the unintended and the unexpected.

Carlotta Corpron, spending her professional life in Denton, Texas, became enamored of the phenomenon of light and the life it brings to forms. Her studies are actually light landscapes. During the 1940s, while teaching art history, design, and photography courses at Texas Women's University, Corpron was also an independent, solitary artist who created a body of abstract work at ironically the same time Laszlo Moholy-Nagy was working with his light studies. Gyorgy Kepes, who met and worked with her during World War II in Denton, notes that Corpron's work, however, goes beyond a mere fascination with form:

She translates these optical events into artistic statements, revealing more than the material substances, more than the surface phenomenon. The reflections from drops of oil that spread as a thin film and produce interference colors similar to the spectral hues of soap bubbles that children and grownups enjoy and admire, and other optical patterns could become metaphors of deeper meanings. In Carlotta Corpron's work they are not merely pleasant patterns, tickling our sensibilities; they have symbolic overtones expressing nature's clarity and order.... Her fundamental aspiration is to bring order into disorder and unity to the manifold, endless variety of visual phenomenon.[50]

Her early photographs of Texas oil storage tanks shot against cloudless skies are experiments in discovering perfect form and shape through light (Plate 5). In "Nature Dancer," Corpron uses her vivid imagination and carefully-placed light to transform the head of Chinese cabbage into a lively dancing creature. "I see things," Corpron says, "I always have. Ever since I was a child I've seen faces and patterns in the clouds." Corpron also experimented with light to reveal the structure of natural forms in her flower studies. In perhaps her most inventive work, Corpron created egg compositions by capturing the images with her camera and then playing with developing the negatives, cropping, enlarging, and overlaying them. "Flowing Light," however, may be her most beautiful picture. Writes Marni Sandweiss:

> The delicate bands of light move effortlessly across the print, gracefully flowing through and around one another in a deep, formless space. The effect is mysterious. The light is still, yet appears to move; it is tangible, yet ephemeral. The plastic onto which the light is reflected is nearly flat, yet the photograph feels as three-dimensional as any of Corpron's photographs of solid forms. In one extraordinary photograph, Corpron has combined all of her concerns for light as it creates design, reveals space, and charts time and motion. In one negative she has succeeded in capturing the very essence of light.[51]

The study of reflected light, therefore, as in the case of Corpron's photographs, operates independently of human will, establishing a mystical bond between the photograph and the world. Even in an apparently documentary photograph, light, the least bodily of substances, helps restore us to the world's body. In the

Figure 5
Carlotta Corpron, "Three Oil Tanks Near Jefferson, Texas"
Courtesy Amon Carter Museum, Fort Worth, Texas

work of Carolyn Vaughan, who has photographed across the Southwest, light forms a bridge between formalist and realist concerns, emphasizing the connection between conception and physicality. In "Desert Camouflage," a dead goat emerges from the light and dark shapes of rocks in the landscape. "Leaf Synchronicity" suggests the real meaning of pattern in nature. Light heightens our perception of textures and timelessness of shifting land masses and rooted trees in "Cottonwood, White Sands, New Mexico." Another New Mexico photographer, Joan Myers, shoots very conventional and seemingly casual shots of the same terrain, which belie its beauty and mystery—traits taken for granted by the contemporary world.

Other current landscape photographers photograph the common or vernacular landscapes which have either suffered from gross stereotyping or are virtually ignored. Liliane De Cock, working as an apprentice to Ansel Adams, deliberately settled on a vision antithetical to Adams' calculated and artistic views of nature. Adams himself claims there is "a magic in seeing and magic in statement, and there is also a magic in the subject; the natural scene, the works of man, and man himself."[52] De Cock photographs without posturing or contriving; her photographs are guileless depictions of barns, windmills, afternoon storms, and other vernacular phenomena. But she uses the full tonal scale of the medium, with emphasis on the somber tones. She prints darkly, as if to make us look again at these landscapes we've come to ignore, and with a luminosity that sustains our view.

Recent work of two other photographers seeks to reinform the viewer about the landscape as a regenerative and religious place. Mary Peck, associated with Gilpin in Santa Fe, works in an almost luminist tradition, emphasizing the idea of sacred place in her New Mexico subjects. A light-imbued fence in "Chaquero, N.M." suggests the life inherent in the most common landscape. In "Mora, N.M.," the light on the grass functions similarly, much in the tradition of Gilpin's platinum and silver printing of depictions of Shiprock, N.M. Diane Hopkins, in the tradition of the photographic pilgrim, has pictured, through emphasis on light and framing, rich details of architectural shrines in Texas and New Mexico. The church in Terlingua, Texas, a religious heart in a vast, desolate country, centered in a ghost town, is comparable to her close-up shot of the graceful angles and adobe texture of Taos church.

The effect of these photographs is to create a discrete space in the photograph analogous to its representation of the world's body. Vernacular and typically religious landscapes both represent an essentially post-modern attitude by women for the need to differentiate space. If the modern world has levelled space, making landscape a utilitarian element for man's development and consumption, these photographs reacquaint the viewer with the meaning of space or resanctify sacred places through photographic means. Historically, the luminist tradition attempted the same effect, as Barbara Novak suggests in *Nature and Culture*. The result is to open the photograph to "God's space" through the creation of discrete space and quietude. Light was the means through which these earlier painters abandoned themselves to the apprehension of Nature: "Only in luminist quietism does the presence of the artist ... disappear. Such paintings, in eliminating any reminders of the artist's intermediary presence, remove him even from his role of interpreter." This quiet tranquility was an attempt to reach a "mystical oneness above time and space."[53]

Linda Connor's treatment of Southwest landscapes provides a final example of contemporary women's landscape photography. Her petroglyph photographs address the current critical impulse in photographic criticism to discourse on linguistic or structural principles which apply to photography. In these photographs, Connor has fixed on the structuralist notion of signs found in American Indian glyphs as they relate to photography's mysterious nature as a linguistically related art form. Jane Livingston writes in *Linda Connor*:

> ... the petroglyph photographs may be seen as reflective images in the extreme, traces of traces, abstract signs referring to other abstract signs. The photograph's usual role as signifier in these works is subtly overturned, because the photo points not to a closed signifier but to another signifier, where signified is obscure, and yet in another sense completely clear.[54]

Connor's photographs thus cancel out the obvious symbolic treatment of nature, the more publicly acknowledged symbols (such as treatments of Rancho de Taos church, for instance) by denotatively neutralizing the modern world's signifiers of signifiers—photography used in this way. Her photographs, like the work of Robert Adams, treat the photograph as a pre-depictive object, a physical bearer of a shadowy trace. This activity, like Talbot's view of photography as the pencil of nature, places the photographer in relationship to landscape in the same way the Native American petroglyphist was: it is simply *making* or *marking*. Taking photographs becomes a ritualistic communion with the land.

If we consider the recent interpretation of men's and women's psychological differences by Carol Gilligan, whose book, *In a Different Voice*, studies contrasting ways of defining and developing morality, then the interrelationships of women photographers and the landscape may come clear. Gilligan argues that men in this culture tend to see the world in terms of their autonomy, whereas women tend to see the world in terms of connectedness. Gilligan suggests that the previously uncatalogued female sensibility offers new guidelines for living in the world, different than the dominant male view. Because of the "nature" of the photograph—its inherent ambiguity and its ability to fix this ambiguity for contemplation— women photographers have utilized this characteristic in varying degrees to depict attitudes about landscape and our relationship to it. In its ability to suspend the transitory state of imagination, photography allows these photographers to address how we imagine the world, our way of seeing it, and our existence in it.

In relating the values of the Southwest region to the larger culture, these photographers manifest the theme of connectedness Gilligan identifies. Women photographers have used socially engaged imagery anchored in the most original formal way to create a new, discrete space for the viewer. They reject such false dichotomies as art/world, expressive/formal, social/personal, mind/body. Furthermore they reveal imagery sometimes described as abstract as, in fact, deriving meaning from bodily awareness of place in the real, contextual world, not in an alienated, timeless, asocial, apolitical, formalist world of bodily and socially repressive art. By re-envisioning the regional landscape, they have come full circle, seeing the world holistically, thus uniting the artificial private and public boundaries that have stereotypically "defined" both men's and women's perception of landscape. In tracing the evolution of women photographers from their early images to the present, we discover that in moving from the private sphere to the public, women as photographic artists have accomplished what Cartier-Bresson writes about in *The Decisive Moment*:

I believe that, through the act of living, the discovery of oneself is made concurrently with the discovery of the world
around us.... A balance must be established between these
two worlds—the one inside us and the one outside us. As
the result of a consistent reciprocal process, both these
worlds come to form a single one.[55]

Women's photography of the Southwest exemplifies formerly uncatalogued female sensibilities, as well as opening possibilities for
new interpretations of our world and new understanding between
the genders.

Notes

1. Quoted in Northrop Frye, *The Educated Imagination* (Bloomington:
Indiana University Press, 1964), p. 23.

2. *The Anatomy of Criticism* (Princeton: Princeton University Press,
1957), p. 48.

3. *Exposure* 6 (Summer 1979), p. 37.

4. See Nathan Lyons, *The Great West: Real/Ideal* (Boulder: Department
of Fine Arts, University of Colorado, 1977), p. 9.

5. Plagens, p. 39.

6. *Artforum*, January 1975, p. 45

7. Anne Tucker, *The Woman's Eye* (New York: Knopf, 1976), p. 3.

8. Margaretta K. Mitchell, *Recollections: Ten Women of Photography*
(New York: The Viking Press, 1983), p. 9.

9. Mitchell, p. 9.

10. Tucker, p. 5.

11. Lyons, p. 10.

12. Amy S. Doherty, "Women in Focus: Early American Women
Photographers," *Picturescope*, 13, no. 4 , 1983.

13. This information was garnered from Richard Rudisell, *Photographs
of the New Mexico Territory, 1854–1912*; David Haynes, unpublished research at the Institute for Texan Cultures, San Antonio, TX; and Jim
Blanch, private study, University of Colorado, Boulder, CO.

14. See Terry Mangan, *Colorado on Glass* (Denver: Sundance, 1975), p.
192.

15. See the Mazzulla Collection, Amon Carter Museum of Art, Fort Worth, TX, for Skolas' work along with the photographs of other western women.

16. In particular, see *The Documentary Photograph as a Work of Art: American Photographs, 1860–1976*, edited by Joel Snyder (Chicago: The David and Alfred Smart Gallery, 1976), pp. 11–32.

17. See the introduction, Lillian Schlissel, *Women's Diaries of the Westward Journey* (New York: Schocken Books, 1982). See also Annette Kolodny, *The Land Before Her: Fantasy and Experience of the American Frontiers, 1630–1860* (Chapel Hill: University of North Carolina Press, 1984), p. 62. *The Land Before Her* chronicles women's creation of an alternative mythology to that Kolodny analyzed in *The Lay of the Land*. The conquest of the virgin land, the rapid deflowering of Eden and the resultant urge to move on to still-virgin territory, the sexually charged process that prompted pioneer men to move again and again, always westward, appears in *The Land Before Her* only briefly, as the backdrop against which pioneer women painstakingly shaped—in letters, diaries, and public writings such as emigrants' guide books and novels—the rich image of the garden of domestic beauty and tranquility. In Kolodny's analysis, the female fantasy in time accepted the wilderness, embracing issues that perplexed and frightened such competent mythologizers as James Fenimore Cooper.

Women perceived also the role of industrialization in the East. As the East changed, so did the fantasy of domestic beauty; in the antebellum decade, Kolodny writes, the prairie home "became the emblematic moral counterweight to impoverished country homesteads or city mansions and tenements alike." In novel after novel, the "scribbling women" cursed by Nathaniel Hawthorne created an "idealized alternative" by which an increasingly urban, industrialized East might be regenerated.

18. See Dawn Lander's "Eve Among the Indians," *The University of Michigan Papers in Women's Studies*, 1976. Lander graphically details the substance of the male view of women on the frontier:

> The Good women on the frontier stay at home, psychologically if not physically. Earlier, I have suggested that the tradition of the American woman's submission to the wilderness experience has the same psychological overtones as the tradition of her submission to sex; her husband has forced her into the wilderness, but she needn't enjoy it, and because she transcends the experience, she is celebrated for her sacrifice. The "wilderness" taboo denies feminine wanderlust and has a dynamic similar to the sexual taboos which deny feminine lust. The home-loving figure is repelled by all forms of wilderness, including sexuality and other peoples. (p. 200)

19. See especially "The sia," *U.S. Bureau of American Ethnology*, 11th Annual Report, 1889–90 (Washington, DC, 1894), pp. 3–157, and "The Zuni Indians," *U.S. Bureau of American Ethnology*, 23rd Annual Report, 1901–1902 (Washington, DC, 1904), pp. 1–634.

20. Quoted in "Some Indian Portraits," *Everybody's Magazine*, Vol. 4 (January 1901), p. 5.

21. Quoted in Jane Cleland O'Mara, "Gertrude Kasebier; The First Professional Woman Photographer, 1852–1934," *The Feminist Art Journal* (May 1975), p. 9

22. Quoted in O'Mara, p. 10.

23. Idem.

24. Karen Brady, "Nothing Was Negative for Photographic Clara," *The Buffalo Evening News*, April 18, 1975, p. 21.

25. Quoted in Marcuse Pfeifer, "Three Women: Carlotta Corpron, Neil Sorr, Clara Sipprell," *Center Quarterly: A Journal of Photography* (April 4, 1983), p. 20.

26. Mary Austin, "Why I Live in Santa Fe," *Golden Book*, October 1932, p. 306.

27. Charles F. Lummis, *Land of Poco Tiempo* (New York: Scribners, 1893), p. 3.

28. Harriet Monroe, "In Texas and New Mexico," *Poetry*, September 1920, p. 328.

29. Robert Coles, *Eskimos, Chicanos, and Indians* (Boston: Little, Brown and Co., 1977), ix.

30. Mary Austin, "Regionalism in American Fiction," *English Journal*, Vol. 21 (February 1932), p. 99.

31. Dudley Wynn, "The Southwestern Regional Straddle," *New Mexico Quarterly*, Vol. 5 (February 1935), p. 7.

32. Wynn, p. 14.

33. Quoted in Paul Horgan, *Erna Fergusson* (New York: Harpers, 1951), p. iv.

34. Quoted in David Vestal, "Laura Gilpin: Photographer of the Southwest, " *Popular Photography*, Vol. 80, 1977, p. 131.

35. Vestal, p. 130.

36. Laura Gilpin, *The Enduring Navaho* (Austin: University of Texas Press, 1968), p. 10.

37. Quoted in "The Questing Photographer: Dorothea Lange," *Dorothea Lange Looks at the American Country Woman* (Fort Worth, TX: Amon Carter Museum of Western Art, 1967), p. 7.

38. Beaumont Newhall, *History of Photography* (New York: Museum of Modern Art, 1978), p. 4 .

39. Newhall, p. 4.

40. Quoted in Newhall, p. 5.

41. Quoted in Newhall, p. 6.

42. Newhall, p. 8.

43. *The American Country Woman*, pp. 35, 36.

44. Quoted in Newhall, p. 9.

45. Quoted in Newhall, p. 10.

46. "Women and Photography: History and Taste," *Artforum* (Summer 1976), p. 33.

47. *The World Within the Word* (Boston: Nonpareil Books, 1979), pp. 316–17.

48. *Earthly Delights, Unearthly Adornments* (New York: Harper and Row, 1978), p. 48.

49. Morris, p. 43.

50. Foreword, *Carlotta Corpron: Designer with Light* (Fort Worth, TX: Amon Carter Museum of Western Art, 1981), pp. 5–6.

51. *Carlotta Corpron: Designer with Light*, p. 9.

52. Introduction, *Liliane De Cock* (New York: Morgan and Morgan, 1973), n.p.

53. Barbara Novak, *Nature and Culture* (New York: Oxford University Press, 1980), p. 102.

54. *Linda Conner* (Washington, DC: The Corcoran Gallery of Art, 1983), n.p.

55. Quoted in Newhall, p. 161.

Pa'i ki'i and Pohaku:
Photographic and Indigenous Values
as Narratives of Change

One of the most recent and fruitful areas of study of indigenous peoples and their cultures has been the critical study of ethnographic photography, largely undertaken by anthropologists or historians of photography and directed toward "documentary" photographs which earlier occupied a minor place within the discipline of anthropology. Recent interest in multiculturalism and cultural revisionism, however, demonstrates that the range of these photo-documents may be most productively understood through interdisciplinary analysis, which attempts to get at interior maps, metaphorical meanings, and perspectives of myth and story. As editor Patricia Johnston notes in a recent issue of *Exposure* magazine: "The strongest studies evince a thorough knowledge of both the culture depicted and the culture depicting. Photographic history must move beyond the analysis of anthropological imagery as simply a generic 'western' view of the generic 'other' to study the specific circumstances of the contact between the photographer and the photographed and the subsequent uses of the images."

Though a spate of current journal articles pursue aspects of Johnston's ideas, they just begin to encompass the basic questions her statement implies and cannot, in their specific focus, address the larger issues at hand. In "Notes Toward a History of Photography in Sierra Leone, West Africa," Vera Viditz-Ward reconstructs the history of native peoples' own photographic traditions. Examining Alaskan groups, Victoria Wyatt shows how native input affected photographic imaging in the early days of photography when the camera's technology required their acquiescence. Another brief study, "Popular Education and Photographs of the

Non-Industrialized World, 1885–1915," suggests how popular forms perpetuated and reinforced well-known stereotypes of race and gender. Implicitly these articles argue that beyond àn "accurate description of faraway people and places or a patronizing or idealizing vision, ethnographic, or documentary, photography must be examined as a venue for study of both cultural practices and conventions of representation.

Considered in light of these two issues, the conjunction of the representation of native identities and the values of the culture holding the camera constitute, for subject, photographer, and viewer, the "photographic encounter," a valuable document of the act of contact. By reestablishing the condition of the photograph, the attitude of the subject, the prevalent photographic conventions, a kind of visual conversation emerges, which may be understood as two-way. Fragments of this conversation have been recorded irregularly by the photographer or assistant, either through notes or interviews, but almost never by the subjects themselves. Even so, in oral cultures reaction and response to photography and photographs exist, adding a contextual understanding to the multiple meanings of the photographic encounter.

One example of this photographic conversation exists in the history of photography in the Hawaiian Islands from 1845 to 1900 in the recorded activities of photographers and their subjects' reactions also recorded in Hawaiian-language newspapers. Remembering that the daguerreotype, the first practical photographic process, was only announced in Paris by Louis Daguerre in 1839, the introduction of photography to Hawaii accompanied the general radical change in the islands introduced by foreigners who, either to spread the Christian gospel or make their fortunes, were influencing the decimation of a population they sought to record. As large numbers of Hawaiians began migrating to the economic centers of Lahian and Honolulu, a competitive economic system was replacing a subsistence and barter economy. By the 1860s the islands were committed to the production of sugar. Laborers were brought to the islands to work on sugar plantations. A strong, centralized government, formed by the Kamehameha dynasty, developed from an absolute monarchy to encompass democratic concepts. The Kingdom survived the bickerings of powerful nations, until it was overthrown by American interests in 1893.

Prior to the introduction of photography, artists' sketches—and later, published engravings—were the only visual record of the islands. Of particular note were the maps and landscapes engraved by Lahainaluna students between 1834 and 1842. Visiting artists often painted portraits of the Hawaiian royalty. For the most part, the common people and the permanent foreign population had no access to personal images until the introduction of photography.

In the islands, the expression pa'i ki'i captured the essence of photography. Pa'i ki'i appeared in the Hawaiian language newspapers in 1856, coinciding with the introduction of photographs on paper in the islands. The term was probably coined by the editor to explain the new phenomenon of photographs on paper. Pa'i meant "to stamp, to print, to impress, to strike with the palm of the hand," and ki'i was the word for picture or petroglyph. Pa'i had been commonly used to describe printing tapa and, later, printing paper in a press. The idea of printing multiple pictures on paper from one negative could easily be equated with the process of printing words (visual symbols for Hawaiians, a people with an oral tradition) on paper. Photographs on paper were only one of many processes promoted by photographers in the late 1850s. Photographs were also available on tin, leather, and glass. Pa'i ki'i became the common expression for photography or photographers, just as paper prints became the standard for photographic images. Initially, pa'i ki'i was synonymous with haole—foreigner or white person. "Na Haole Pa'i Ki'i O Kakou," "Our Haole Photographers," proclaimed a headline in one newspaper. Many photographers came to the islands from California, where not only was competition keen but the decimation of fires in San Francisco in the 1850s, had encouraged them to look for new markets. A logical step and a new frontier, the islands were at least a stopover on the way to Asia, Australia, and other Pacific countries.

As might be expected, Hawaii produced few early native Hawaiian photographers. The first was apparently John Meek, Jr., who was taught by a haole photographer, Charles Burgess. With his brother-in-law, Horace Crabbe, Meek bought out Burgess in 1867. They advertised, claiming their Hawaiian ancestry: "We ask that you come down to our studies since we are local kids from Hawaii." Because of severe economic problems brought about by the drop in sugar prices in the next two years, they had to sell out;

nevertheless, the existence at one time of their "several hundred choice negatives" raises important considerations about the role of photography in cultural dialogue.

Most recent critical study of historic cultural representation of this sort, whether categorized as ethnographic, documentary, or popular—for example, studio or tourist photography—has assumed a cultural imperialism. Keith McElroy argues that "of all professional and amateur photographic imagery, geographic and ethnographic photography, which has yet to be systematically treated by historians of photography, comes closest to revealing the essence of the era of international imperialism (1885–1915)." Unlike earlier periods of colonialism, however, this period saw the advent of new practical systems of photomechanical reproduction which permitted the public to share a sense of participation in imperialist activities through an explosion of profusely illustrated popular publications. Therefore, the information patterns invented at the turn of the century remain part of the perceptions held in common by both industrialized and non-industrialized peoples. Our inadequate understanding and lack of theoretical tools for dealing with these images, and the secondary manipulations which used them to shape our shared vision, is a continuing threat to understanding in a world community locked in the consequence of the imperialist competition. Though McElroy uses the term imperialist to denote a late 19th- and 20th-century economic and political system used by the industrialized nations to exploit the peoples and resources of non-industrialized areas of the colonial world, his definition may be expanded to how photographs of the non-industrialized world were manipulated by interests in the industrialized nations to produce a vision reduced to terms of race (labor) and commodities. As more recent arguments by Hawaiians and other Native American activists address the long-term consequences of imperialist imagery, we have come to understand that commodified images of paradisal peoples and places in the 20th century continues the colonial and imperialistic mindset.

Possibly the most provocative point of McElroy's and other critics' analyses is the pervasiveness of this imagery in the perceptions of both the outsider and the insider. Even as pa'i ki'i evolved linguistically from an assumption of the photograph metaphorically connected to the pictograph, so the power of this connection forever joins the subject's identity and the conventions and philosophy of representation. It is no wonder that throughout the history of photography, its purveyors have characterized its meaning as "mirror with a memory," "windows and mirrors," "the pencil of nature." And it is no wonder that one of the lasting effects of colonization felt by native peoples in general is the effect these images rendered largely by foreigners still have on native identities.

An equally significant consideration of the effect of photography on self-image is the debate about representation, which has been addressed eloquently by Simone de Beauvoir over fifty years ago. Beauvoir recognized the connection of women's subordinate status to the cultural dialogue between the "one" and the "other"—the dominating culture and the minority. In terms which describe both the stereotyping and the coopting of female and ethnic identities, de Beauvoir assessed feminine self-image within a patriarchy:

> ... As variable, contingent, and mutable as the concepts of femininity and masculinity may be—a function of discourses and not of biology—the former is inevitably positioned as Other, the latter invariably as the One. Thus, whether feminine Otherness is celebrated and valorized, or perceived as a structure of oppression and subjugation, its prevalence as an apparently universal social and cultural given has not been disputed.

When considering the prevailing passive position women have occupied historically as subjects of imaging—both in the popular and fine arts—the question of representation becomes particularly interesting when women as "other," minority, or as subordinates negotiate the cultural prescriptions of themselves as authors. Feminist criticism addressing the construction of identity recently has turned from an analysis of differences to an undercutting of the premise of a unified identity. Rather than argue the dissimilarities of women's radical alienation from the dominating culture, as exemplified in language and other symbolic systems such as the visual arts, critics have redirected their inquiry into the process, the act of articulation. They link through analysis the production of identity and meaning to subjectivity. Therefore, when women native artists, such as photographers, represent themselves and their culture, the various critiques of the sign and representation imply at least an implicit consideration: how may the other be the one? How may the woman native artist reclaim identity without acknowledging the power of stereotypic material by working with it? And beyond these considerations, how does the native woman depict uniquely, not as a spokeswoman for "culture" or for a unified cultural identity?

Because the answer to this question is bound up, in part, in the ambiguous nature of the photograph, the production of revisionist work by native photographers often necessarily embraces the art/artifactual qualities of photography to reconstruct identity and meaning. One example of a contemporary Hawaiian photographer's efforts to join photojournalism, oral storytelling, and ancient wisdom to dispel stereotypes of "the other" is the work on Hawaiian sacred stone formations by Lahe'ena'e Gay. Called Pohaku, these stones and their pre-contact sites are sacred spaces of living history, indeed for Hawaiians, living beings, and thus a part of family genealogies. Hawaiian scholar John Dominis Holt writes: "In these rocks you find a kind of energy. It can be imbued with certain powers from an aumakua, an ancestral god.... When certain people die, their spirits go into a rock. This is the remnant we have of the old culture. Whatever is left should be protected."

During the past seven years, Gay has photographed and catalogued 2,400 pre-contact Hawaiian stone sites, including secret burial caves, temples, fishing shrines, and stone deities. One reason for her mission is that these sites are being lost at an alarming rate: as many as 30 sites a year are looted, mangled, or destroyed by development. One estimate indicates that 85 percent of Hawaii's cultural materials have already been lost. There is a market for Pacific art both because of the ease with which looters can expedite the Hawaiian finds and the vogue of the art because it is so rare. A wooden or stone image may go for half a million dollars today.

Claiming access and information from the kupuna, the elders who know the history of the stones and their locations, Gay traces her own genealogy and dreams to the stones as she narrates her photographs at the museum exhibition. Yet Gay believes, as do the Hawaiians about language, that truth comes not from the mouth but from the heart. As a guardian of the stones, she believes the stones will talk to your heart, and she relates one such experience upon finding a once-dreamed-of stone in a cave on the Big Island five years ago. The Pohaku may also be the foundations of sacred sites, such as heiau or temples. As the stones of these temples are considered to be alive, they are set in the place of honor in

Lahe'ena'e Gay: "Pohaku: Through Hawaiian Eyes"
from the exhibition at the Bishop Museum, April 24, 1992—
September 20, 1992. Permission by the author.

Hawaiian homes, sometimes given offerings and food. More than to photograph, then, Gay says the purpose of her work is to communicate the foundation and core of the stones themselves. After hundreds of years of pule (prayers), dreams, and aspirations having been spoken to the stones, the Pohaku takes on a life, a soul of its own. The elders say that if one places his hand on a sacred site, one can feel a heartbeat; the movement of ethereal blood as it moves through the veins of each water-worn pebble or lava-formed stone. Gay concludes: "Knowing that these sites are alive, that they have a soul, a spirit, is a first step. Our Kupuna say Pohaku represents our grandparents, being the dignity and wisdom of the past. They are also our Keiki (children) who are the faith and hope, a guiding light through the darkness of an uncertain future. To continue to scar, rob, or destroy our Pohaku is to bring our existence close to extinction."

Beyond the philosophical and spiritual arena of Gay's work is her unique performance mode. Representation for Gay occurs not only in the photographic and interpretive (textual) work—in photo, titles, and interviews or catalogue, textual material—but in her own style as storyteller and interpreter. At the opening of her show at the Bishop Museum, she was in attendance several times giving "talks" in the three galleries of photographs. Dressed in a suede explorer's hat, chic, colorful pants and top, adorned in Hawaiian shells and jewelry, she cajoled, harangued, and chanted to a compliant, following audience about Hawaiian culture as she led the group from photograph to photograph. The performance was a curious combination of western style and academic argument to strong matriarchal teachings. Claiming relation to the alilli (high) class of Hawaiian ancestors, she further promoted herself as photographer and cultural interpreter by claiming special permission to photograph sites and talk with kapuna elders.

Response within the Hawaiian community was very mixed. Mirroring the positions of the varying sovereignty groups, criticism ranged from total rejection of Gay's credibility to silence on the matter. The local haole press, museum staff, and audiences were enthusiastic, however. For many non-Hawaiians, seeing the sites in photographs, learning some of the legendary stories about the religious places and stones was a needed beginning in bridging cultural ignorance. Nevertheless, the specter of Gay as a bogus interloper arose during the show quite possibly because she had lived for a long period on the mainland and was professionally trained. Therefore, her claims to exclusivity of knowledge about the sites rang false to some local Hawaiians.

Whether prophet or fabulist, Gay's presentation as representation raises crucial questions about the issue of self-image and image-making for native women. As both woman and minority, her style, no matter how individual or unique, was connected to larger cultural issues—ironically, ones she claimed to seriously and conscientiously address. In the case of Gay, she was questioned most severely by native Hawaiians who were offended, not by the artistic work itself, but by her oral interpretation. The example of this woman artist exemplifies the difficulty of negotiating the margins of women as subjects and authors. Expectations of her as an "Hawaiian" woman posed a set-up both in terms of "the other" and "the one." Probably Gay's style was an effort to bridge the conventional attitudes of the dominant and subordinate. In fact, her authority as an Hawaiian woman photographer claimed dominance in her work and verbal articulation about it. She therefore reversed the hierarchy of values between eastern and western and indigenous, yet suffered criticism from the people she claimed not only to represent but to be ethnically descended from.

Part of Gay's difficulty in negotiating the margins of expectation rests on the history of the commercialization of indigenous imagery. Probably one distasteful element for local critics was her advertisements for herself. In the midst of communal appeal, she announced the sale of photographic prints of the sites she had argued to be so private and special. Photographic replication, commercial gain both appeared to argue in opposition to Gay's cultural advocacy. Though it can be argued that she intended the opposite—to make available new powerfully accurate images of a tourized and idealized "haole" Hawaii—some critics felt the sting of financial gain in her personal and artistic display.

In her "Paradise Recycled: Photographs in Samoa in Changing Contexts," Allison Devine Nordstrom posits a model of the commercialization of an image. She shows how commercial photographs, originally made for private use, were eventually used in travel and so-called scientific articles, which often inaccurately identified and represented the subjects for the periodical's larger intent. The example of this cache of photographs, originally made in 1891 in Apia where Samoans sat for family portraits, wedding

pictures, and presented photographs of themselves to esteemed
visitors, were therefore translated to other contexts in cultures
where they were reduced to generic signifiers of the exotic and the
other. Appropriations of this sort have constituted, according to
Bernard Smith, not only a preconceived idea of Pacific peoples and
places connected to earlier depiction by European tourists,
painters, and travellers' tales, but ultimately a blending of the
usually distinct stereotypes of the noble/ignoble savage. Users of
early Pacific photographs showed the ability to hold both ideas
simultaneously, or alternately. The same image could be understood either way the circumstances required.

One example of the "use" of people and places is the appropriation of an untitled photograph by Thomas Andres of a Samoan
woman which was later engraved and used to accompany an article, "The Lotus Land of the Pacific," in *Harper's New Monthly Magazine*. In this new context, the photograph was retitled "The Mer-
riest, Sauciest Little Maid," and visually reinforced the roman-
tic/exotic/erotic theme of the article. Likewise, the nineteenth-century landscape images of the tropics followed generic formulas
and functioned interchangeably. Like today's conventions for picture postcards and illustrated tourist brochures, a few palm trees
and a beach were sufficient markers of paradise to authenticate it
and confirm expectations. Thus, a portrait of a bare-breasted girl or
a tattooed man, for example, even if taken at the request of the sit-
ter for private use, can serve, once it finds its way into the marketplace, as pornography, a tourist novelty, a documentation of
"racial types," or an anatomical record. The same photograph can
be used as proof of a visit, proof of a political point, a paean to the
passing glories of a vanished race, a justification for economic exploitation, or an affirmation that a particular person or event not
only existed but was of sufficient importance to merit a photograph. Photographs are used in books and magazines both for the
selective information they contain, and to decorate the text. As certain images and types of images are used repeatedly, they become
markers, the primary purpose of which is to signify the place in a
quick and efficient shorthand that requires little real seeing. Photographs that appear to contradict the generally accepted ideas of a
place are dismissed as inaccurate, anomalous, or unimportant. As
is the case with similar images from other places dominated by the
imperialist nations of the West, early photographs of Samoa were

used in ways that reflect the attitudes held by the colonizers towards their subject people.

Because of the pervasiveness of this shorthand of signifying and seeing Hawaiian people and places, it would be easy to completely dismiss the value of contemporary ethnic photographic work, let alone the sacrality of their subjects. However, such a body of photography seeks to engage both native and non-native viewers in the photographic encounter, utilizing systems of expressed meanings each may read and understand. Historian Greg Denings, whose book on the Marquesas islanders and their decimation entitled *Islands and Beaches*, notes:

> Culture is consciousness externalized. The actions, roles, the expressed relationships, the artefacts, the regularized behaviour that constitute culture are all vehicles of meanings that are both expressed and read. To know a culture is to know the system of expressed meanings. To know cultures in contact is to know the misreadings of meanings, the transformation of meanings, the recognition of meanings.

In his metaphor of islands and beaches, Denings further argues that because this description is a model for the ways in which human beings construct their worlds and the boundaries between them, encounter and survival becomes a process of renegotiating boundaries when a culture loses its metaphors, its guides to understanding.

The role of the ethnic response in contemporary photography in Hawaii is not only to reclaim boundaries for cultural preservation but to transform the colonizer/outsider as well. Such photographers as Shuzo Uemoto, Renee Iijima, Gaye Chan, John Morita, Kimo Cashman, Anne Landgraf, Mark Hamasaki, Karen Kosasa, and Stan Tomita transpose the stereotypic, romantic, racist views of people and place as they question the cycles of appropriation which continue to destroy authentic experience and meaning.

More, women as subjects and authors, as in the case of photographer Gay, critic Allison Devine Nordstrom, and the "anonymous" Samoan woman, continue to exemplify these negotiated boundaries of gender and ethnicity. In one of the stories of the coming of Captain Cook to Hawaii, reminiscent of the pattern of the Marquesas islanders' fate, Marshall Sahlins says of the workings of the Hawaiian worldview: "Hawaiian history repeats itself, since only the second time is something of an event. The first time it is a myth." In the storied anticipation of a god on the fatal arrival of Captain Cook, Hawaiians ironically prepared themselves for what became their partial undoing. His "second coming" was sanctioned as a truth. For Hawaiian and ethnic photographers today, photographic retelling—as second seeing—as cultural encounter may ultimately be the most compelling and transforming for the ethnic or native photographer whose own identity may be reclaimed.

In the case of even a controversial Gay, retelling through photographing is a secondary event, constituting a truth—"an event" or reality. Even if authenticity continues to be disputed in a world always conscious of referentialness, reclaiming imagery remains an important act against cultural extinction.

LITERATURE
Poetry and Place

An Interview with Maxine Kumin

Maxine Kumin was born in Philadelphia and received her B.A. and M.A. degrees from Radcliffe·College. She has lectured in English and American poetry at Princeton, Brandeis, Columbia, Tufts, and has served as a faculty member at the Bread Loaf Writers' Conference in Vermont.

Author of a number of books of poems, four novels, children's books, collected essays, she was awarded the Pulitzer Prize in 1973 for Up Country: Poems of New England. *For many years a resident of Newton Highlands, Massachusetts, a suburb of Boston, she now resides with her husband year-round on their farm in New Hampshire.*

SA: A lot of people refer to you as an optimistic or positive poet. Do you see yourself in that role?

MK: No, I don't think I am an optimistic writer. I think that pulling back and retreating to live on the farm and attempting to live at least partially in a self-contained or self-sufficient world reflects my dismay about the world. I choose not to live so much in it. I don't have a very happy view of human nature. You don't have to look very far to see the kind of destruction we are capable of. And I think that my poetry reflects that.

SA: Do you think, then, that people confuse the natural world and those who write about it—writers such as yourself, Frost, Thoreau, for example—with optimism?

MK: I think so, yes. People see pastoral poetry as gently bucolic; it's serene. Really, the natural world is full of the same kind

of cruelties as the human world, except that it's more acceptable because it is part of the ecosystem.

SA: And easier to retreat to? One senses you feel caught sometimes between the two worlds—the natural and the human.
I'm thinking of that line from your poem "Amanda's Eyes"
where you say to the mare, "take away all that is human."

MK: Yes. That's a very specific poem about a specific incident.
And the person in the poem was Anne [Sexton]. But in a
moment of despair, or bereavement, or anger, to get back to
that world of just the daily rounds of looking after the beasts
is a great salvation. I was very criticized by one critic for that
line, "take away all that is human." But I guess, if you can't
relate to animals, you can't enter into that feeling.

SA: I marvel at your ability to communicate that sort of salvation—the daily tending to the animals—along with certain
hard truths about them and us. In the poem, "Excrement,"
for instance, you are in one sense illustrating a truth and, in
another, you are simply moving manure from one pile to
another.

MK: Now that's an "up" poem, an inspirational poem. That's
about as inspirational as I can get.

SA: And yet, I associate that poem with an earlier one, "Heaven
as Anus."

MK: I seem to be turning into some kind of coprophile.

SA: Like Swift; an excremental vision. Really I was thinking of
your humor. Whether your poems are predominantly
"dark," as in "Heaven as Anus," more upbeat, as "Excrement" is, they derive a certain force from the humor.

MK: Well, I like to combine grotesqueness and humor. I think
they go together. They are very subtle and unexpected, and
they keep colliding. That's the saving thing. To be able at
least to smile, if not laugh. It's a way of putting up with the

world. A way of enduring. Certainly not controlling it, but a way of saving yourself.

SA: Ironically, we keep talking about salvation, and the title of this most recent book of poems is *The Retrieval System*. Many of these poems, like earlier ones, illustrate your interest in the generations.

MK: Very much so. I wish I had more material to work with. There's so little that's left that's come down to me. I think I've just about exhausted it.

SA: That same critic who criticized your line in "Amanda's Eyes" might be surprised to read this line from the title poem of your collection: "Fact: it is people who fade, it is animals that retrieve them."

MK: Yes, the lives of animals we love remind us of others. Not necessarily just the faces, as in that poem, but the actions, the personalities, so that they almost seem to be lost people reborn.

SA: It would be nice if it were true, wouldn't it?

MK: Well, yes. I think if I could come back in the next life, I would come back as a ...

SA: A what?

MK: Probably a Morgan horse. Something very sensible and strong. Certainly not a flighty thoroughbred.

SA: I've always wondered what precisely it is about horses that so attracts you. They're so primary to your work.

MK: Yes, I am trying very hard not to write any more poems about horses. And there are a great many water poems. In fact, when my first book was reviewed the critic said, "Maxine Kumin seems to be amphibious." But about the horses—I ask myself that, but then I bounce away from it, maybe because I don't really want to know. But you need only go through the pages of a popular magazine, say this week's *New Yorker*, and count how many horses appear in line drawings, cartoons, articles, to see how they pervade our cultural patterns. I don't know particularly what the attraction is: I suppose part of it is mastery. You know, schooling a young horse, or reschooling a horse that has been abused in some way and regaining that animal's trust. I think it's fascinating. Now I don't know why it is fascinating. Partly, I guess it is because 1 don't have any grandchildren, and this is an outlet for my affection and energy.

SA: Did you grow up around horses?

MK: No, I didn't. I was a city child. We were the kind of family that *had* dogs, which is to say that they came and went in various sad ways. As a child, animals were always following me home. The affection for horses began because we lived in Germantown outside of Philadelphia. It was a safe city in those days, and nobody thought much about what kids did. By the time you were eight, you had wheels and you could go places on your two-wheeler, and we were always winding up in the park watching people ride the horses. I agitated to take riding lessons at the local stables. In those days, they had no arena; they didn't teach you anything. You went alongside the guy who took you out on the lead line six or seven times, then he undid it, and you were on your own. But I used to ride, and I used to hang out there, muck out, and help with the evening feed, and get home and catch hell for it, and all that sort of thing.

That's where it started. It was just an obsession that never faded. When our Number Two daughter was about ten, she went to stay with an old college chum of mine out in the country. They had horses, and they were very serious about horses. She learned to ride, and then, of course, we all were hooked. We went out to buy one pony, and we ended up— oh, it's a long story. We ended up with two ponies because the two were only being sold as a pair. Eventually, she went to college, sold her ponies, and left behind a mother just wild about horses.

SA: Was it your love of horses that took you to the farm?

MK: No, I don't know where that comes from. It was just always there dormant. We lived in a suburb of Boston when our kids were in public school and then we bought derelict property in New Hampshire and used it as a summer place and then, pretty soon what was happening was I was going up in May. And then I was staying later to harvest, and our last young one left the fold, and there really seemed no reason for us to continue that city rat-race. My husband finally took the plunge, and he quit his job, and we moved up there and decided we could freelance. And that's what we've been doing ever since.

SA: How long?

MK: We've been there year-round for four years.

SA: Has this affected your work in any way?

MK: Well, I suppose like the horses and the love of swimming, poetry is a direct outgrowth of this consuming interest. For instance, I have gotten terribly interested in vegetables, having started a vegetable garden tentatively many years ago. I never knew anything, and now every year I love trying to grow things I haven't grown before. For example, bok choy, which is something like a swiss chard with a long, sweet, celery-like stalk. You can substitute it for celery in all sorts of things. Last year I grew an old-fashioned type of black bean. I get all these seed catalogs, and it's a real fix for me to look at them. And vegetables take on more and more kinds of meaning for me. I think I have a lot more vegetable poems coming. It really is a miracle. I haven't gotten over my total fascination. It continues to surprise and delight me.

The thing about modern language is we've gotten away from our origins. We really are not aware of what comes out of the soil. Everybody with two inches of earth ought to grow something. My husband is more of a realist and keeps explaining to me that we will not solve our distribution problems by encouraging people to have vegetable gardens. But it is much more energy efficient, for instance, to grow potatoes in your backyard. It's so easy to grow potatoes hardly anyone does it. You don't even need to turn the soil over. You just lay down old mulch hay, spoiled hay, and you put the cut eyes down on the mulch and dust the whole area with sulphur, cover it over with mulch hay and go away. And you don't have to touch it until it's time to harvest.

SA: How do you coordinate your work at the farm with your writing each day?

MK: During the growing season there is no point in my trying to write because the growing season and the competitive trail riding season take our time. The riding season picks up in May and runs until October. There is slack time after we get the garden in. Then from October to May is a tight writing schedule. I do chores and then go to my desk. Particularly in winter it's easy to do that because it doesn't warm up to entice you out-of-doors until about 1:00. In winter either we ride or we cross-country ski at about 1:00 or 2:00.

SA: So you balance the physical requirements of running the farm with your writing?

MK: I find I can't write effectively more than a few hours. I think it is better not to force it past that period. And I am a slow, painful, retarded kind of writer. If I get a dozen finished poems a year, that's a very fine year. Once in a while, I get a "given" poem—one that goes right down my arm, through my fingertips, and onto the paper. Once I got one at Bread Loaf and wrote it on an envelope while sitting there listening to a fellow poet read. I wrote it right out. I think I might have changed a line or two. It's my New England puritan belief— you know, salvation through grace and all that—that if you work and suffer enough that you will, every once in a while, get a "given" poem.

SA: Speaking of "given" poems, your life and writing hinges so on the physical world, yet many of your poems refer to or come from dreams, don't they?

MK: Yes, I dream a great deal about traveling because that's one of my anxieties. You know, the dream in which I miss my bags or my connections or I'm running to catch a plane or something. But the other half of my dreams are concerned with physical activities, like riding horseback or skiing. Then there's the matter of a poem like "My Father's Neckties." That was one of those curious instances when a dream surfaced remembered almost totally in the morning and it traveled around in my head all day nagging at me to discover its importance. I didn't understand the dream until I wrote the poem. When I wrote the end of the poem, I knew what the dream was saying. Sometimes, I feel we find what we are thinking—oftentimes as an act of salvation.

SA: There's that word again. Salvation. So many of your poems strike me as "religious" in some broad definition of the word. In *The Retrieval System*, for instance, many of the poems are about the soul.

MK: Yes, many of the poems suggest I am looking for the soul as if it were some organ in the body. It hasn't come under the scalpel yet, but it's in there somewhere. Behind the pituitary gland or something. All these generations of sloppy surgeons haven't found it yet. As I go through middle age, I think I am increasingly interested in thoughts of our own mortality. And playing around with this idea of the soul. I'm not a believer. But the soul is like a little vestige, and I'm trying to find it.

SA: I remember when I heard you read an early draft of "Body and Soul," you had a marvelous reference in there—the "quarter pound soul"—which you later altered in the finished poem. How do you make such decisions?

MK: Well, you might remember I felt that, unfortunately, the reference might suggest a popular hamburger advertisement. I did love the idea. I got it from an article about a doctor who weighed his patients after death and found them a quarter pound lighter and thus deduced that the escaping soul constituted the loss of weight. I try to have a "Pal of the Desk"— some fellow writer critique my work. Of course, Anne used to do that. She had a way of fingering a bad, spongy poem. I still trade off things with Bill Meredith, though he is so busy, I have shown things to my friend Carole Oles. I wish I had more people. Don Hall and I did trade off a few times last year. He is a neighbor of mine.

SA: What about forms? Are they a "salvation," a way of working through problem areas?

MK: I have my own students work through all the basic forms so that they then can reject them. And I feel in my own work that I use forms and abandon them, then they resurface. For instance, in *The Privilege* I wrote a whole cycle of sonnets. Then I went on to something else.

SA: You mentioned students and traveling. Aren't you doing a lot of workshops and teaching now? Does this contribute to your own writing?

MK: For one thing, let's look at the cold facts. It's a living. To do writers' conferences, give readings, etc. And that's become important. It also provides a balance for me because I can go for weeks at a time without any of that social intercourse which we all need. And I like getting out into groups And I am particularly enjoying working with more women. The older I get, the more important those relationships with women become. It fascinates me to see what's happening. When Anne and I were struggling to become housewife poets and a male editor said "I really wish I could print that but I printed a woman last month," we were so much a part of our culture that it didn't occur to us we were being had. And I look now and I see the wonderful grit that young women have. It's beautiful and I'm glad I am observing it.

SA: Do you think then, that there's been a blurring of that distinction "woman" poet?

MK: I think we're getting there. We have a long way to go.

SA: It seems to me you accomplish both—write poems perhaps only a woman would write and be interested in reading, yet write about things like horses, the farm, etc., for a wide audience. You survey a wide world.

MK: Yes, thematically there are the so-called "womanly" poems. But I do try to reach a wide audience. Most certainly. As for the experience of being a "woman" writer, I can relate a little story that I am sure is a common experience for women writers. I was writing in a corner of the bedroom, my kids were about seven or eight before they understood that the rest of the world didn't have afternoon rest periods. On this particular day, my middle child was very cross with me. I don't know what I had done. We were all in our rooms having our "rest" period. I was working on my poems. Under the door came an envelope. Inside there was a note written in an obviously disguised foreign hand which read: "Dear Mrs. Kumin: I think your stories are terrible, your poems are worse. I hope they never sell. Signed: A Well-Wisher."

SA: Your family figures largely in your work. But I recall only one poem about your son.

MK: I don't know why he hasn't inspired any other poems except "For Daniel: On the Highways of Your Mind." I am very close to him in a way, but it doesn't approach the closeness of a mother and daughter.

He occasionally visits us at the farm. And we still have our intense Scrabble games to the death. That's a family thing. Christmas Dan gave us a deluxe Scrabble set. He does view his mother as eccentric and does tease me a great deal. He watched my evening routine one day with the horses, getting them hayed and watered. The cat came down and the dog, as they always do, to monitor my proceedings. The last thing I did was take a can of sunflower seeds out to the birds so that the small birds could get them first the next morning before the jays. After observing all this, he said to me, "Mom, I got a great idea for you. It will short-cut this whole proceeding." I thought he was serious. "Why don't you just feed the birds to the cat and that will be two less things to feed," he said. I think he views with a certain amused condescension his aging parents. We are called by the children "those two eccentrics" quite frequently.

SA: What about your husband? Do you try out your poetry on him?

MK: Never. We made a pact years ago that I never would have to put a comma in or read any of his technical papers. And I would never try out my work on him, and it works out very well. We are entirely compatible working with our animals, skiing, doing projects around the place. I mean I will lend him some typing paper, and we do trade stamps back and forth.

SA: You say you don't know where you are going now with your poems except, perhaps, to the vegetable patch?

MK: Well, I have exhausted a great many of my former themes. I read Nancy Friday's book *My Mother Myself*, and I was going to do a group of poems called the Nancy Friday poems— "The Female Phallus," "The Lactating Father," etc. She keeps raising, in an ironic way, all these possibilities. And it's sort of a fascinating thing. So I have been playing with that.

But *The Retrieval System* strikes me as so final. I don't see where I can go after *The Retrieval System*. I just have to wait patiently. I have to do as Rilke counsels: "await with patience the birth hour of a new clarity."

Red Earth:
The Poetry of Alice Corbin Henderson

> After the roar, after the fierce modern music
> Of rivets and hammers and trams,
> After the shout of the giant,
> Youthful and brawling and strong
> Building the cities of men,
> Here is the desert of silence,
> Blinking and blind in the sun—
> The old, old woman who mumbles her beads
> And crumbles to stone.
>
> *Red Earth*, 1920

So wrote Alice Corbin Henderson as she opened her third book of poems, far from the "hog-butcher" of the world, that literary landscape of Chicago where she had made her early reputation as critic, scholar, and poet. Admirer of the "barbaric yawp" of Whitman, advocate of the *vers libre* of Pound, Sandburg, and Frost, she found her own new voice in another American Place—Santa Fe, New Mexico—where she fostered a literary community as the new poetry matched the experience of a neo-primitive setting. At first glance, little of Alice Corbin's childhood background would seem particularly to ready her for the extremes of the southwestern environment—the sun, silence, and adobe later rhapsodized by fellow New Mexican Charles Lummis. Born in St. Louis, Missouri, on April 16, 1881, she was educated in schools in Illinois, Missouri, and Virginia where standard training meant reading American poets Longfellow, Whittier, Lowell, and English poets Wordsworth, Tennyson, and Browning. The popular verse of her day stressed the melancholy moods of nature, homespun sentiment, and the poet's subjective reactions. Not surprisingly, her first book of po-

115

ems, *Linnet Songs*, published in a limited edition of fifty books in
1898 by Wind-Tryst Press when she was a junior in high school,
echoed the popular and traditional poets she had read.

Yet a hint of Henderson's skill and philosophical bent distin-
guishes some of this youthful verse, which was done with the encouragement of her English teacher, Harriet C. Brainard, later the
wife of William Vaughn Moody and an active member of the arts
community in Chicago. In the poem "Death," Henderson asks to
be buried not beneath the romantic bower of a weeping willow
tree, but "upon the boundless prairie ... beneath the tangled
grasses ... And where the stars of heaven's moorlit sea/That cold,
indifferent rays shall over me shed,/ When I am dead."[1] Along
with religious and family subjects, a poem entitled "Milton," and
one addressing solitude, Henderson showed an early awareness of
the lullaby, the Negro song, and the ballad as fertile sources for
poetry.

No doubt the death of her mother of tuberculosis in 1884 and
her consequent moves among family members also influenced the
attitudes of the young poet. Having entered the University of
Chicago in the fall of 1899, Henderson, because of chest inflamma-
tion, later went south to Sophie Newcomb College in New Orleans
in the winter of 1902. Exposure to new customs and to the rich
black folk traditions in the South must have impressed the Midwest girl, as did the valuable experience at the New Orleans *Times-
Picayune* where she worked as a reviewer and savored firsthand
the vibrant newspaper world that stood in such a contrast to a
young woman's standard education. Back in Chicago, where she
wrote reviews for the *Evening Post* and the *Chicago Tribune*, she met
William Penhallow Henderson, an art instructor from Boston who
had traveled widely in Europe. Married on October 14, 1905, the
couple found themselves in the midst of a literary and artistic revival in Chicago.

The two collaborated on Henderson's next two books, one a
book of plays for children written during her pregnancy before
their daughter Alice's birth on January 27, 1907. Her husband supplied the woodblock illustrations for that text, *Adam's Dream, and
Two Other Miracle Plays for Children,* and color lithographs for the
next, a translation of *Anderson's Best Fairy Tales.* The royalties from
this book enabled the Hendersons to travel to Europe in 1910—yet
another experience that influenced both their work. When they re-

turned in 1911 after touring Italy, France, Spain, and Holland, Alice had a second book of poems and William, a collection of European sketches to enliven his exhibits and lectures. *Spinning Woman of the Sky* appeared in December 1912. The collection of thirty-three poems reflected Henderson's classical interests, the use of universal symbols such as the earth, sky, sea, moon, and stars, and symbols to signal moods, as well as religious and contemporary themes. Still derivative, the collection nevertheless demonstrated some of Henderson's breadth. Four of these poems appeared the same month in the new magazine, *Poetry*, aligning her with the "new poetry"—work which reflected her painterly sensitivity to light and color. Named associate editor of the magazine, a position she occupied until 1922 alongside editor Harriet Monroe, Henderson matured as a poet as a result of her work as an editor and critic. Writing on subjects as diverse as Japanese poetry, aboriginal verse, "lazy criticism," cowboy poets, English critics, and science and art, Henderson was abreast of the new poetry movement in America, its antecedents, its myriad expressions.

Her advocacy of the poetry of Carl Sandburg led to his recognition and publication and a lifelong friendship. Monroe credits her with discovering Edgar Lee Masters. Ezra Pound continued to praise Henderson's astuteness throughout the decade: "Alice was the only intelligent element ... my only comfort during the struggle," he wrote of the battle for the recognition of avant-garde poetry.[2] In *A Poet's Life*, Harriet Monroe recalled the characteristics that made the accomplished Henderson so respected:

> Her round face with its smiling Cupid mouth, blue eyes, and impertinent little nose, never prepared one for the sharp wit which would flash out like a sword. She was a pitiless reader of manuscripts; nothing stodgy or imitative would get by her finely sifting intelligence, and we had many a secret laugh over the confessional "hot stuff" or the boggy word weeds which tender-minded authors apparently mistook for poetry.

Characteristic of Henderson's thoroughness—and wit—she circled the word "blue" in her copy of the book and wrote in the margin, "BROWN!"

In 1917, when *The New Poetry, An Anthology* edited by Monroe and Henderson appeared, the Imagist position was clearly defined in Monroe's introduction and illustrated in the collected poems which included T.S. Eliot's "Portrait of a Lady," Wallace Stevens' "Peter Quince at the Clavier," and poems by Henderson demonstrating that quality Carl Sandburg called "the urge for the brief and the poignant."[3] The effect of the piercing lyrics and philosophy of Bengali poet Rabindranath Tagore, an early visitor to the *Poetry* office in 1912–13 before he won the Nobel Prize for Literature in 1913, also is evident in Henderson's poems, which display an oriental direction of vision, a simplicity of diction, yet a delicacy of feeling. In "Love Me At Last," she writes:

> Love me at last, or if you will not,
>   Leave me;
> Hard words could never, as these half-words,
>   Grieve me:
> Love me at last—or leave me.
>
> Love me at last, or let the last word uttered
>   Be but your own;
> Love me, or leave me—as a cloud, a vapor,
>   Or a bird flown,
> Love me at last—I am but sliding water
>   Over a stone.

What could have been a very standard love lyric, Henderson transforms in the last two lines.

In an earlier declaration of the Imagist creed (*Poetry*, March 1913), F.S. Flint argued that the group attempted to return to the classic principles of poetry exemplified in the work of Sappho, Catullus, and the medieval François Villon. Here Henderson achieves what Monroe also called "modern" in Imagist verse: the restoration of that direct relation between the concrete and the emotional, discarding the abstract verbosity of, say, the Victorians. As Monroe wrote in her introduction to *New Poetry*:

> In looking at the concrete object or environment, it [this poetry] seeks to give more precisely the emotion arising from them.... Great poetry has always been written in the language of contemporary speech, and its theme, though legendary, has always breadth and direct relation with contemporary thought, contemporary imaginative and spiritual life.[4]

Far from revolutionary, then, Henderson's poems, as well as others in this collection, were restorations, influenced by the classic Greek poets, Italian sonneteers, French symbolists, and Eastern writers, returning poetry to its organic, hence "modern" source.

But if Henderson's poems in this volume showed a philosophic and stylistic maturity beyond that of her earlier collections, the critic's cry was still very much alive, as illustrated in her letter to Harriet Monroe after moving to New Mexico with her husband and daughter in the spring of 1916:

> Out here, against these hills and in quietness, one is apt to get a perspective on many things.... I very much fear that Cinderella is going back to her ashes, and that she may feel more comfortable there than in her automobile—that this supposed popularity of the art is a good deal of dust, or rather, that when the dust clears away, not much may remain. By that I mean especially that one sees so much stuff passing itself off as poetry that is nothing of the sort. The need for a perfectly fearless high standard was never greater than it is at the moment.

And she concluded, speaking of the volume *New Poetry*, just received from Monroe: "some stuff has no business being there (including some of mine)."[5]

This new perspective gained in New Mexico signaled yet another period of growth for Henderson, with twofold cause. Suffering from tuberculosis, which had brought her to Sunmount Sanitorium in Santa Fe, she no doubt came with a sense of joy and pain—exuberance about the "Red Earth" country, as she called it, and a new firsthand look at the native sources of culture, folklore, and poetry she had studied in Chicago and championed in *Poetry*; pain from her illness, a kind of leavening agent that allowed her to see the new landscape and its people, their joys and sorrows, more realistically. By 1920, when she collected the New Mexico poems into *Red Earth*, she would write with a wisdom and understanding in "Rain-Prayer":

> A broken ploughed field
> In the driving rain,
> Rain driven slant-wise
> Over the plain.
> I long for the rain,
> For farmlands and ploughlands
> And cornlands again.
> O grey broken skies,
> You were part of my pain!

Here, also, living in a land that was as minimal as it was expansive, Henderson realized other salient premises of Imagism. In her 1917 introduction to *New Poetry*, Monroe advocated the study and use of other languages "to find out what poetry is." She noted that poetry existed before the English language began to form itself out of other languages and that it now exists in forms of beauty among faraway peoples who have never heard "our special rules."[6] In *Red Earth*, Henderson turned from her work as scholar and critic on aboriginal, black, and cowboy folk sources to that of practitioner.[7] She attempted to match the organically imposed rhythms of Spanish, Mexican, and Native American song with the stylistic process of exteriority, remaining detached and objective so as to approach authenticity. *Red Earth* is the culmination of Henderson's formal education and the restoration of the very qualities advocated by Imagism in the actual experience with "aboriginal" sources.

Chiefly powerful in these poems is Henderson's understanding of place as expressive of folk experience, an experience she believed generated a primitive understanding of life which made culture possible. As in the case of Padraic Colum's *Wild Earth and Other Poems*, which Henderson had enthusiastically reviewed and compared to Yeats' use of primitive Celtic song, *Red Earth* signaled the creation of a southwestern poetic idiom to explore a new imagery. Time itself was a major theme, and the geology of the land laid bare to view, along with the brilliant sunlight, native flora and fauna, and Spanish-American, Indian, and Anglo responses to the region. While there was a temptation among the new Anglo emigrés settling or visiting New Mexico during this time to rhapsodize or romanticize the theme of antiquity, Henderson understood well the enigma of "mother earth." As John Gould Fletcher explained:

> Mother earth—tierra madre—is what the Spanish-Americans call it; and in that phrase is so much that most Anglo-Saxons cannot understand. In New Mexico mother earth is most often a harsh mother, since so much is desert—layer upon layer of mother-earth and all of it strange; as strange, faraway, remote, and fiercely individual as China or North Africa.... Break a branch of pinon and let its resinous sap stick to your fingers, or dig a new water-ditch through this crumbling red soil if you would know why New Mexico earth is mother-earth. It clings as it yields.[8]

Having written a poem entitled, "Acequia Madre," Henderson
could write of the land's hold on the imagination in "Three Men
Entered the Desert Alone":

> And his spirit sang like a taper dim
> As the slow wheel turned on the desert's rim
> Through the wind-swept stretches of sand and sky;
> He had entered the desert to hide and fly,
> But the spell of the desert had entered him.

And in her poem "In the Desert," she characterizes the fatal, yet
beautiful quality of this landscape, echoing Tagore's "In the Garden":

> I have seen you, O king of the dead,
> More beautiful than sunlight.
>
> Your kiss is like quicksilver;
> But I turned my face aside
>   Less you should touch my lips.
>
>   ...
>
> But the warm field, and the sunlight,
> And the few years of my girlhood
> Came before me, and I cried,
> *Not Yet!*
> *Not Yet, O dark lover!*

So strong is Henderson's identification with place, the way life is
bound to earth and sky by gestures filled with religious meaning,
that she writes in "From the Stone Age":

> Long ago some one carved me in the semblance
>   of a god.
> I have forgot now what god I was meant to
>   represent.
> I have no consciousness now but of stone, sun-
>   light and rain.
>
> The sun baking my skin of stone, the wind lifting
>   my hair;
> My thoughts are of stone,
> My substance now is the substance of life itself;
>
> Since I am a stone
> I have no need to remember anything—

> Everything is remembered for me;
> I live and think and dream as a stone....

Perhaps the most dynamic quality of this collection is Henderson's brilliant use of the image. As in the case of painters of the period who utilized the photograph as a bridge between the actual event and their somewhat idealized vision of a ceremony or person, Henderson renders the central image in each poem as that connection, mirroring the moment, linking writer and reader to the event. In her "Notes" to *Red Earth*, she indicated that poetry to the Indians was not description but a mirror of the nature in which they lived and worshiped. In praising the lasting quality of her "Imagist" poetry, Fletcher noted her ability to make the "language and the thing ... one."[9] Pound maintained that the intellectual and emotional complex generated by capturing this "instant of time" implied a system of desires plus memories which exert a dominating influence upon personality.[10] Having written a critical article on "Art and Photography" in which she discussed the realistic and interpretive elements of Robert Frost's poetry, Henderson understood the implication of the image. Able to create a series of portraits—tableaux—she makes the moment resonate, as in "Juan Quintana":

> The goat-herd follows his flock
> Over the sandy plain.
> And the goats nibble the rabbit-brush
> Acrid with desert rain.
>
> Old Juan Quintana's coat
> Is a faded purple blue,
> And his hat is a worn brown;
> And his trousers a tawny hue.
>
> He is sunburnt like the hills.
> And his eyes have a strange goat look.

Of the instant intuition the image provides, she once mused that no greater peace could be felt than in the contemplation of a tree. In "Sunlight," she writes:

> The sunlight is enough,
> And the earth sucking life from the sun.
> Horses in a wide field are a part of it,
> Dappled and white and brown;
> Trees are another kind of life,

Linked to us but not understood.
(Whoever can understand a horse or a tree
Can understand a star or a planet:
But one may feel things without understanding,
Or one may understand them through feeling.)
The simple light of the sun is enough.
One will never remember
A greater thing when one dies
Than sunlight falling aslant long rows of corn,
Or rainy days heavy with grey sullen skies.
Not love, not the intense moment of passion,
Not birth, is as poignant
As the sudden flash that passes
Like light reflected in a mirror
From nature to us.

Thus each of these poems, with its flash of image, becomes a ceremony in words. In the natural rhythms of the Native American and Hispanic folk forms, Henderson caught a motion that carried her thoughts to their logical conclusions. John Gould Fletcher later praised her poetry as able to encompass two worlds in this process—"the world of ordinary discourse, and a second world which is merely suggested by the words, far wider and fuller, lying in contact with the first world but yet detached from it."[11] As in the case of the ceremonies she mirrored, the poem was at once representational and symbolic. Henderson continued to love the red earth country and to sift from it impressions that gave her a new and authentic voice as a writer. Ruth Laughlin noted that:

Alice Corbin's appreciation of New Mexico grew deeper each year. She collected a fine library of southwestern books and studied New Mexico history, Indian myths, Penitente ritual, and folk legends and customs of her Spanish-American and Indian neighbors. She was always eager to get first hand information from such authorities as Edgar L. Hewett, Paul A.F. Walter, E. Dana Johnson, Charles F. Lummis, Nina Otero Warren, Kenneth Chapman, and Harry Mera. She delighted in Howard Thorpe's early reminiscences and encouraged him to write his collections of cowboy stories and ballads.[12]

If *Red Earth* was the culmination of a mature personal expression for the poet, her collection and editorship of *The Turquoise Trail, An Anthology of New Mexican Poetry* in 1928 signaled the re-

sult of the region's influence—and of hers—on a number of outstanding writers. Noting that New Mexico represents a distinct
atmosphere from that of any other part of the country, Henderson
identified the great fund of Indian poetry, Spanish folksongs and
poems, and cowboy songs as the three native sources of poetry influencing the writers in her anthology. "It is not the purpose of this
collection to present literal translations of Spanish folk-plays or
poems, or of aboriginal verse, or anonymous cowboy songs, which
have been collected elsewhere," she wrote, "but to show how
much the traditional background and the soil itself have influenced the work of contemporary poets in New Mexico."[13] Only
three "native" New Mexicans were included, but the presence of
Yvor Winters, Carl Sandburg, Willa Cather, Edgar Lee Masters,
D.H. Lawrence, and others testified to the "subliminal influences
of soil and atmosphere" Henderson found "as new, as liberating as
it is primal."[14]

Not surprisingly, Henderson also called the volume a record of
companionships. Her great gift as collector and critic is evident in
the astute introduction; her talent for recognizing the best in people is inherent in the anthology. Haniel Long called her a gentle
critic. "She took the position of allowing a poem to grow in its own
right like a plant. Her attitude towards a new poem, or a new aspect of a friend's psyche, was one of welcome," he said, remembering the informal poetry readings that began with Witter Bynner,
Lynn Riggs, Spud Johnson, and Long during the 1920s. Affection-
ately named "The Rabble" (short for the Rabelais Club because of
their often Rabelaisian mood), the group expanded and interacted
through the years in the Poets' Roundups, readings to raise money
for the Southwest Indian Arts Fund, and the Writer's Editions, a
self-publishing venture designed to foster the growth of American
literature through regional publishing. Indeed, like Mabel Dodge
Luhan in Taos, Henderson in Santa Fe greatly encouraged what
Edgar Lee Hewett once characterized as the major influential trend
in the state: "Art has rescued this state from the commonplace and
made it conscious of its own fine character," he noted.[15]

In her final volume of poems, *The Sun Turns West* (1933), one of
the three first Writer's Editions (which also included Haniel Long's
Atlantides and Peggy Pond Church's *Foretaste*), Henderson wrote
autobiographically, using the uniqueness of her New Mexico home
to reflect on her past. Part I of the collection centers on memories of

her childhood; Part II celebrates distinct moods in twelve short
lyrics; Part III contains a series of enigmatic pieces called "Divided
Thoughts"; Part IV, "Another Spring," celebrates the creative
power of life and death. Though the poems are not as boldly original as her New Mexico poems, they nevertheless are among Henderson's finest, demonstrating her ability to create a sense of
reverie. Still striking the memorable and thoughtful image, Henderson writes in "Evening":

> By the smoky tide of evening
> The sands are running out to the sea,
> And an old man sits by the wharf
> With his pipe gone out on his knee.
>
> The sun behind his shoulders
> Is the measure of his desire
> For the sea, which is only long
> Lacking the old-time fire.
>
> Color streams over the water
> Like many flaming oils;
> On the brown sea beach of evening
> The fishermen fling their spoils.

Experimental, the effects of these poems often are provocative, as
in "The Wave":

> There is no means of knowing
> Why it is I love you.
> You are like a rose with three petals,
> Like a lake without stars.
>
> In your eyes
> My love returns to me
> With its own reflection.
>
> II
>
> Oh, what a liar,
>   with deceiving words!
> For when have the eyes found beauty
> Without in some way searching for the wave
>   that tumbles backward?...

Models of compression, these poems illustrate Henderson's
ability to execute what Pound cited as the highest achievement of
Imagist poetry—to make the image a key to the emotional and intellectual complex. In "The Wood," the image keys a complex of

memories connecting the periods of the poet's life, a rich psychic source:

> I walked through that wood where the winds were
> Warm as from a prairie heated by the sun,
> And thought that I should fall and be buried
> There in the heaped fragrance of pine-cone and sun;
> But the wind turned, and my mind changed
> And I became a sea whereon waves ran
> Over another sea like iron or glass,
> Through which I saw that wood where the winds were
> Warm with the pine-scent and sun-steamed grass.

T.M. Pearce said of Henderson's fourth and final book of poetry: "The title certainly refers to the turning of time, the fading of life's intensity and power. *Red Earth* in 1920 is a living animated painting of the Southwest; *The Sun Turns West* in 1933 is a living, animated portrait of Alice Corbin Henderson."[16]

But if Henderson noted the turning of time when, at 51, she published her last volume of poems, she persisted in her energy to write in prose about community, ceremony, and song. Having written a "Foreword" to a collection of songs, *Spanish Folksongs of New Mexico*, arranged and transcribed by Mary R. Van Stone in 1928, she gathered verses she had written for her children and grandchildren into *A Child's Bouquet* in 1935, Mary Morley setting them to music. In 1936 and 1937, she served as editor-in-chief of the New Mexico project for the American Guide Series, contributing the essay on literature which astutely demonstrated her knowledge of native, conquest, and regional works. She was active in planning the Coronado Cuarto-Centennial, and could even jest with historians as she echoed a familiar ballad by François Villon about their uncertainties:

> Where were Senecu and Socorro?
> Where Quivira—I'd love to know!
> Where, oh where, did De Vaca Wander,
> In, or out, of New Mexico?

But perhaps the most beautiful of Henderson's final writings was *Brothers of Light: The Penitentes of the Southwest* (1937), an account of the Hendersons' journey to Abiquiu, where they witnessed the Holy Week rites of the lay order which arose from the third order of the Franciscans. Having been earlier a collector of *al-*

abados, Henderson's prose study of the Hispanic Catholic hymns and ritual and her husband's woodcut illustrations are a creative demonstration of scholarship and beauty. Underlying the essentially literary presentation, including collected ceremonial hymns, are genuine research and fine typography. Poet and painter combine to create an informal yet solid account that demonstrates the power of the artist as interpreter. One line attests to the poetic brilliance of Henderson's prose: "These shrill sounds of religious fervor suddenly lifted above the bare desert have the effect of poising the single soul against space."

Indeed, in Henderson's best writing she achieves this same effect for the reader. Though noted by John Gould Fletcher as one of the best Imagist poets, highly praised by Pound, and recognized by Padrai Colum as creating "lasting" poetry, Henderson nevertheless remains sadly underrated. But for even the untutored reader who may not recognize her significant contribution to modern poetry or her pioneering work as editor, folk-collector, mentor, "group person," as Long called her, the poems still speak powerfully of tierra madre and her philosophy that life has a continuity with all that comes before and after the personal interim. As the poem "Prayer-Wands" shows, she was herself, in her friendships and her writings, that "middle" interim for others, providing a creative link:

I

I have dreamed of the thunder-birds,
The great ones of the sky.
Riders upon painted horses
Lifted me up.
I was one of them.
We chased the sorrel deer.

Now I am become as the least among you,
As grass on the prairie,
As dust on the earth.
And lest I grow proud, I strip myself,
And sit naked and dirty
So that the spirit may not forget.

...

Thinking over the old times gone,
My mind is hard to me.

Earth has a middle, like this stone,
Worn round on the mesa-top
From looking at the sun.

Holding this rock,
My mind pierces inward.

...

The old gods are gone
With our Lost Others.

...

My mind follows them,
And soon my body
Burrowing downward and inward
Will come to the Middle World
Where all seeds wait.

Notes

1. *Linnet Songs* (Chicago: Wind-Tryst Press, 1898), n.p.

2. Quoted in Witter Bynner, "Alice and I," in "Alice Corbin: An Appreciation," edited by Witter Bynner and Oliver LaFarge, *New Mexico Quarterly Review* 19 (1949): 42. Readers should note that the poet signed her poetry, "Alice Corbin, " and her prose with her full name; for the sake of simplicity her full name will be used throughout this essay.

3. See T.M. Pearce, *Alice Corbin Henderson* (Austin: Steck-Vaughn Company, 1969), for a concise treatment of Sandburg and Henderson's professional relationship.

4. Harriet Monroe and Alice Corbin Henderson, eds., *The New Poetry, An Anthology* (New York: The Macmillan Co., 1917).

5. Quoted in George Dillon, "A Note on Alice Corbin Henderson and *Poetry*," in Bynner and LaFarge, *New Mexico Quarterly Review*: 44.

6. "Introduction," *The New Poetry*, p. v.

7. The reader may want to examine the following articles in *Poetry* magazine that reflect Henderson's critical opinions and focus: "Poetic Prose and Vers Libre" (Vol. II), "Art and Photography" (Vol. VI), "Japanese Poetry" (Vol.VII), "Aboriginal Poetry" (Vol. IX), and "Cowboy Songs and Ballads" (Vol. X).

8. Witter Bynner and Oliver LaFarge, "Alice Corbin and Imagism," *New Mexico Quarterly Review*: 49.

9. Ibid.

10. See Pearce, p. 9.

11. See Meredith Yearsley, "Alice Corbin Henderson," *American Poets, Dictionary of Literary Biography* (Detroit: Gale Research Company, 1986), p. 168.

12. Witter Bynner and Oliver LaFarge, "Santa Fe in the Twenties," *New Mexico Quarterly Review*: 66.

13. Alice Corbin Henderson, ed., *The Turquoise Trail, An Anthology of New Mexico Poetry* (Boston and New York: Houghton Mifflin Co., 1928), p. xi.

14. Ibid.

15. Alison Dana and Margaret Lohlker, eds., "Introduction" to "Artists and Writers: A List of Prominent Artists and Writers of New Mexico," *Santa Fe New Mexican*, June 26, 1940.

16. Pearce, p. 35.

Bones Incandescent:
Peggy Pond Church

When I first met Peggy Pond Church in 1980 in her home on Camino Rancheros in Santa Fe, I knew her only by reputation. Although author of the best-selling memoir, *The House at Otowi Bridge*, she was chiefly a poet. "The First Lady of New Mexico poetry, who should be in all poetry collections," W. David Laid wrote in *Books of the Southwest*, in his review of *Rustle of Angels*. In 1984, having published her final of eight volumes of poetry, Peggy won the Governor's Award for Literature. Fifty years before, Elizabeth Shepley Sergeant prophesied in *The Saturday Review of Literature* that here was "a pristine young poetess ... probably the first real New Mexican to produce a book of undeniable poetic promise out of her region and her life." The Longmont Award, granted for the outstanding merit of *The House at Otowi Bridge*, and the Julia Ellsworth Ford Foundation Prize for her humorous children's tale, *The Burro for Angelitos*, certified that a graceful stylist was at work, even in nonfiction. First among the writers published by the Rydal Press in the Writers' Editions during the 1920s and 1930s, Peggy's accomplishments as a poet began along with a flowering of New Mexico arts and letters. Playwright Lanford Wilson, when asked to summarize the best books of 1982 for the *New York Times Book Review*, instead lauded *The House at Otowi Bridge*, which he had just discovered as "one of the most wonderful and surprising books" he'd read in years.

What I didn't know that summer day in 1980, as a representative from the University of New Mexico I arranged for the gift of Mrs. Church's papers to the school, was how much I knew of the poet through her poetry. Years later, at her memorial service in November 1986, I was astounded by the variety and number of people in attendance at St. John's College who had come to honor her after her death. Her long-time friend, Corina Santistevan, later noted: "Her friends cut across borders of age, race, religion, culture, and profession. Young people were at the services, as well as old men and some friends since childhood, including an archaeologist, teachers, and librarians. It was a roomful of a great variety of people who spoke lovingly about Peggy." Most spoke about her through her poems or memories of some story associated with them. One young woman told of working for a tree service, cutting down an old, failing willow which Peggy later regretted killing and so wrote a poem about it. In her sadness for the forlorn tree, Peggy hung an old hat on its few remaining branches. At the Society of Friends' service, the family distributed a last statement left by the poet which contained this coda from her "Elegy for a Willow Tree":

> Now I, old willow tree from which the birds have fled,
> through whose branches the sap no longer rises
> leave my own vacancy on the waiting air.

Memories of these aspects of her personality, plus her special gift for irony and warmth, sifted through the afternoon in quoted lines, stanzas committed by and to the heart. Somehow the range of poetry—seventy years of it since she published her first poem in 1915—and the complexity of life were reflected in the diversity of the audience. Yet, when contemplating writing her autobiography, she recognized the difficulty of assessing either poet or poetry. (Late in life she was advised by her friend Lawrence Clark Powell, professor emeritus at UCLA, to tell her life through the poetry.) In a letter to May Sarton—one of several in a correspondence that lasted from 1948 to 1986—she remarked that a young woman had been by that day to look through her files, expressing interest in writing her biography. "But who?" Peggy asked in the letter. "Which poet? Which Peggy?"

The reader of this volume of poems certainly mines a rich and intriguing biography, but also a study subtly drawn, one that contains more than references to the personal life. When asked about her poet's credo, Peggy once replied, "It's the land that wants to be said." She wrote perceptively about the Southwest landscape, not as background or setting but as experienced essence. Love, marriage, family, war, and the woman writer were equally her subjects, yet in each case, as May Sarton observed in another letter to her, she was utterly "controlled, not confessional." Of her *The Ripened Fields: Fifteen Sonnets of a Marriage*, Lawrence Clark Powell noted: "Peggy Pond Church is one of the few poets to grace the Southwest—I mean poets, not versifiers with which the region abounds. Her emotions are deep, her language controlled. She sees the landscape with the far sight of history and also with the preciseness of a knowing observer of the nearby."

Hers is a story as rich as the history of New Mexico itself, the poetry sophisticated because of its experiential and universal appeal. "Sensory, yet celestial" Peggy called the achievement of fellow New Mexico poet Haniel Long; her life and consequent art also has that kind of resonance. Born December 1, 1903, in Watrous, New Mexico, then the territory of New Mexico at the locale known as Valmora, she represented the fourth generation of her family to feel the pull of the earth. Peggy not only marks the early Watrous flood as significant in her young life, but remembers that the search for place was continuous. In the 13 years from kindergarten through high school, she attended several different schools, never more than two years in any one of them. But growing up summers on the Pajarito Plateau, the outdoor life—the beauty of the canyons and mountains, the mysteries of the Anasazi Indians—permanently influenced the precious, yet shy, girl. The opportunity for free and independent discovery, riding horseback, hiking, or observing the evidence of ancient societies influenced Church's solitary, almost transcendental, love of nature and offered a rare chance for her to experience the wilderness in ways most girls of that period could not. In the winter of 1917–1918, she attended Santa Fe High School, her only year of schooling in New Mexico, except for six months at a convent in Albuquerque when she was eight. Guided by a governess at ages eleven and twelve, she learned the names of wildflowers and mesas and began to feel a love for poetry. Her mother also recited aloud to the children, particularly from the *Child's Garden of Verses* and Kipling's *The Ballad of East and West*. Her first poem was published by *St. Nicholas* magazine when she was still in her teens. In high school at Hillside School in Connecticut, she won an *Atlantic Magazine* prize of $50 for a poem. She spent two years at Smith College beginning in 1922, leaving in 1924 to marry Fermor Church, a young man from Washington, Connecticut, who had come out to teach at the Los

Alamos Ranch School. As the first faculty wife at the school, Peggy
found the isolated mesas anything but dull. Tracing the myriad
"roads to utterness," far from the tyranny of the clock, telephone,
or even the calendar, she wrote poetry throughout these years at
the school where the Churches reared three boys. In 1943, the
school was commandeered by the federal government for the
Manhattan Project and the development of the atomic bomb.

During the early 1930s, Peggy became interested in Jungian
analysis. During this time she studied her dreams and began a
kind of introspection that lasted, as reflected in a series of journals,
throughout most of her life. After her two initial books of poems
(from which several of the poems originally appeared in the *Atlantic*, *Poetry*, and *Saturday Review*), Peggy's reflectiveness led to a
much different voice in her third volume of poems, *Ultimatum for
Man* . The family moved to Taos in 1943, and in this book Peggy
examines the consequences of war and destruction juxtaposed
against personal lives. In 1948, she became a member of the Society
of Friends, attended meetings, and published in the Quaker journal, *Inward Light*. Her interest in the psychological continued at
Berkeley, where Ferm lived in 1956. During this period, Peggy also
wrote *The House at Otowi Bridge*, beginning the memoir after Edith
Warner's death in 1951. *The Ripened Fields*, sonnets on her marriage, was published in 1957 and demonstrated many of the personal concerns the poet experienced in regard to that relationship.

After moving back to Santa Fe in 1960, the couple remained
involved in the life of the city as well as in the rich area of life they
particularly shared together—their hikes, retreats, and drives
through the heart of New Mexico and the Southwest. Peggy began
research on Mary Austin, another famous Santa Fe resident whom
she had known briefly in the early 1930s. She attended lectures at
St. John's College by John Holt, Robert Bly, and Joseph Campbell,
as well as seminars on Pablo Neruda, Whitman, Thoreau, and
Yeats. In 1975, Ferm died of a brain tumor. After this loss, Peggy
brought out *New and Selected Poems* in 1976, *The Lament at Tsankawi
Mesa* in 1980, *Rustle of Angels* in 1981, and her final volume, *Birds of
Daybreak*, in 1985. She continued her correspondences with poets
May Sarton and Denise Levertov, editor Roland Dickey (who had
published *The House at Otowi Bridge*), Lawrence Clark Powell, and
her Taos friend, Corina Santistevan. Shortly before her death, she
began close scrutiny of her journals (some she had burned in the

1930s). What remained were rearranged in collections called "The Terminal Journal" (about the death of her husband), "Pajarito" (nature writings), "Poli" (the record of her relationship to her dog), and daily journals kept since the 1950s. While attending seminars on Greek tragedy as well as lectures at St. John's, she continued her intense musical interests and reading, was interviewed for radio programs and magazines, and honored with autograph parties and awards. On October 23, 1986, she took her own life according to the precepts of the Hemlock Society, of which she was a member.

Though Church maintained throughout her life that she was not a "member" of the Santa Fe writers' group which achieved some renown during the 1920s and 1930s, she nevertheless read at the "Poets' Roundups" and knew members of this group, including Alice Corbin Henderson, Mary Austin, and Haniel Long. There is at least an implied influence and place for her among these older writers who established a kind of writers' colony in New Mexico. Despite New Mexico's rich Spanish and Mexican literary tradition, when the first influx of Anglo writers to Santa Fe and Taos began, artists such as Mary Austin bemoaned the lack of a wider audience and more conscious recognition of New Mexico's native literary sources. "One confidently predicts here," she wrote, "the rise, within appreciable time, of the next great and fructifying world culture." Another émigré, author, archaeologist, historian, and journalist, Charles E. Lummis, rhapsodized about the Southwest in the opening paragraph of *The Land of Poco Tiempo:* "Sun, silence, and adobe—that is New Mexico in three words.... It is the Great American Mystery—the National Rip Van Winkle—the United States which is *not* the United States." Harriet Monroe, editor of the little Chicago magazine, *Poetry,* continued this line: "Why go to Greece or China? This Southwest, which is but one chapter of our rich tradition, is our own authentic wonderland—a treasure-trove of romantic myth—profoundly beautiful and significant, guarded by ancient races practicing their ancient rites, in a region of incredible color and startling natural grandeur."

More recently, Robert Coles in his *Eskimos, Chicanos, Indians* offered a somewhat more scientific explanation for this same response: "At the altitude of high northern New Mexico, the air has lost one-fourth its weight; it is low in carbon dioxide and oxygen and has therefore also lost its capacity to refract or diffuse light." But even the social scientist waxed poetic: "The hazy, somewhat softened, even blurred vision of the coastal plains or the prairie gives way to a clear, bright, almost harsh, sometimes blinding field of view. Air that an outsider has come to regard as transparent suddenly becomes translucent—so sharp, so clean, so light that one feels in a new world possessed of new eyes." Indeed, for the Anglo newcomers of the 1920s and 1930s, exotic, light-charged New Mexico was a spiritual place of new vision. Embracing this place and its multicultural heritage as their lost roots in a depersonalized America, they created a body of work containing folk materials and professing a literary potential. Moreover, many of these newcomers had the sophistication and training to tap these resources. Working as editors and collectors, with connections to the eastern establishment, they attracted other famous writers and artists to come to the Southwest, including Carl Sandburg, Vachel Lindsay, Witter Bynner, and Ezra Pound. In 1928, Alice Corbin Henderson, assistant to Harriet Monroe at *Poetry* magazine, edited *The Turquoise Trail: An Anthology of New Mexico Poetry*, which included Peggy Pond Church along with thirty other poets. Among them were Mary Austin, Witter Bynner, Paul Horgan, Spud Johnson, D.H. Lawrence, Haniel Long, Mabel Dodge Luhan, and Eugene Manlove Rhodes. With the advent of the "Poets' Roundups," supported by Alice Corbin, Peggy, Witter Bynner, and Haniel Long, public readings and publications through the Writers' Editions gave voice to a body of poetry along with the growing publication of translations, novels, and literary and social science journals. By the end of the 1930s, a sixteen-page "Southwest Book List for 1938–1939" named eighty-eight writers "living in and about Santa Fe," with 280 adult and juvenile titles that they had produced, in which Church was included. The ultimate purpose of the Writers' Editions, "a cooperative group of writers living in the Southwest," was to see that "regional publication would foster the growth of American literature."

Along with the discovery of the Southwest as an exotic, art-inspiring region, often romanticized, writer Erna Fergusson noted that it was also a testing ground, a hard country, forbidding and challenging. She writes in *Our Southwest*:

> The arid Southwest has always been too strong, too indomitable for most people. Those who can stand it have had to learn that man does not modify this country; it transforms him, deeply.... It is wilderness where a man may get back to

the essentials of being a man. It is magnificence forever rewarding to a man courageous enough to seek to renew his
soul.

Indeed, rather than particularized as uniquely regional in its
folklore, geography, and ancient history and peoples, this Southwest possessed, in common with all dynamic places of the heart,
qualities both local and universal. In their assessment of the effect
of this landscape on literature in *Southwest Heritage*, literary historians T.M. Pearce and Mabel Major noted two themes that have
emerged from this territory:

> The recurring motif in the poetry of the Southwest is the
> timelessness of Nature, the antiquity of the Indian and Span-
> ish civilization of the region, and the recentness of the white
> man in this old land, together with the briefness of the indi-
> vidual life. The poet looks at a rock covered with inscrip-
> tions, a piece of ancient pottery, the dim painting of hands in
> a cave, a circle of trees where a house has been and no house
> is, an age-old road, and writes of the twin deities, Perma-
> nence and Evanescence.

Experiencing directly these themes, as well as the individual's
quest for spiritual growth, Peggy Church embraced the Southwest's noted extremes, experiencing the cycles of flowering,
drought, and migration that have left us Chaco, Mesa Verde, and
Hovenweep. Primal experiences of flood and drought are key to
her life. Moreover, she grew up in a landscape but was dispossessed of it—she lost that which had succored her childhood and
young womanhood. During one of the particularly challenging
periods in her life—1932–1934—after losing her father to brain
cancer, suffering a schism in her marriage, and confusions about
her own destiny, mentor and poet-friend Haniel Long encouraged
her to focus on poetry The act of writing not only renewed her creative, positive life, but reconnected her as maker of metaphors,
symbols, and parables, with the cycles of self. Writing in 1985 the
"Afterword" to Long's prose poem, *The Interlinear of Cabeza de Vaca*
(originally published in 1936), she linked the meaning of the poem
to the poet's development in the landscape. Like the Spanish explorer, who through deprivation and hardship came to know himself and his fellows by "shedding his skin," so Long discovered in
himself the ability to feel for others. She writes:

Without straying in any important detail from the historical account, Long makes the matter-of-fact Spanish soldier's journey an adventure of inner transformation, an adventure in the invisible realm of the human soul. "What can describe a happening in the shadows of the soul?" his Cabeza de Vaca wonders at the beginning of the *Interlinear*. What Haniel saw in the rugged Spanish soldier was, I am convinced, a reflection of his own inner journey. He was a poet who took the soul seriously in the same way Keats did who called the world "a vale of soul-making," and once wrote, "I began by seeing how man was formed by circumstances— and what are circumstances?—but the touchstones of his heart?—and what are touchstones?—but the provings of his heart?—and what are provings of the heart but fortifiers or alterers of his own nature?—and what is his altered nature but his Soul?"

Nature and one's nature for Church are intimately bound. As she revealed in her assessment of how the role of the poet relates to themes and images in Long's poem, the choice of such native, folkloristic subjects is an act of autobiography, containing within it elements of an older history—archetypal, primordial events in the "place" of the self. She notes that Long, like his Cabeza de Vaca, had his own shipwreck—a breakdown, a descent into the darkness of self—which necessitated his relating in a new way to others. Noting that Keats, whom Long read, also wrote about the poetic nature, she maintains what brought Long out of his black period was "losing himself in another human being and thus becoming aware that there is something in all of us, not the combative and possessive ego, through which we are able to share life and wholeness with another." She explains:

It seems to me that the *Interlinear of Cabeza de Vaca* might be a portion of Haniel Long's autobiography, an account of transformations that had taken place in his own journey through the vale of soul-making. He has recreated Cabeza de Vaca in his own image. It is the image of the poet who has emerged from the wilderness of self with an understanding of the Invisible not learned from books or teachers but from the provings of the heart.

The same observations may be made about Church's poetry. While she writes often directly from experience, with awe and zeal, in an effort to hone the beauty of the moment or to apply it to some corresponding personal awareness, her focus on particulars of the land and people results in an ecstatic attention, at once holistic. Another "regional" writer, Eudora Welty, describes how place animates the writer's philosophy and style:

> It may be that place can focus the gigantic, voracious eye of genius and bring its gaze to point. Focus then means awareness, discernment, order, clarity, insight—they are like the attributes of love. The act of focusing itself has beauty and meaning; it is the act that continued in, turns into meditation, into poetry ... the question of place resolves itself into the point of view.

Losing oneself in this love for the landscape also makes for new discoveries. Place and poetics in Church's work are significantly linked. She began the habit of writing as an exorcism of her shy self when she was a girl, and this habit took shape in the beating out with her fingers on a tabletop formal rhythms of poems she had read and heard. From these more formal constructions, we see her moving to experimentations with controlled free verse, more "natural" rhythms. She has said that it is chiefly sound that gives birth and then meaning to a poem, that a "poetic ear" is key. "I had a good ear for it. I heard it and read it out loud. Before radio and television and movies, what we had was the drama of the landscape." When asked how, specifically, this drama affected her voice, tone, and meaning, she added, "I have listened endlessly to the Rio de los Frijoles." Likewise, Church read a number of poets for their language, the way in which sound makes meaning. She was influenced by her study of Blake, Yeats, Eliot, Rilke, Neruda, Thoreau, and Wordsworth. Her formal education in poetics reflects a poetry whose meaning is shaped by landscape. Reading Neruda and Rilke in their original Spanish and German, she commented that she took greatest note of words that defied translation, whose sounds in their native tongue remained key. Thus, form for her became a matter of response, at once mysterious, even evanescent, yet permanently shaped. After the Manhattan Project, she commented that to make sense of her uprootings and the larger questions of world safety, harmony, and peace, she "looked for patterns." In her poems, which treat the ideas of universal community, the sanctity of sacred places, even the poet's aging ("like a shipwreck," she once called it), her own homing pattern is evident: "I write to keep things from getting lost," she said.

Another key to Church's ability to write personally, yet universally, is her gender and her attitudes about the woman artist. Lawrence Clark Powell recognized in *The Ripened Fields* "a finer distillation" than Meredith's *Modern Love* because she had a "woman's sensitivity ... rather than bitter, at last accepting and serene." He continued in his assessment to note that this quality helped assure her "a place in our literature beyond the regional." Typically, the conflicts for the woman who is writer have been thought to create a schism within the self—a disjunctive position between societal expectations and personal desire that often contributes to anything but the "accepting and serene." Church, though never really a careerist, experienced many of the contrarieties of being a creative woman. Adrienne Rich (in *Adrienne Rich's Poetry*) writes insightfully about the conflicts between the ego necessary to creativity and the traditional expectations of womanhood:

> For a poem to coalesce, for a character or action to take shape, there has to be an imaginative transformation of reality which is in no way passive. And a certain freedom of mind is needed—freedom to press on, to enter the currents of your thought as a glider pilot, knowing that your motion can be sustained, that the buoyancy of your attention will not be suddenly snatched away. Moreover, if the imagination is to transcend and transform experience it has to question, to challenge, to conceive of alternative, perhaps to the very life you are living at the moment.... So often to fulfill being a female being by trying to fulfill traditional female functions in a traditional way is in direct conflict with the subversive function of the imagination.

Rich sees a direct conflict between love—how it is traditionally defined by culture—and the ego necessary for creativity, achievement, and ambition, which often is at the expense of others. Likewise, May Sarton sees the conflict similarly within the woman artist, "who becomes one at her own peril." Sarton explains that the conflict is between the central value of relationship which puts her at odds with the necessary ego, the imagination:

> I think where it is harder to be a woman is when the woman is also an artist and thus torn apart between life and art in a way that men are simply not. A young man goes to college and goes into a career and marries right on the trajectory he has designed in college. The young woman who wants to

write, say, and goes to college and then marries, if she has children, for about ten years or more suddenly is thrown back into a life of domesticity where most of her energy, must go into the home. The artist is buried.... Personal relations do not eat at men in the same way, it seems to me. They are not primarily nurturers and women, even single women, are.

In her nonfiction studies of the lives of two creative women—Edith Warner in *The House at Otawi Bridge* and Mary Austin in *Wind's Trail*—Church indirectly mused about this creative dilemma as she also thematically reflected her personal struggles with it in some of the poems. In Warner, she saw the ability to unite the seemingly disparate, to link lives significantly together through the wells of "woman's wisdom," gentleness, and sensitivity, even to face death serenely. On the other hand, Church believed that ultimately Mary Austin gave over her own woman's self to an omnivorous ego—through sacrificing her tenderness, which granted perception, deep feeling, and a love of the landscape. For Church, then, ego and imagination are not synonymous. Rather, she advocates that women, as connected as they are to primal sources, have a unique wisdom to bridge the outer and inner worlds, rather than suffer what is traditionally viewed as conflict. As she wrote of Long's loss of ego as necessary for his transformation as a man and poet, so she champions woman's "natural" ability to be reborn in the "loss" of self. In "Lines for a Woman Poet," written for May Sarton, she first admires the woman poet, riding like a falconer into battle with the singing bird on her shoulder:

> I know that bird. I know that falcon eye,
> those beating wings that drive it toward the sun,
> the whirling plunge of light and the curved beak
> and how it tears the heart to drink the blood,
> the living blood on which its song must feed.

She continues by acknowledging the "gods' indifference to our mortal pain," naming the throes of Daphne and Leda. She says:

> We cannot soar
> like birds toward the sun. We must endure
> the weight of winter and the darkened moon,
> not like Van Gogh who was devoured by light
> until his brush bled fire.

But far from the mere, simplistic, silent suffering in order to make the poem, is the woman's own unique strength, her ability to relate, connect, save, and unite, beyond the egoistic approach:

> Let the fierce phoenix go with his sharp cry
> toward the flaming sun, oh mythical bird
> that would consume your heart. Lie down, lie down
> now among roots and leaves and let your eyes
> be dark as the closed child's and let the mole
> speak his blind wisdom to your folded hand.
> Birth is not had by willing.
> Let the rose unfurl, in time like air, what summer knows.

Unwilling to reduce the mysteries of the woman artist or the self to the classic babies-or-books argument, Church also does not see the birthing image of the poem here as a "passive" motherhood. She is perhaps closer to Rilke in her assessment of the wells of creativity and how they relate to being a woman when she quotes him in her journals, "I await the birth hour of a new clarity," which is Rilke's line about the coming of the muse. Church sees the muse as an androgynous source. In an exchange of letters on this matter with May Sarton, she says the muse is like an "electric current," an "epiphany" sparked by person, event, or thing, and that when he has been male, she later realized he was but "an incarnation of the inner being." Influenced by Jungian thought, Church ultimately related creativity to the striving for balance between the male and female parts of the self. The uniqueness of being a woman artist, however, was the ability to seize upon the poem as an act of relatedness and relationship rather than lone ego. Even the conflicts—her quoting of Yeats, for instance, "the quarrel with ourselves makes poetry"—she thought essential to tenderness and nurturing. Whether geological or psychological, Church's poems most often unite the inner and outer worlds as well as the parts of the self: "I realize the important things to me have been the epiphanies.... Usually, for me, things seen, rather than things done. I have never forgotten—I must have been between five and six—a brilliant cowslip growing at the center of a bog in a cow pasture, my longing to approach it, barefoot as I was, but not daring for fear I'd be sucked down into the bog. But the cowslip is still there, inside. Decades later, reading *The Secret of the Golden Flower*, I was reminded."

Reading Church's poetry, one cannot ignore the primal quality of the dominant image, event, or experience. Much like the imagist group of poets she tangentially was acquainted with in New Mexico (the work of Pound, Corbin Henderson, and Harriet Monroe), meaning in Church's poems often begins with the values of rhythm and tone as connected to the image. Form then arises from the poet's meditative awareness of values in the world and within. Rather than a documentary realism, however, Church accomplishes through the image a *translation* of experience—indeed the value of that experience that imparts a keener sense of being alive. Proust advocated in *The Past Recaptured* that it is underneath these little-recorded details—images, say, of nature, domestic life, a marriage—that reality is hidden:

> ... the grandeur in the distant sound of an airplane or in the lines of the spires of St. Hilaire, the past contained in the savor of a madeleine ... they have no meaning if one does not extract it from them.... The grandeur of real art is to rediscover, grasp again, and lay before us that reality from which we become more and more separated as the formal knowledge which we substitute for it grows in thickness and imperviousness—that reality which there is grave danger we might die without having known and yet which is simply our life.

For Church, this translation from the simple image, keenly observed, to the essence or value of that image echoes one of Webster's definitions of *translation*: "being conveyed from one place to another; removed to heaven without dying." Her intense focus goes beyond mere self-expression rooted in the ego. These poems are self-explorations intensely wrought, bodied-forth, and magical, so that self expression and revelation of the world are one and the same. As these poems vary in structure and kinds of revelation, they energize the understanding, signify the poet's dedication to change, to grow, to see things anew. Church's cumulative effect on the reader was what Thoreau, whose works she studied, advocated in his notebook, Thursday, Dec. 10, 1840:

> I discover a strange track in the snow, and learn that some migrating otter has made across from the river to the wood, by my yard and the smith's shop, in the silence of the night. I cannot but smile at my own wealth when I am thus reminded that every chink and cranny of nature is full to

overflowing—that each instant is crowded full of great events.

Such poetry that translates and relates, is likely organic and revolutionary, so that in this collection of Church's poems we discern not simply the static, realistic image, but the search for a form to accommodate meaning and thus the connection the poet makes in the act of writing between inner and outer worlds. In writing "to keep from getting lost," the poet activates the paradox common to all art. For Church, these images, these objects activate the very self "lost" in the service of this dedication. As she commented to Sarton in regard to her life, "solitude is a way of waiting for the inaudible and the invisible to make itself felt."

Like most lyric poets, Church tends to want to write a longer narrative and thus implies in the repeated motifs, themes, and images the connections between poems. If, then, the poem serves as a study in inner autobiography—symbolic event in the poet's life—then taken together this collection constitutes a narrative, a story of that life. Church saw connections between her writing and external events. Often she would leap up during a conversation and read a poem to make a point. She also held that plot or action was what activated the primordial or archetypal image so that, taken together, these poems make a symbolic story. Like Jung, she believed that art consists of the unconscious activation of an archetypal image. The artist's unsatisfied yearnings reach back to a "voice" or what Jung called the collective unconscious. The artist discerns the psychic elements that play a part in the life of the collective.

Church, who said she was "up to her ears in mythology" (as well as listening to the Rio de los Frijoles), richly taps both sources. Denise Levertov, in describing this "rhythm of the inner voice of the poet," explains this gift further:

> What it means to me is that a poet, a verbal kind of person, is constantly talking to himself, inside of himself, constantly approximating and evaluating and trying to grasp his experience in words. And the "sound" inside his head of that voice is not necessarily identical with his literal speaking voice, nor is his inner vocabulary identical with that which he uses in conversation. At their best sound and words are song, not speech. The written poem is then a record of that inner song.

Treating as she did the shifting issues which caused conflicts between the old and the new, Church reconciles, as Jung advocated, the insight of the artist and the needs of society, the pattern of her poems a bridge between both.

As Church once said about Haniel Long's poetry and life as poet, the "finding" of one's life is a heady experience that one desperately wants to share. "It is as though one held in one's hand the mustard seed that might become the greatest of all trees and longs to summon all the birds of the air to shelter in it." In the quest for the enriched and shared life in the poem, the reader may feel as she did when describing the search for the seldom-given, almost perfect poem: "It is as though, walking among sand grains on an ancient riverbed, we come upon the perfectly formed crystal of which all others are only approximations." With these poems, stones that they are—birds, bread, stones—we hold in one hand the warm remnant of a mountain. Haniel Long once wrote Church: "You know how for a poet everything is a symbol and we write only for those who will understand us." Church's gift is such that she makes poets of us all.

HUMOR
Literary, Periodical, Political

Marietta Holley:
The Humorist as Propagandist

Walter Blair was quite right in calling Marietta Holley a propagandist.[1] Born on the family farm in Jefferson County, New York, in 1836 where she lived until her death in 1926, she confronted the nineteenth century's most urgent issues in the twenty novels which span a 41-year career. Racial and religious questions, women's rights, temperance, fashion, manners, travel—all were scrutinized by her crackerbox philosopher, Samantha Allen, whose wisecracks and button-hole logic entertain and edify the reader.[2] All also derive from Holley's central concern: if women could just get the vote, they could gain control of their lives and positively affect political decisions. Of course women did get the vote, and despite an immense popularity that earned her one reviewer's sobriquet as "the female Mark Twain," Holley's topicality and her formula novels made her a literary antique only ten years after her death.[3] For the reader who has the benefit of retrospect, Holley is unique among women writers of her day. Not only did she address crucial issues with a comic approach, but she used the language of humor to popularize the feminist stand generally unpopular with the mass audience because of its shrill or intellectual rhetoric. Samantha Allen, from rural Jonesville, spoke in a dialect her audience could identify with. Her rustic homilies were grounded both in a religious respectability and in everyday experience which made credible and simple the arguments for women's rights. More important, Holley discovered in humorous language not merely a proselyting agent for causes, but a means for exposing and challenging the overriding sentimental views which kept women from seeing themselves realistically.

149

When Holley published her first novel, *My Opinions and Betsey Bobbett's* (1873), she was immediately successful because she wrote in a tradition already popular with the mass audience. Sold by subscription by American Publishing Company salesmen, the novel was in the style of the Literary Comedians who used language extraordinarily (figurative language, malapropisms, exaggerations, understatement) and the Down Easters whose common-sense characters spoke dialect. Holley drew Samantha Allen in direct line from Ben Franklin's Silence Dogood, Benjamin Shillaber's Mrs. Partington, and Frances Whitcher's Widow Bedott. But there was an important difference. Samantha is indeed a wise fool like Mrs. Partington, remarking to Horace Greeley that the only Darwin she knows is Darwin Gowdey, a "natural fool"; but she also is the "hero" of the Samantha books. I say hero because she is strong, wise, active, self-reliant, a leader, organizer, adviser—all the characteristics usually exhibited by the male protagonist. Moreover, she has none of the so-called feminine shortcomings. She's not helpless, sickly, jealous, or sentimental. Yet she is a good wife and mother and is active in domestic and community affairs. What Holley had up her sleeve in combining these "male" and "female" characteristics is partially clarified in a remark she made in the article, "How I Wrote My First Books":

> ... at that time decidedly unfashionable, my first sketches were full of women's suffrage.... I thought that it would soften somewhat the edge of unwelcome argument to have the writer meekly claim to be the wife of Josiah Allen, and so stand in the shadow of a man's personality.[4]

Thus, all of the Samantha books are authored by "Josiah Allen's Wife," whose "unfashionable" judgments were accepted as sound for two other reasons. Holley made Samantha respectable according to the values of the period by making her religious. Holley also managed to "put a good deal of our common human nature into the characters," thus making her husband, Josiah, spinster Betsey Bobbett, as well as Samantha, strongly identified with ideas and real people.[5]

These last two accomplishments best enabled Holley to succeed in creating Samantha's dichotomous role of male and female traits, for in Betsey Bobbett and Josiah, Holley created straw men who were humorously felled by Samantha's example. Throughout this novel (as in the others), Samantha, by virtue of her horse sense, experience, morality, and her ability to apply these to problems in the home and the public world, is the paradigm of good behavior. However much the reader may laugh at Samantha for some of her gullible statements as he would Mrs. Partington, primarily he laughs with her at the other characters. That is, Holley manages to make the butts of her jokes her philosophical targets. And through the foibles exposed in Josiah and Betsey Bobbett, Holley systematically destroys the very virtues of womanhood her audience believes in and replaces them with the more realistic model of Samantha.

Betsey Bobbett and Josiah Allen represent the polarities of men's and women's spheres which so influenced behavior in the nineteenth century. Betsey Bobbett is Jonesville's ugly spinster, who writes sentimental poetry and pines to Samantha to assuage her singleness. Long of nose and short on experience, Betsey easily represents the extremes of the idol of womanhood. Though never married, she lauds this state by emphasizing a woman's worthlessness without it. Her poems are based on other sentimental models and hence in their artificiality represent Betsey's complete identity with the genteel heroine—shy, innocent, dependent, sentimental. In her pretension to education, she drops her r's as in this excerpt from the poem "Women's Speah," whose sensibilities speak for its author:

> Yes, wedlock is our only hope,
> All o'er this mightly nation;
> Men are brought up to other trade,
> But this is our vocation.
> Oh, not for sense or love, ask we;
> Our watchword is to married be,
> That we may be supported.
>> Chorus—Press onward, do not feah, sistehs,
>> Press onward, do not feah.
>> Remembeh wimmen's speah, sistehs,
>> Remembeh wimmen's speah.[6]

Josiah Allen, on the other hand, though he certainly loves Samantha, represents the characteristic ideas of men's sphere or the public life. Josiah articulates the popular sociological, religious, and political arguments of the nineteenth century, all which maintain and perpetuate such ridiculous characters as Betsey Bobbett.

That is, Betsey, in her ludicrous behavior mirrors the disastrous results of Josiah's arguments about women's natures even as Josiah, who mimes ideas without examining them and is dogmatic and short-sighted, is anything but the ideal husband Betsey would like to have. In a classic argument with Samantha, Josiah reiterates the traditional arguments about women that should keep them out of the public sphere. First he says they are physically weak, then that the law should protect their dependent dispositions, and finally that they are angels and thus deserving of protection from the public sphere.

The consequences of Josiah's stand and the willingness of Betsey Bobbett to pursue it, however ludicrously, were the worries of other feminists, like Susan B. Anthony and Francis Willard, because these beliefs made women powerless. Given the problems of abuse from drunken husbands or men irresponsible in various ways toward their families, Ellen Dubois outlines a very real power struggle in which, as the public and private spheres polarized, the family as a social institution lost its clout:

> Although the family continued to perform many important social functions, it was no longer the sole unit around which the community was organized. The concept of the 'individual' had emerged to rival it. In the nineteenth century, we can distinguish two forms of social organization—one based on the new creature, the individual, the other on the family.... These overlapping but distant structures became identified respectively as the public sphere and the private sphere.... Adult women remained almost entirely within the private sphere, defined politically, economically, and socially by their familial roles. Thus, the public sphere became the man's arena; the private woman's.[7]

Dubois goes on to point out that the temperance movement was able to muster great support from the very women defined by the experiences of the home because that movement appealed to women in terms of this environment, whereas the feminist movement was a "guerilla" fringe.[8] Susan B. Anthony and others almost defeated their causes by failing to recognize their audience:

> The very thing that made suffragism the most radical aspect of nineteenth century feminism—its focus on the public sphere and on the nonfamilial role for women—was the cause of its failure to establish a mass base.... The lives of

most nineteenth century women were overwhelmingly limited to the private realities of wifehood and motherhood, and they experienced discontent in the context of those relations.[9]

Add to this outline of women's sphere (the role of women and the changing influence of the family) the cardinal virtues of True Womanhood—the code for women's behavior within this sphere—and the meaning of Holley's selection of characters becomes clear. According to Barbara Welter, the tenets of True Womanhood were piety, purity, submissiveness, and domesticity.[10] But piety was the value which linked the rest together. Said the writer in the *Young Ladies' Literary and Missionary Report*, in religious vineyards you may labor without the apprehension of detracting from the charms of female delicacy."[11] Caleb Atwater indicated in *The Ladies' Repository* that religion complements submissiveness: "It is exactly what a woman needs, for it gives her that dignity that best suits her dependence."[12] As for domesticity, Mrs. S.L. Dagg noted religion as being a substitute for intellectual pursuits "that clash with … domestic duties."[13] Hence Samantha can as cannily quote scripture for the sake of argument as she can turn raw experience into insight and evidence. Her language and the logic it disseminates is religious and domestic and firmly roots her in her audience's mind as a member of the private sphere whose wisdom comes from that quarter.

From this vantage point, then, Samantha begins to debunk the very tenets her audience believes in by showing the principles of True Womanhood to be unrealistic, debilitating, and false. Holley accomplishes this on two levels: she dramatizes the ironic differences between action and expression, and she has Samantha use her domestically-grounded wisdom to expose illogical positions. For instance, each time Betsey opines the characteristics of the True Woman or suffers Samantha to listen to yet another genteel verse, Samantha is at work. The hot kitchen stove, darning, gathering wood, and other housewifely chores contrast Samantha's real situation—that is, marriage, wifehood, motherhood—with Betsey's artificial notions. "Men do admire to have wimmen clingin' to 'em, like a vine to a stately tree, and it is indeed a sweet view," Betsey says one day to Samantha who has finished her morning's work and is doubling carpet yarn. Samantha counters with a typical extension of the metaphor, which, carried to its logical end, proves

Betsey's comment illogical. "So 'tis," says Samantha. "I never was much of a clinger myself. Still if females want to cling, I haint no objection. But as I have said more'n a hundred times if men think that wimmen are obleeged to be vines, they ought to feel obleeged to make trees of themselves, for 'em to run up on" (p. 237). This pattern of testing the expression of ideas against reality (action and experience) or against language based on the observable reality of the domestic sphere comes full circle when Samantha reiterates Betsey's basic vine/tree philosophy to a potential husband Betsey is pursuing. "Are you willing to be a tree for Betsey?" Samantha asks. His answer confirms Samantha's argument. Without a word, he escapes to the barn.

Another example illustrating the discrepancy between the premises of True Womanhood and reality occurs in Samantha and Josiah's classic argument on women's suffrage. Josiah posits that women are too weak to go to the polls, and Samantha chooses a familiar strategy in rebuttal: she takes him literally. "You may go into any neighborhood you please, and if there is a family in it, where the wife has to set up leeches, make soap, cut her own kindlin' wood, build fires in winter, set up stove-pipes, drown kittens, hang out clothes lines, cord beds, cut up pork, skin calves, and thatched straw with a baby lashed to her side—I haint afraid to bet you a ten cent bill, that that woman's husband thinks that wimmin are too feeble and delicate to go to the polls" (p. 265). The full effect of Samantha's tack is best illustrated at the end of this scene. Josiah has argued that because women are angels, they are *too good* to vote with men. Then, when Samantha admonishes him to bring her some wood from the woodpile, he says, "I would get some this minute Samantha but you know jest how hurried I be with my spring's work, can't you pick up a little for this forenoon? You haint got much to do have you?" "Oh no," says Samantha in an ironic tone, "nothin' at all, only a big ironin', ten pies and six loaves of bread to bake, a cheese curd to run up, 3 hens to scald, churnin' and moppin' and dinner to get. Jest a easy mornin's work for an angel." The scene and debate ends when Josiah promises to get the wood tomorrow, and Samantha thinks to herself: "I said no more, but with lofty emotions surging in my breast, I took my axe and started for the wood pile" (p. 98).

Within this pattern of juxtaposing expressions against experience or verifying arguments by concretizing them, as Samantha does with Josiah's statement about angels, Samantha excels at developing her own arguments from the ground up. That is, she uses domestic metaphors, images, or instances—verifiable reality—and derives her philosophic truisms from them. She ironically practices what a character in *The Other Girls* (1873) says, "The best and brightest things I ever thought have come into my head over the ironing board or the bread making."[14] This is ironic because the tenets of True Womanhood which keep Samantha and women behind the ironing board are the very ones debunked. About suffrage and its relationship to piety and purity, Samantha says, "I don't know as it [women voting] would be any more public business, than to sell Episcopal pin cushions, Methodist I scream, or Baptist water melons, by the hour to a permiscuus crowd" (p. 226). About domesticity and submissiveness as they relate to suffrage, she says:

> Wimmen find time for their everlastin' tattin' and croshain.'
> They find plenty of time for thier mats, and thier tidys, thier
> flirtations, thier feather flowers, and bead flowers, and hair
> flowers, and burr flowers, and oriental paintins, and Grecian
> paintins, and face paintins. They spend more time a frizzin'
> thier front hair than they would to learn the whole constitu-
> sion by heart; and if they get a new dress they find plenty of
> time to cut it all up into strips, just to pucker it up and set it
> on agin ... but when it comes to an act as simple and short as
> puttin' a letter into the post office, they are dreadful short on
> time. (pp. 227–28)

As for women's nature, Samantha strikes one of her best domestic metaphors: "You may shet a lion up for years, in a room full of cambric needles and tattin shettles, and you can't get him to do anything but roar at 'em, it haint a lion's nature to do fine sewin. And you may tie up a old hen as long as you please, and you can't break her of watin' to make a nest, and scratch for her chickens" (p. 239). Yet, Samantha carefully builds with her domestic language an argument that provides that women's blind compliance to the activities of their sphere have limited their natures. "If God had meant that wimmen should be nothin' but men's shadders, he would have made gosts and fantoms of 'em at once," she says. "The very reason why men's talk as a general thing is nobler than wimmen's is because they have nobler things to think about ... when did you ever know a passel of men to set down and spend a whole afternoon talkin' about each other's vest, and mistrustin' such a feller painted; fill a women's mind with big, noble sized thoughts, and she won't talk such little back bitin' gossip as she does now" (pp. 230–31).

What Samantha's domestic experiences allow her to argue is not an end to housekeeping, church work, and typical female activities, but a balance between the private and the public spheres and an *application* of the training the private sphere gives women. During the course of the novel, Samantha illustrates these two points by successfully arguing for women's rights with a diverse group of people—a free-love lecturer, an unmarried woman who lectures on the joys of marriage, Ulysses Grant, Dr. Mary Walker, and Victoria Woodhull—and by traveling to New York to see Horace Greeley. In her discussion with Greeley—a reiteration of the popular antisuffrage arguments—Samantha suggests that women are capable of entering into public life precisely *because* of their domestic training. Here, Samantha manages to convert her domestic metaphors to public affairs and the White House, which is in need of a good "house cleanin'." Arguing against Greeley's statement that nature made men rulers she says:

> Nature made queen bees Horace. Old Nature herself clapped the crown on to 'em. You never heard of king bees, did you? Industrious equinomical critters the bees are too. The public duties of that female don't spoil here, for where will you find housework done up slicker than hern?... Where will you find a better calculator than she is? No dashin' female lobster-esses pullin' the wool over the eyes of her Senators. No old men bees gaddin' round evenin's when their confidin' wives think they're abed dreamin' about their lawful pardners—no wildcatishness, and smokin' and drunkenness, and quarrelin' in her Congress. You can't impeach *her* administration no how, for no clock work ever run smoother and honester. In my opinion there has a great many men set up in their high chairs that would have done well to pattern after this Executive female. (pp. 284–85)

The ease with which Samantha slides from the natural world to the home to the public world is emblematic of how handily Holley would resolve the double standard of the private and public spheres. But more than just argue for the vote, it's clear that Holley intended to awaken her audience from their complaisant endorsement of hollow values. And though she uses a language that the mass audience of women would be familiar with, she often advocated what was good for the goose was good for the gander. In one argument about rearing children, Josiah tells Samantha that their daughter Tirzah Ann can't go to the circus but son Thomas Jefferson can. Samantha's retort transfers the values of women's sphere to men's: 'The Lord made Thomas Jefferson with jest as pure a heart as Tirzah Ann, and no bigger eyes and ears, and if Thomas J. goes to the circus, Tirzah Ann goes too ... purity and virtue are both masculine and feminine gender ... God's angels are not necessarily all she ones" (pp. 115, 117). Furthermore, if Thomas J. goes with the boys for a smoke and a chew, Samantha plans to buy Tirzah Ann a pipe.

Despite the distinctive attention to women's suffrage in this Holley novel and others, the modern reader can appreciate several less topical characteristics of Holley's work. For one thing, the novels are written by a woman—that is, the character Samantha is a writer who in the prefaces explores all the doubts and chagrins of the nineteenth-century woman writer. Moreover, Holley, who was a dedicated writer of genteel poetry and a correspondent with Whittier and Longfellow, explored in humorous language a less sentimental and more realistic fictional world in which women could examine themselves. Holley's success is one reason why humorous writing became a legitimate method by which women writers could explore personal, social, and political absurdities. This new role gave subsequent writers a new power far removed from their earlier decorous or didactic writing. When women became humorists they could develop wider ranges of style. And, in becoming the tellers of the jokes, like Holley they had new opportunities for more dynamic characters and identities. Most of all, as Holley did with her persuasive domestic language, female humorists as entertainers relate in a unique way to their audiences. Walter Blair says that "Samantha did more for the cause of women's rights than many hard workers ever accomplished by serious speeches and arguments."[15] One could argue that Dorothy Parker, Phyllis McGinley, Jean Kerr, Erma Bombeck, Frank Lebowitz, Nora Ephron, Rita Mae Brown, and the string of humorists that follow godmother Holley have done the same for their own causes.

Notes

1. *Horse-Sense in American Humor* (Chicago, 1942), p. 238.

2. For a complete list of Holley's novels and a brief discussion of her many subjects, see Katherin Blyley's dissertation, "Marietta Holley," University of Pittsburgh, 1936.

3. See *The Critic*, 1904, p. 6 for a short comment and photograph.

4. "How I Wrote My First Books," *Harper's Bazaar*, Sept. 1911, pp. 404–5.

5. "How I Wrote My First Books," p. 404. Holley also notes the reluctance of readers to acknowledge that a woman wrote the book—an unmarried woman at that who might not be expected to write so cogently about married life.

6. Marietta Holley, *My Opinions and Betsey Bobbett's* (New York, 1873), p. 184. All subsequent references will be to this edition and will be quoted parenthetically in the text.

7. "The Radicalism of the Woman Suffrage Movement: Notes Toward the Reconstruction of Nineteenth-Century Feminism," *Feminist Studies*, Fall 1976, p. 64.

8. Dubois, p. 69.

9. Dubois, p. 68.

10. Barbara Welter, "The Cult of True Womanhood," *American Quarterly* 18 (1966): 151–74.

11. *Second Annual Report of the Young Ladies' Literary and Missionary Association of the Philadelphia Collegiate Institution* (Philadelphia, 1840), p. 20.

12. "Female Education," *Ladies' Repository and Gatherings of the West: A Monthly Periodical Devoted to Literature and Religion*, 1 (Cincinnati), p. 12.

13. *Second Annual Report*, p. 26.

14. *Horse Sense*, pp. 238–39.

15. *Horse Sense*, p. 239.

Comic Columnists Since the Civil War: Evolutions in the Vernacular Voice

In 1886, newspaper editor Charles F. Rudolph, working with eight-column home print in a tumble-down adobe in the Texas Panhandle, announced the birth of a new trailhead town with this salutation: "The *Tascosa Pioneer* tips its beaver to the people of the Texas Panhandle on this fair June morning and settles down to business." For Rudolph, who liked to tip a bottle as well, business consisted of the frontier journalist's usual fare of news, weather, gossip, and ads like this one for Dunn and Jenkins Saloon: "A most deservedly popular resort," whose owners are "particular about their brands and propose to set no 'pizen' before you." A business less lucky in the changing fortunes of the cowtown earned this valediction: "The Hard Times restaurant has gone out of business. It was not altogether hard times that did it." In his column "Cupid's Victims," Rudolph detailed a more predictable vocation: "The marriage bells have jingled hereabouts for the past two or three months. There is a growing impression that this business will come to an abrupt halt, however, on account of material becoming scarce." Rudolph wrote of "hen fruit," in the market, the arts "terpsichorean," pony express riders lost in blizzards and ice men who hoped for a slow thaw. In his report of a hail storm, "many an unlucky calf, pig, and chicken turned its toes to the daisies." Moreover, when the same was true for some gunslingers, and Tascosa, with its own Boot Hill cemetery, a violent cowboy strike, and visitors like Billy the Kid, got a rough reputation, Rudolph chided: "Tascosa has not had a man for breakfast in a week." Boosting the farmers, he just as glibly deadpanned: "People build a country, not cows."[1] Such folksy wisdom, like the better-known work of Mark Twain, Artemis Ward, or Bill Arp, not only typifies the journalist's use of humor to achieve a rapport with his audience from the post-Civil War period to the turn of the century; it illustrates a trend that continues to the present day as well: the country journalist transferred the vernacular and style of the oral tradition to the news page. When newspapers and magazines were departmentalized, the comic columnist assumed this role of the storyteller. A brief look at representative columnists illustrates how the column, in its evolution, has translated characteristics of the oral tradition into an urban voice in an urban landscape.

As in its use as a mouthpiece for Benjamin Franklin's Silence Dogood, the newspaper, from colonial times to the turn of the century, was a repository of native American humor, entertaining, cajoling, instructing readers—indeed, appealing to them by keeping them close to their oral tradition. Despite repeated pronouncements by such observers of American life and wit as Mrs. Trollop, James Thurber, and Melvin Maddocks that American humor was dead, like God, or George Burns, it continued to reappear in various forms—perhaps most continually in newspapers, and later, in magazines. Of humorous journalism after the turn of the century, Norris Yates says, "Between 1900–1920 the humorous column of the urban daily, conducted in each case as the personal organ of one writer, grew to become the most important single medium of American humor."[2] During this period the sons of Charles F. Rudolph moved East—that is, journalists who got their start in the Midwest or West found the urban centers appealing: Eugene Field moved from Denver to Chicago; Franklin P. Adams, from Chicago to New York. Vestiges of earlier frontier journalism survived: Alfred Henry Lewis of Arizona wrote his "Old Cattleman" stories for the Kansas City *Times* and *Star*, and Louis T. Stone's "Winsted Liar" column recorded the behavior of the Winsted animals—a cow who gave ice cream in the winter and a bulldog who hatched out a setting of eggs. But, in general, the two strains of folk humor most popular in newspapers and periodicals during the nineteenth century—southwest humor and Down East humor—became a hapless country cousin in the city. George Ade in *Fables in Slang* (1899) and *More Fables in Slang* (1900) pulled the crackerbox out from under the common sense oracle by using this character's traits to expose not the superiority of rural horse sense but the seediness of small town life. Ade describes one farmer with a Whiskbroom set of whiskers. "If you had thrown a Pebble into this Clump," Ade writes, "you would have scared up a Field Mouse and a couple of Meadow Larks."[3] And out in Mark Twain country—San Francisco—Gillette Burgess wrote not of blue-tongued jays or buckshot-swallowing bullfrogs, but of a purple cow in his magazine *The Lark*. So the period was a transitional one. Writers moved East; better-educated audiences supported a variety of humorous periodicals including *Vanity Fair*, *Punch*, and *Life*; humorous journalists increasingly made their fortunes in the city and the syndication of their columns made national the influence of their environment. And if, as Walter Blair suggests, oral story-telling "caused both skill and assiduity to come into play" and affect the "style, structuring, and the characterization of the written story,"[4] then the on-going tale-swapping at the Whitechapel Club in Chicago and the Algonquin in New York combined with older oral tradition to influence the column's content, style, and voice. The column—the "personal organ" as Yates calls it—continued to identify the humorous columnist as storyteller amid the more objective reporting of other sections of newspapers and magazines. This voice could be varied by the shape of the column itself, which could allow older forms—the frame tale, for instance—to be utilized. But most of all, these older forms proved adaptable to the changing values in an urban setting.

An example of this adaptation in this transitional period is columnist Don Marquis. Apprentice to Joel Chandler Harris as a columnist for *Uncle Remus's Magazine* and admirer of Eugene Field, Marquis was familiar with Field's notion that the East threatened the roots of native humor and Harris's belief that the vernacular voice was unique. Harris wrote: "The vernacular is part of Americans' personality. It belongs to their history, and it seems in some ways to be an assurance of independence and strength, or sanity and wisdom, of honesty and simplicity."[5] Thus, when Marquis created his cockroach correspondent—archy—who laboriously typed out his reactions to contemporary social subjects such as strikes, psychic powers, and prohibition, as well as philosophical subjects, he created an animal menagerie reminiscent of Harris's fables. Yet archy, who parades with Mehitabel the cat, Warty Bliggens the toad, Freddy the Rat, and a number of other critters including spiders, a lady bug, lightning bug, flea, and cricket, through Marquis's *The Sun Dial* (1912–1922), narrates his fables from a unique position: he is a free-verse poet reincarnated in a bug body. And a cockroach body at that. This dilemma Marquis uses to create a central tension and an urban fable. As archy says in "the open spaces": "one trouble with/ cockroaches is that they/ do not get/ out into the open/ air enough/ even the tumble/ bugs play golf/ and it keeps/ them serene and/ wholesome...."[6] The morals to such fables, often woven into archy's halting lower case free verse or climaxing some pieces, typify the confusion of the urban life. In his first exchange with the columnist, made by throwing himself head-first off the typewriter carriage onto the keys, archy writes:

> expression is the need of my soul
> i was once a vers libre bard
> but i died and my soul went into the body of a cockroach
> it has given me a new outlook on life
> i see things from the underside now
> thank you for the apple peelings in the wastepaper basket
> but your paste is getting so stale i cant eat it
> there is a cat here called mehitabel i wish you would have
> removed she nearly ate me the other night why dont she
> catch rats that is what she is supposed to be for
> there is a rat here she should get without delay[7]

Certainly, there is the traditional lesson about mankind to be learned from beastly mistakes. Warty Bliggens, for instance, fancies that toadstools were designed just to protect him from the elements and that he is the center of the universe; "similar/ absurdities/ have only too often/ lodged in the crinkles/ of the human cerebrum,"[8] archy writes. The lightning bug glows so brightly as he is flattered by a gallery of animals that mehitabel spots him and eats him. But, more so, the moral of these beast fables is disturbing, indeed, confusing. Mehitabel, transmigrated from an Egyptian princess, thinks of herself as a lady, but blandly resorts to drowning her kittens when her chronic affairs with itinerant Toms tie her down. "Artists shouldn't have offspring," she says.[9] Thus, the natural world—the mirror of man's world—is out of joint. Archy rewrites Aesop's fables: "The meads must be made safe/ for sheepocracy," he has the wolf tell the sheep. "And so jollying her along," archy reports, "with the usual human hokum/ he led her home/ and the son of a gun/ did not even blush when/ they passed the mint bed/ gently he cut her throat."[10] Archy rewrites

natural history as well, and he indicates in "what the ants are saying" an ironic way in which the meek will inherit the earth:

> it wont be long now it wont be long
> man is making deserts of the earth
> it wont be long now
> before man will have used it up
> so that nothing but ants
> and centipedes and scorpions
> can find a living on it [11]

Along with this adaptation of the fable to the experiences of
city life, Marquis reflects archy's dilemma in his language. Because
of his lower case life, archy attempts to articulate his underside
view as a language of experience much like the crackerbox oracle
used the vernacular to suggest the superiority of commonsense
truth to formal learning. But archy vacillates between his despair
over his bug body and his consequent associates (that is, bugs who
do not speak his language) to disdain for man. "i pass it on to
you," he writes the columnist one day, "in the hope that you may
relay it to other/ human beings and hurt their feelings with it ...
the only reason i tolerate you is because/ you seem less human to
me than most of them."[12] Thus, he speaks in a language both col-
loquial and poetical. He embodies the conflict between education
and rube knowledge historically funny to Americans. Moreover,
neither extreme of language allows him to solve the problems of
his urban existence. His struggle with language best illustrates this
fact when in "CAPITALS AT LAST" he manages to transcend his lower
case existence when one day he chances to lock the shift key. Writing in rhymed verse, he lyrically soars beyond the vernacular until
a lurch by hungry Mehitabel releases the key and sends him scur-
rying for his life into the typewriter. The situation dramatizes how
the schism in archy's life—the poet's soul in the cockroach body—
effects a duality in his mode of expression. Rather than reflect the
positive values Harris enumerated as synonymous with the vernacular experience, or the values touted by the crackerbox character whose mis-mastery of language suggested common sense,
archy's fables reveal only one constant byword: survival.

Despite Marquis's being closest to native American sources
during the '20s, another urban columnist successfully combined
certain elements of oral storytelling with urban attitudes and experiences. Robert Benchley, a New Englander, contributed to

Franklin P. Adams's "The Conning Tower," and flowered as a columnist on *Vanity Fair*, the *New Yorker*, and later as a filmmaker. Benchley excelled in the monologue, the format for mock lectures, self-help essays, reviews, and various commentaries on life and literature. At first glance, his character, the Little Man, seems antithetical to the crackerbox character popular at the turn of the century, for the Little Man is victim of enemies as diverse as French pastry, inter-office memos, and hay fever. Yet, if the narrator has not the control of his world as the common sense character did by utilizing everyday experience as a motto, he has one way of surviving: he tells the story of his own victimization. In "The New Bone-Dust Theory of Behavior, Is Your Elbow All It Should Be?," "The Correspondent School Linguist," "Why Does Nobody Collect Me," "The Social Life of the Newt," he masters Mark Twain's age-old classic point of making the storyteller the focal point for the listener rather than the story. In Benchley's case, the "I" of the monologues engages the reader by being both joke and joker. Benchley's character battles bathroom slippers that insist on shuffling away from him under the bed; he recommends in "The Menace of Buttered Toast" that "you get out of bed, go into the kitchen in your bathrobe, cut three slices of whatever happens to be in the breadbox (usually cake), and toast it,"[13] and suggests in preparing the ground for a garden to use dynamite. A trip to the dentist he entitles, "The Tooth, the Whole Tooth, and Nothing But the Tooth."

Yet, when the reader examines Benchley's use of language and structure, though the narrator dissembles himself, he is so tyrannized by the domestic and technological and, even, natural scene, that he borders on quiet hysteria. Benchley's use of another Twain trick—straight from the oral tradition—dramatizes the Little Man's haplessness. The structure of the shaggy dog story, recommended by Twain as one of the funniest modes of storytelling, is carried to crazy extreme. Benchley's character bumbles his way through parenthetical thoughts, digressions, meaningless allusions, and even transposition of words and phrases with the outward acumen of a scholar. Of course, the feigned erudition is deflated by tangled words and nonsensical phrases which facilitate the heart of the shaggy dog story—the anti-climax. For instance, in "Political Parties and Their Growth," he says:

During the early years of our political history the Republican Party was the Democratic Party, or, if you choose, the Democratic Party was the Republican Party. This led naturally to a lot of confusion, especially in the Democratic Party's getting the Republican Party's mail; so it was decided to call the Republicans "Democrats" and be done with it. The Federalist Party (then located at what is now the corner of Broad and Walnut streets and known as "The Swedish Nightingale") became, through the process of Natural Selection and a gradual dropping-off of its rudimentary tail, the Republican Party as we know it today.[14]

Benchley's persona gets so bumfuzzled that he often is a Mr. Malapropism calling Mark Twain Mark Clemens in "Tiptoeing Down Memory Lane" and finally dubbing him the author of that story about the "Drunken Frog of Calvados County." Part of the charm of Benchley's anticlimactical narrator is his urge to tell all—to think out loud as in this excerpt from "Cell-formations and Their Work":

In about 1/150000 of a cubic inch of blood there are some five million cells afloat. This is, as you will see, about the population of the City of London, except that the cells don't wear any hats. Thus, in our whole body, there are perhaps (six times seven is forty-two, five times eight is forty, put down naught and carry your four, eight times nine is seventy-two and four is seventy six, put down six and carry your seven and then, adding, six four three, one, six naught, naught, naught), oh, about a billion or so of these red corpuscles alone, not counting overhead and breakage.[15]

Unlike the earlier version of the shaggy dog story, narrated, say, by Mrs. Partington to illustrate some common sense truth, Benchley's shaggy dog stories demonstrate not truth but neurosis. Likewise, the Little Man's vernacular is not grounded in experience that makes for solid judgment, but in experiences that taunt, challenge, and ultimately defeat. The only strength the narrator has is in *knowing* he is defeated from the beginning. The self-ironist—the character who can make fun of himself—bests no one, but at least he's telling the joke on himself. Language, then, is the key to surviving.

Today, some fifty years after the beginning of the Marquis-Benchley heyday, the urbanization of America and its accompanying situations still give an impetus to columnists' humor, to their creation of narration, structure, and style. Characteristics of oral storytelling continue to surface, but more than ever the column is a linguistic environment fashioned by the columnist to accommodate the influence of literary skills for a chiefly urban public. The experiences that contributed to frontier folk humor hardly are duplicated in the city, that is, hearty individualism and other such traits that made for a ring-tail roarer or a shifty Simon Suggs exist seldom on the slick pages of *Esquire*, the *New Yorker*, or the *Village Voice*. Walter Blair has noted that with the death of Will Rogers in 1935, no witty oracle has emerged since as a prominent humorous character. Yet, if no one character emerges, various narrators do to carry on the familiar theme of survival, among them a number of women columnists who collectively appeal to a wide audience with their "Little Women" image. For instance, Erma Bombeck writes in her book "If Life Is a Bowl of Cherries, What Am I Doing in the Pits?":

> I heard a story about a research rat recently that makes one pause and reflect. The rat's name was Lionel. He was a pro. He had everything tested on him from artificial sweetners to bread preservatives to foot fungus viruses to brutal subway experiments and survived them all. A researcher figured he was something of a Superrat ... an immortal who could sustain life no matter what the odds.
> The researcher took him home as a pet for his children. Within three months, this indestructible rat was dead.
> It seems that one day the rat was taken for a ride in the car with the teenage son who had a learner's permit. The rat died of a heart attack.
> That's what this book is about. Surviving.[16]

Survival for Bombeck means more than physically conquering dirty clothes hampers, overcharged Visa cards, or pet anacondas. Yet, her tales are decidedly physical—almost like the roguish world of the Southwest humorists. Like Benchley's Little Man, she is made the butt of countless experiences. In "The Varicose Open" she describes herself attempting to master the feat of picking up the ball: "Gripping the racket, I forced the ball to the inside of my foot where it rolled over the foot and toward the net. I cornered it and started inching the ball up my leg, but lost my balance and fell into the net. Approaching the ball once more I accidentally kicked with my foot, and in a crouched position, I chased it to the corner of the court, slamming my body into the fence."[17] Again, like Benchley, the difference is that she is the narrator. Yet, unlike Benchley, her weapon is the well-turned phrase. To her son, who is trying to teach her how to pick up the tennis ball and chides that they'll spend a few more weeks on that before trying to learn the game, she counters: "Now let me tell you how to pick up the towels in the bathroom. You simply bend your body in the middle, grasp the towel firmly between...."[18] In almost every situation, Bombeck, the victimized mother, really comes out on top because of her glib retorts or the control she exerts as a narrator. Often her lists of feats and defeats read like a tall tale. And these exaggerations give her clout as the victim since (1) they are no surprise to her, and (2) she reinforces her chosen status as wife, mother, and chief bottle-washer by surviving these most heinous victimizations. For the reader, she lists self-help treatises such as "Replacing the Toilet Tissue Spindle" and "Operating the Clothes Hamper." She describes situations seemingly out of control:

> On Sunday, she dragged the brood to church. The baby chewed up two verses out of the hymnal, one child followed a rolling dime all the way to the altar, and the third stole a sponge from the Holy Water font. The minister stood at the door, and said: "You should be thankful the good Lord is looking after you."[19]

But, unlike Benchley's neurotic character, language never fails her. Her vernacular voice comes from a woman who consistently keeps a dirty house and knows it. As she notes in one piece, "not even an orthodox worrier, " as she calls herself, can survive a week when things go right. The car starts, she finds a place to park in front of the supermarket, Angie Dickinson looks a little fat that night on t.v., and she cooks a dinner no one had for lunch. She tells her husband, "Do you know that yesterday I went into the boys' room and their beds were made? The bad times I can handle. It's the good times that drive me crazy." But, with relief, just at that moment they hear a car turn into the garage and make the "sickening scrape of a fender when it meets an immovable wall. Things are looking up," Bombeck concludes. That is, losing is the way the Little Woman wins. She counts coup with each defeat because, along with her narrator, the audience anticipates and identifies with the absurdities of family life and suburbia, and sees the victim as heroine for surviving such challenges.

Not as widely known as Bombeck, who appears in over 700 newspapers as a syndicated columnist, Nora Ephron nevertheless appeals to a higher-brow crowd with her column in *Esquire* and other pieces for ladies' magazines. Ephron, rather than dramatize situations in her monologues, is more analytical and confessional, yet still uses the anticlimaxes, humorous word play, and metaphorical language of the folk humorist. Ephron's folk, however, are strictly urbanites. The vernacular, consequently, is shaped by this well-bred, well-educated woman whose style brings together a conversational flavor with a literary manner. Some examples: "We have lived through the era when happiness was a warm puppy, and the era when happiness was a dry martini, and now we have come to the era when happiness is knowing what your uterus looks like"; a consciousness-raising group is like "running a soap opera"; she asks Linda Lovelace, "Why do you shave off your pubic hair in the film?" to which she replies, "it's kinda hot in Texas"; Julie Nixon Eisenhower is described as "a chocolate-covered spider."[20]

But when Ephron talks about herself, as in the case with previously discussed self-ironists, she is identified as storyteller and subject functioning in a highly-controlled linguistic environment. The best example is her ever-popular essay, "A Few Words About Breasts," which begins calmly with a statement about androgyny in the first paragraph only to end in that paragraph with these remarks:

> Even though I was outwardly a girl and had many of the trappings generally associated with girldom—a girl's name, for example, and dresses, my own telephone, an autograph book—I spent the early years of my adolescence certain that I might at any point gum it up. I did not feel like a girl. I was boyish. I was athletic, ambitious, outspoken, competitive, noisy, rambunctious. I had scabs on my knees and my socks slid into my loafers and I could throw a football. I wanted desperately not to be that way, not to be a mixture of both things, but instead just one, a girl, a definite indisputable girl. As soft and as pink as a nursery. And nothing would do that for me, I felt, but breasts.[21]

Thus, Ephron as narrator survives in a world of glib style. In a more sophisticated manner than Bombeck, she is aware of the power of pace, a surprising one-liner, a well-placed word. Thus, despite the neurotic concern she expresses over flat-chestedness and late-blooming in this essay, she has us enthralled as much because of style as subject-matter. Note this last paragraph and its stinger:

> After I went into therapy, a process that made it possible for me to tell total strangers at cocktail parties that breasts were the hang-up of my life, I was often told that I was insane to have been bothered by my condition.... And my girl friends, the ones with nice big breasts, would go on endlessly about how their lives had been far more miserable than mine. Their bra straps were snapped in class. They couldn't sleep on their stomachs. They were stared at whenever the word "mountain" cropped up in geography. And *Evangeline*, good God what they went through every time someone had to stand up and recite the Prologue to Longfellow's Evangeline: "... stand like druids of eld .../ With beards that rest on their bosoms." It was much worse for them, they tell me. They had a terrible time of it, they assure me. I don't know how lucky I was, they say.
>
> I have thought about their remarks, tried to put myself in their place, considered their point of view. I think they are full of shit.[22]

Hence, in its evolution from folk journalism to newspaper column to syndication in nation-wide newspapers and popularity in class magazines, the comic column has been shaped by the style, structure, and characterization of the oral tradition as it was reinterpreted in an increasingly urban environment. Characters, such as Marquis's archy, gradually disappeared with the appeal of the personal narrator who, like Benchley, more directly expressed the attitudes and conditions of readers. In Bombeck and Ephron, the narrator is fully identified with the author, and the older forms, such as mock oral, shaggy dog, and beast fable, are replaced by a strictly linguistically-hewn environment, which, unlike the Benchley persona and archy, the writer controls in a literary manner. Thus, educated writing has merged with the vernacular resulting in a distinctively urban style perhaps most extremely illustrated in the columns of Fran Lebowitz in the *Village Voice* and *Mademoiselle* magazine. In the attempt to play the role of town wit, Lebowitz is much more self-conscious than either Bombeck or Ephron and relies much more on literary conventions for her cuteness than on hard experience which is the root of the vernacular voice. Experience is translated from even the physical struggles of suburbia Bombeck likens to frontier overland journeys to the second-hand experience of books and observation. Consequently, Lebowitz' voice is detached and predictable. In some ways, however, she plays an urban crackerbox, whose observations can be pontificated from a position of experience with city life and an over-conscious style which exposes the dangers of this experience. What has happened, then, in this evolution of the comic columnist, is the older forms of storytelling once expressing positive values in the nineteenth century are utilized to express just the opposite values in the twentieth century, as in Marquis and Benchley, and Ephron. For instance, the shaggy dog story in Benchley represents not control of the audience's attention, but the neurosis of the narrator. Despite the trend of contemporary columnists to create a linguistic environment in which they can control the laughter as they continue to direct themselves and others, one commonality with the oral tradition continues to exist. The vernacular voice provides, as Joel Chandler Harris suggested, if not positive values, at least a sense of security. It is the voice of survival.

Notes

1. *The Tascosa Pioneer*, Archive and Manuscript Collection, Panhandle-Plains Historical Museum, Canyon, Texas, n.p.

2. Norris W. Yates, *The American Humorist: Conscience of the Twentieth Century* (Ames: University of Iowa Press, 1964), 14.

3. George Ade, *Fables in Slang*, quoted in Walter Blair and Hamlin Hill, *America's Humor* (New York: Oxford University Press, 1978), 38.

4. Walter Blair, *Native American Humor* (Chandler Publishing Co., 1960), 75.

5. Joel Chandler Harris, quoted in *Native American Humor*, 143.

6. Don Marquis, *Archy and Mehitabel* in *The Best of Don Marquis* (New York: Garden City Books, 1939), 3.

7. Marquis, 34.

8. Marquis, 14.

9. Marquis, 70.

10. Marquis, 42.

11. Marquis, 160.

12. Marquis, 118.

13. Robert Benchley, 'The Menace of Buttered Toast," in *The Benchley Roundup* (New York: Delta, 1954), 323.

14. Benchley, quoted in *America's Humor*, 429.

15. Benchley, quoted in *America's Humor*, 430.

16. Erma Bombeck, *If Life Is a Bowl of Cherries—What Am I Doing in the Pits?* (New York: Fawcett, 1971), 13.

17. Bombeck, 83.

18. Bombeck, 83.

19. Bombeck, 52.

20. Nora Ephron, *Crazy Salad* (New York: Knopf, 1975), 68.

21. Ephron, 3.

22. Ephron, 4.

Emily Dickinson's Crackerbox Humor

In a letter that illustrates her finest sensibility, Emily Dickinson wrote to friend and associate editor Doctor Holland of *The Springfield Republican*: "Who writes those funny accidents, where railroads meet each other unexpectedly, and gentlemen in factories get their heads cut off quite informally? The author ... relates them in such a sprightly way, that they are quite attractive."[1] I say "finest" sensibility, not only because sentimentality is absent in Dickinson's remark, but because her sense of humor and aesthetic sense are kin. "Tell the truth but tell it slant," she would later say. In her letter, the words "unexpectedly" and "informally" provide that certain slant readers encounter in Dickinson's poetry—that jarring of the mind which Emerson in his essay "The Comic" (1843) says the idealist experiences when he examines reality. "His perception of disparity," Emerson says, makes "the eyes run over with laughter"[2]: "It affects us oddly, as to see things turned upside down, or to see a man in a high wind run after his hat, which is always droll. The relation of the parties is inverted—hat being for the moment master, the by-standers cheering the hat."[3] Dickinson's perception and expression of inversion has led critics to call this propensity "wit,"[4] "riddle,"[5] or "metaphysical mirth."[6] But Dickinson's taste for train wrecks and unceremonious decapitations—cultivated in her reading habits and in "seeing New Englandly"—makes Constance Rourke right: she is a comic poet in the American tradition.[7] Specifically, in many of her humorous poems a crackerbox persona plumbs comic modes to tell the truth slant.

Beginning with George F. Whicher, Dickinson scholars document the effect of her reading on her wit. In *Emily Dickinson's Reading*, Jack L. Capps gives two chapters to colonial and contemporary and to newspaper and periodical materials in order to demonstrate the poet's eager perusal for information, recreation, and gossip.[8] In his chapter, "American Humor," Whicher details in particular the periodicals: "Next in importance to the Bible in determining the mental climate of Emily Dickinson's formative years was *The Springfield Republican.*"[9] Copied and published alongside Irving, Bryant, Poe, Longfellow, Holmes, Hawthorne, and Whittier in the paper were "Mrs. Caudle's Curtain Lectures" from *Punch* and favorite American specimens from Johnson J. Hooper, author of the popular *Adventures of Simon Suggs*, William T. Thompson's *Major Jones's Courtship*, New England favorite Seba Smith's Major Jack Downing letters, burlesque interviews by "Jonathan Slick" (Ann Stephens), odd character sketches from *The Yankee Blade*, and other mock sermons, tall tales—in short, a variety of native American wit. Dickinson delighted in this humor, for she imitated the mock sermon, funny Valentine, and humorous story while at Mount Holyoke Seminary and wrote for the humorous manuscript magazine *Forest Leaves* at Amherst Academy. An early letter indicates her mastery of the "screamer" technique, even as it mentions one of the most popular crackerboxes of the day, Mrs. Partington. Emily chides her uncle Joel Norcross for not writing:

> You villain without a rival, unparalleled doer of crimes, scoundrel, unheard of before, disturber of public peace, "creation's blot and blank," state's prison filler, *magnum honum* promise maker, harum scarum promise breaker—oh, what can I call you more? Mrs. Candle would call you a gentleman, that is altogether too good Mrs. Partington, "a very fine fellow," neither does this apply.[10]

As others of her letters show, Dickinson's appreciation of a Mrs. Partington type was due to its correspondence to Dickinson's own terse and tart Yankeeness. She wrote in a letter: "No one has called so far, but one old lady to look at a house. I directed her to the cemetery to spare expense of moving."[11] The author of such a sentiment could not fail to appreciate Mrs. Partington's cool expediency coupled with a false tug of the conscience when she directs Ike to drown some kittens. "I'll take the chill off the water," she says. "It would be cruel to put them in stone cold."[12] Never mind that Dickinson despised cats and threatened to drown Vinnie's "pussies" herself. As Whicher, Thomas H. Johnson, and Richard Chase so convincingly show, Dickinson suffered greater disjunctions than that. The fact of her inheritance of a religion that had lost its powers of revelation, of her domination by a father—Squire

Dickinson—whose aristocratic aplomb was lessened by a burgeoning democracy, of her capacity for love never quite requited, of her
tutelage under under critics like Thomas Higginson whose poetics
were obtuse to her own, all contribute to her comic vision. Emerson explains how such disjunctures figure into comedy:

> The presence of the ideal of right and of truth in all action
> makes the yawning delinquencies of practice remorseful to
> the conscience, tragic to the interest, but droll to the intellect.
> The activity of our sympathies may for a time hinder our
> perceiving the fact intellectually, and so deriving mirth from
> it: but all falsehoods, all vices seen at sufficient distance, seen
> from the point where our moral sympathies do not interfere,
> become ludicrous. The comedy is the intellect's perception of
> discrepancy.[13]

So Dickinson, whose physical and psychological detachment from
the world facilitated the distance Emerson speaks of, could control
the absurd flux of her universe by objectifying it comically in verse.
Or as filmmaker Charlie Chaplin maintained: long shot for comedy, close-up for tragedy. Thus Dickinson could write a poem
about a very common occurrence—the landing of a balloon—in
which the last line is a deadpan of the author's intent:

> Their liquid Feet go softly out
> Upon a Sea of Blonde—
> They spurn the Air, as 'twere too mean
> For Creatures so renowned—
>
> The Gilded Creature strains—and spins—
> Rips frantic in a Tree—
> Tears open her imperial Veins—
> And tumbles in the Sea—
>
> The Crowd—retire with an Oath
> The Dust in Streets—go down—
> And Clerks in Counting Rooms
> Observe—"'Twas only a Balloon."[14]

This poem, along with several others that feature a gallery of
village and national types and local events, is an excellent example
of Dickinson's crackerbox humor. The first two stanzas, with their
exaggerated and fantastic images, suggest a tall tale. The "Liquid
Feet" of the "Gilded Creature" that move over a "Sea of Blonde"
are quickly undercut by distinctly human and, as such, devastating

qualities. The creature "so renowned" spurns the air, ironically the very territory it is made for. The consequence of its puffed-up pride follows: frantically straining to avoid its fate, the "imperial Veins" are torn open. The final stanza of the poem, though not precisely proverbial, completes the description of the exaggerated first part of the poem, as the Gilded Creature tumbles into the sea and the crowd resorts to cursing its loss of entertainment. The "clerk mind" tells it as it is: "'Twas only a Balloon." Dickinson has constructed an anecdote in the crackerbox tradition that lives through exaggeration and understatement. The capitalization and punctuation further suggest the crackerbox's propensity for misspelling and bad grammar despite a pretension to knowledge evident in the elevated diction. For instance, in the first stanza the dashes are inconsistent with the other two stanzas, causing a seemingly ridiculous enjambment: "retire with an Oath/ The Dust in Streets...." But consistent with the change in punctuation is the exclusively vernacular level of the last stanza, whereas, in line three of the first stanza, the vernacular ("'twere too mean") and the elevated diction are mixed. The linking of these alterations suggests a "wise fool" has been at work here as we are set up by the earthy last stanza for the last pithy line. Ironically, "'Twas only a Balloon" recalls the earlier "'twere too mean," making logical what appeared to be the work of a rube. Both the pretentiousness of the balloon and the pigeon-hole pragmatism of the clerks are found wanting. This is true especially if the reader acknowledges another character in the poem—the narrator. As ignorant as this narrator seems to be, he nevertheless expounds unexpected or unwanted truths from behind his mask of inferiority.

Though it is likely that in the above poem Dickinson was having a little fun with a *Republican* article dated three years before which commented on a balloon's ascension, "It almost seemed like the translation of the prophet Elijah," Dickinson's implied persona comments on drunken preachers, genteel ladies, gossips, neighbors, and the self like other crackerbox characters.[15] A transposed metaphor, surely the error of a fool, carries the meaning of this poem to its past, inquiline word:

> The Leaves like Women, interchange
> Sagacious Confidence—
> Somewhat of nods and somewhat
> Portentous inference.

> The Parties in both cases
> Enjoining secrecy—
> Inviolable compact
> To notoriety.
>
> (987)

Less harmful than these gossipy dames is the town drunk who, because of the crackerbox's missed rhyme in the last four lines, is safely oblivious to "Honor" for one more day:

> The Ditch is dear to the Drunken man
> for it is not his bed—
> his Advocate—his Edifice—
> How safe his fallen Head
> In her disheveled Sanctity—
> Above him is the sky—
> Oblivion bending over him
> And Honor leagues away
>
> (1645)

Not so for the victimized parishioners who must face either the fire and brimstone or the liberal preacher. The crackerbox innocently pictures the former in impossible terms: he "scalps your naked Soul—" (315). The latter earns a proverbial phrase: "He preached upon 'Breadth' till it argued him narrow" (1207). But the local genteel ladies earn the crackerbox's kindest regards, even if he does use a word in the third line that erotically connotes hair:[16]

> What soft—Cherubic Creatures—
> These Gentlewomen are—
> One would as soon assault a Plush—
> Or violate a Star—
>
> (401)

Other than sheer entertainment, the import of the above examples is explained in this comment on the crackerbox role by Norris W. Yates:

> The crossroads oracles carried on the tradition of the court fools and jesters in satirizing their readers in an era when the common man was the uncrowned king, at least in the official mythology. Too, they could, at the same time, flatter the people by giving them a sense of superiority over the unlettered or conceited rube even as this hayseed told them their faults. However, any criticism would tend to be directed at the fictitious oracle rather than at the real but shadowy

writer behind him. Thus the writer could criticize his readers
up to a point but still amuse and hold them.[17]

But, one could argue, isn't it illogical for a poet with few published poems in her lifetime to fret about audience? Why the
mask? Though the crackerbox brand of humor is not discussed,
critics do see Dickinson's humorous guise as fit for certain of her
proclivities. John Wheatcroft in his article on her "serious view of
humor" argues that at its simplest level Dickinson's humor is the
mind at play.[18] Paul Anderson notes the comic vein as a means of
control.[19] Dr. John Cody believes that her "poetry does not so
much represent the sublimation of love, as is generally supposed,
as it does the sublimation of rage."[20] Beyond these considerations,
however, I think Dickinson's crackerbox is a Yankee adaptation of
the Puritan self. By that, I mean the crackerbox's attitudes and
characteristics are those of the secularized Puritan. The Puritan's
technique for introspection, as exemplified by Jonathan Edwards,
was the talent of every shrewd Yankee who could objectify and
analyze his subtlest inward feelings. Outward conditions could be
controlled by this inward consciousness. As George Whicher says,
"For him [the Yankee] the mind was its own place, and in alliance
with infinite power could surmount any tangible obstacles."[21]
Thus, for Dickinson the poem was the stage upon which the mind
could play out its feelings, objectify and analyze them for the audience of self. In this sense, the crackerbox takes on a different dimension. Certainly, he is the "reputable" character who attacks
those who threaten integrity by their dishonesty, pretentiousness,
or carelessness. But once Dickinson uses him to question such
"absolutes" as God's will, he seems subversive. Dickinson's
cat/banker/burgler God, her "Papa above," illustrate this angle.
Yet such a God, who indicts lovers by disparaging communication
or makes of man a mouse, deserves a hoax and the most extreme
form of the Yankee nature—the trickster—that Richard Dorson describes:

> The Yankee appeared as a scheming knave and fertile
> prankster who matched his wits against a suspicious world,
> both for business and pleasure. Ingrained in the Yankee fable
> lay the conception of a wily, cozening trickster, poised under
> a mask of ingenuousness and seeming good will for a
> shrewd deal or act of mischief.[22]

As Hamlin Hill and Walter Blair say in *America's Humor*, this Yankee was first and foremost a trickster, but not a criminal. It would seem that just such a character is needed to combat a God whose promises are only fulfilled through death. Thus, in the mock prayer, "'Heavenly Father' take to thee" (1461), the persona says that God "In a moment contraband" with his own "candid Hand" "Fashioned" "The supreme iniquity"—man. The persona flatters the creator only to reveal the trick of such feigned flattery by ending with an apology for God's "own Duplicity." In "Papa above" (61), the persona converts the idea that "In my Father's house are many mansions," to that of a mouse and a rat in "seraphic Cupboards." In fact, in a whole canon of "religious" poetry, Dickinson has her crackerbox, if not fool God, at least expose Him for what He is.[23]

This brings us to one final consideration of Dickinson's crackerbox humor. In the wise fool's dealings with mere mortals and the Most High, he mediates between the extremes that are the hallmark of the tension in Dickinson's poetry—what Edmund Burke in his *Philosophical Enquiry* (1757) called the sublime and the beautiful. The homely metaphor, the wise saw, the revelation of noble thoughts through the vernacular—even the enigmatic term "wise fool"—are humorous ways of combining the petite with the grand or the terrifying with the familiar. On a simple level, we see that such combinations either domesticate the horrifying or make astonishing the minute. This characteristic runs throughout Dickinson's poems as exemplified in an early poem, "A little east of Jordan" (39), in which the "little" of line 1 deflates the pomposity of the event and Jacob, termed "A Gymnast," asks that he be allowed to leave off wrestling in order "To Breakfast." Similarly, in "The gentian weaves her fringes" (18), the Christian burial service is parodied: the presiding clergyman is "An aged Bee," the funeral parlor a garden, the Son a "Butterfly," and the Holy Ghost a "Breeze." In "The Bible is an antique volume" (1545), written and re-written toward the end of her life, Dickinson calls the Holy Spirit the "Holy Spectres," the enlightened writers "faded men," "Satan," "the Brigadier," Judas "the Great Defaulter," David "the Troubadour," and Eden "the ancient Homestead." In another late poem, "Elijah's wagon knew no thill" (1254), Abraham is told to sacrifice his "Urchin" son Isaac, for God is characterized as a "Mastiff" who needs the sacrifice of human blood in order to be flattered and placated. In "'Heavenly Father' take to thee" (1461), written late, the religious lyrics became a mock prayer juxtaposing "the supreme iniquity"—man—against the supposed "father" who in fact fashioned "In a moment contraband" sinful man. The implication is that the narrator—the moral child—recognizes God's "own duplicity": that if "We are Dust" we are, after all, made in His image. Thus Dickinson jousts with conventionally awesome and common items by mixing or exchanging their characteristics.

If we return to Emerson's explanation of the comic and consider it in terms of Dickinson's religious background, an Edwardian Calvinism, we may note how this crackerbox comedy serves an aesthetic (as in poetics) end. Burke, Edwards, and Emerson all share a similar aesthetic and philosophical theory. Burke and Edwards both borrowed from Locke a part of their theory of the sensations. Emerson and Edwards both were moralists who thought that harmony, wholeness, and the consenting together of parts approximated the Godhead. Beauty is a result of this consent of being to Being, as Edwards called it in his "A Treatise Concerning Religious Affections." The sixth sense for Edwards was a religious one which makes man whole with God. Likewise, Emerson affirmed the Whole: "Nothing is quite beautiful alone; nothing but is beautiful in the whole."[24] For Edwards, the "dissent from being" was deformity, the region of devils.[25] But if we remember Emerson's definition of comedy, what is irreligious for Edwards is, in Emerson's terms, the pre-requisite of the comic: man because of his reasoning faculty finds delight in perceiving the discrepancy between the parts and the Whole. Taking this one step further, Burke noted two extremes in the "whole": the sublime and the beautiful. The leading passion of the sublime was self-preservation which contended against the sources of the sublime: pain, sickness, death, fear, obscurity, power, infinity, magnificence, and suddenness. The leading passion of the beautiful, on the other hand, was a sense of society expressed in the love of man or woman and whose source was pleasure. Pain and pleasure could be joined in a "relative pleasure," Burke said, which he called *delight*. Thus, terror can cause delight, Burke said, because "the passions which belong to self-preservation turn on pain and danger; they are simply painful when their causes immediately affect us; they are delightful when we have an idea of pain and danger without being actually in such circumstance."[26]

In these terms, as sticky as they are, the crackerbox ultimately functions psychologically. What delights, for Dickinson, is that irreverence that challenges a hidebound Calvinist God. Seeing the distorted, the discrepancy, is for Edwards and his tribe a dissent from being. Yet this delight also is a "relative pleasure" which unites the insular self with society. It turns on the "idea" of pain and anger without actually subjecting one to the fray. Hence the crackerbox—that dramatizer of disparity for the sake of unity—is as essential to Dickinson's poetics as her poetics are to her psyche. For Dickinson, neither the Puritan religion nor science nor transcendentalism could serve as a system. Only the realm of the imagined self—of the imagination—seemed true. In this sense, the crackerbox persona was the role of the poet imagined.

In England, Burke's philosophical treatise was put into practice in the Gothic novel where the atmosphere of the sublime dramatized the moral ambiguity of the villain-heroes and an anti-clerical plot. In America, it was expressed by the young woman whose fear made her whistle like a boy in a dark graveyard and say, "Nature is a Haunted House—but Art—a House that tries to be Haunted." Why the mask? "The Truth must dazzle gradually/Or every man be blind."

Notes

1. George F. Whicher, *This Was a Poet* (New York, 1939), p. 181.

2. Ralph Waldo Emerson, "The Comic," in *The Portable Emerson* (New York, 1946), p. 206.

3. Emerson, p. 212.

4. Charles R. Anderson, *Emily Dickinson's Poetry: Stairway of Surprise* (New York, 1960), pp. 3–4.

5. Dolores Dyer Lucas, *Emily Dickinson and Riddle* (DeKalb, IL, 1969).

6. Paul W. Anderson, "The Metaphysical Mirth of Emily Dickinson," *Georgia Review* 20 (Spring 1966), p. 72.

7. *American Humor* (New York, 1931), p. 267.

8. Jack L. Capps, *Emily Dickinson's Readings* (Cambridge, MA, 1966), pp. 101–43.

9. Whicher, p. 170.

10. Whicher, p. 177.

11. Whicher, p. 178.

12. P.B. Shillaber, "The Cats and Kittens," quoted in Walter Blair, *Native American Humor* (San Francisco: Chandler Pub. Co., 1960), p. 267.

13. Emerson, p. 206.

14. Thomas H. Johnson, ed., *The Poems of Emily Dickinson* (Cambridge, MA, 1951). All further references to Dickinson's poems appear in parentheses following the quotation and refer to the system of numbering adopted by the editor.

15. C. Anderson, "Emily Dickinson Looks at the American Scene," *New England Quarterly* (June 1958), p. 165.

16. The definition in *The American Heritage Dictionary of the English Language* (1969) reads, in part, "having a deep, thick pile ... irregularly from *pilus*, hair."q

17. *The American Humorist: Conscience of the Twentieth Century* (Iowa, 1964), p. 22.

18. "'Holy Ghosts in Cages'—A Serious View of Humor in Emily Dickinson's Poetry," *American Transcendental Quarterly* 72 (1964), p. 96.

19. Paul W. Anderson, p. 80.

20. John Cody, *After Great Pain: The Inner Life of Emily Dickinson* (Cambridge, MA, 1971), p. 415.

21. Whicher, p. 163.

22. Quoted in *America's Humor* (New York, 1978), pp. 183–84.

23. See poems 18, 59, 357, 413, 437, 597, 1479, 1545, 1612, others.

24. Quoted in Whicher, p. 164.

25. Leon Howard, *"The Mind" of Jonathan Edwards: A Reconstructed Text* (California, 1963), p. 72.

26. *A Philosophical Enquiry into the Origin of Our Ideas of the Sublime and the Beautiful*, ed. J.T. Boulton (New York, 1958), p. 32.

The Widow Bedott Meets Samantha Allen: The Role of Female Humorists

In the preface to her first book, Marietta Holley had her crackerbox character, Samantha Allen, tell husband Josiah that a voice had instructed her to write a book on "wimmen's rights." As Samantha says: "This skairt him worse than ever—I could see, by his ghostly countenance—and he started off on the run for the camfire bottle ... but he could see by my pale but calm countenance that I was not delirious any and he knows I have got a firm and cast iron resolution." But Josiah gets the last word in, almost, when he counters: "Who will read the book when it's rote, Samantha?" Who indeed? Twenty years later, Stinson Jarvis, writing in the "Open Letters" column of the November 1892 *Century* magazine, seemingly answered this question with one of his own: "Why, in literature, are there no female humorists?" Possibly Jarvis had escaped the high-pressure tactics of American Publishing Company salesmen, or his high-brow tastes excluded popular books from his definition of literature, for Samantha's book did get written (even if she tells us it was chiefly because she promised Josiah he wouldn't have to pay people to read it). And it was read: *My Opinions and Betsey Bobbet's* launched a forty-two year career during which Holley would never be without a publisher. In 1887 her *Samantha at Saratoga or Racing After Fashion*, like Frances Whitcher's *Widow Bedott Papers*, which was still being published thirty years after her death, was a "better seller." In 1892, the year of Jarvis' query, Funk and Wagnall's advanced Holley $14,000 for *Samantha at the World's Fair* (1893). So when the Widow Bedott met Samantha Allen—and they did meet on parlor tables and in the popular imagination during a common time of popularity—they ranked their creators among the most beloved of nineteenth-century humorists.

Nevertheless, Jarvis' letter indicates what a rare achievement this popularity was for these writers by explaining conditions that negated female humor:

> Our sister, so far, is compelled by her nature, to make idols and ... she is too much in earnest over her devotion to them to lapse into what would seem to her to be frivolity. Whether erected rightly or wrongly, these idols become a part of herself, and must be propped up at any cost. If, in spite of all her effort, some other power throws them down, or if they throw themselves down, she may become bitter, or sad, or savage, or religious—but never humorous.[1]

A quick scan of the typical "female" writing of the period verifies Jarvis' contention: religious biographies, didactic seduction novels, even satiric feminist essays all exemplify the seriousness with which these writers and their audiences regarded such idols. Not only that, but, as Jarvis continues, this seriousness had its drawbacks. "Their picturesque passion for reverential wonderment," their inability to acknowledge human weakness in any way except to condemn it, both result in vanity, a lack of reason, and an unwillingness to admit to any disillusioning truth. On the other hand, men suffer no such debilitating qualities because, unlike women, they "learn by education that they know nothing," form a fellowship upon the ground of mutual loss, and make a sport of absurdity. In other words,

> man's humor is the outcome of his capacity to see truth, or at least discern untruth, and thus to make comparisons. Accustomed since childhood to find the sawdust dropping out of everything ... he ceases to allow his early and more effeminate passion for something to adore and idealize to override his growing desire for truth.[2]

Though he intimates that idealizing is both a feminine and an immature quality, Jarvis also suggests that experience, more than nature, determines the ability to discern truth, indeed, that experience can be an antidote for one's nature. It follows, then, that humorists like Twain, Ward, Billings, Shaw, Shillaber and others—men widely experienced—would debunk, in their female characters, the "nature" nurtured on limited experience. But the fact that Whitcher and Holley ridiculed these qualities also suggests that they first had to laugh at themselves, for, as Jarvis says, "as long as women cannot break their idols or suffer injury when these get broken, just so long they will never produce humor."[3] In part, this ability came from broadening experiences, both personal and historical, for the combined careers of these humorists—1846–1914— spanned a major period of transition and reform in women's roles. In part, it came from a realization as writers and readers of that period's fare of "women's" literature that the language that reflected and shaped women's vicarious experiences was one of seriousness, sentiments, and artificiality. It was a language that not only created unrealistic idols, but provided no means for criticizing the discrepancy between the real and ideal. Whitcher and Holley found the language of popular humor—Down Eastern and Literary Comedians—appropriate not only for parody of this genteel sensibility and its values, but for creating a fictional world antithetical to that known by and about most women. Furthermore, each writer created two distinctly different female characters—the adder-tongued widow and the common-sense Samantha. Since both were writers, their use of language allows the reader to explore their natures, motivations, identities—something no doubt their creators were vicariously grappling with.

I

Before Whitcher and Holley popularized the Widow and Samantha, there were other funny females, but none who tapped native American sources while focusing on a leading female character. We remember Sarah Kemble Knight (1666–1727) for her spirited sallies into proletariat life outside her native Boston; Marcy Warren (1728–1814) wrote a series of political plays satirizing contemporary Boston; Susanna Haswell Rowson (1762–1824) and Judith Argent Murray (1751–1820) wrote comedies expressing moral and social values.[4] But these were imitative: most mimed English comic modes, the authors not only rare as humorists but as women who wrote. When that "damned mob of scribbling women," as Hawthorne called them, did appear on the scene, they captured a market polar to that of the writers of Native American Humor. Though in growth these two types of popular literature parallel one another, social changes would further insulate them from each other. Ellen Dubois explains the distinct separation of "family" and "society" that constituted these changes:

> Although the family continued to perform many important social functions, it was no longer the sole unit around which the community was organized. The concept of the "individual" had emerged to rival it. In the nineteenth century, we can distinguish two forms of social organization— one based on the new creature, the individual, the other based on the family.... These overlapping but distinct structures became identified respectively as the public sphere and the private sphere.... Adult women remained almost entirely within the private sphere, defined politically, economically, and socially by their familial roles. Thus, the public sphere became man's arena; the private woman's.[5]

So in the popular imagination developed a mirror of the polarization of men's and women's experiences. Men and women did share family life, but women, lacking the secular experience of the public sphere, lacked also the impetus to record their private world in any other than serious terms. Men, on the other hand, developed in their popular literature a way of dealing humorously with the myths, traditions, and rich language of the world of the family and of the individual, though they wrote increasingly of the public arena. Ironically, this native American humor early threatened the sensibility of high-brow critics, the very ones likely to praise the serious and genteel writing of women. Women who wrote popular literature thus developed none of the duplicity of sensibilities that men did. This literature for men provided alternative entertainment and oftentimes criticism of their own genteel tradition. Women's literature, on the other hand, was singular; the sensibilities of popular and high-brow literature were the same. Like the insulated experience of the private sphere, it offered no means for examining itself. Hawthorne, almost alone among critics, could see the long-term threat of the scribbling mob. Not only did they threaten his magazine market, a market for serious writers, but their writing was inferior; they wrote "like emasculated men."

Yet despite the truth of Hawthorne's judgment, there were reasons for this spineless literature and these reasons explain why a literature so lachrymose in subject and style was so popular. One would suppose that the vitality of the family offered ample native elements for the lady writer. After all, the Yankee peddlar did come to the home, the comedy of manners so popular with English audiences occurred in American villages, and Native American dialects were spoken over the kitchen as well as the tavern table. The simplest answer lies in the sheer kinesiology of the private and public spheres. When, because of this dichotomy, the family no longer was the only unit of social organization, women guarded even more tenaciously their source of identity and power—their familial role. The hallmark of this role, which Barbara Welter has amply described in her article "The Cult of True Womanhood: 1820–1860," consisted of four cardinal principles: piety, purity, submissiveness, and domesticity. Each principle demands not only a dedication to superiors—God and man—but an identity grounded in collective responsibility, not the individual. The only respectable movement into the public sphere, then, was not one that would give vent to the recognition and use of native materials. The only acceptable movement for women from the private to the public sphere was religious, ironically because it did not divorce women from the other three virtues of True Womanhood. Said the *Young Ladies' Literary and Missionary Report*, in religious vineyards, "you may labor without the apprehension of detracting from the charms of feminine delicacy." Moreover, in religion (or piety) lay the fulcrum for all biological, social, and philosophical attitudes about women. Dr. Charles Meigs explained to a graduating class of medical students that women were *naturally* religious: "Hers is a pious mind. Her confiding nature leads her more readily than men to accept the proffered grace of the Gospel." Caleb Atwater, Esq., indicated in *The Ladies' Repository* that religion complements her submissiveness: "It is exactly what a woman needs, for it gives her that dignity that best suits her dependence." Furthermore, as Mrs. S.L. Dagg noted, religion should be a substitute for any "intellectual pursuits that clash with her domestic duties." She should instead do religious work "which promotes these very duties." Her thoughts, activities, physical and psychological reality thus defined by strict moral precepts, woman and her sphere were immobilized by the same attitudes that made them idols. Barbara Welter explains:

> The nineteenth century American man was a busy builder of
> bridges and railroads, at work long hours in a materialistic
> society. The religious values of his forebears were neglected

in practice if not in intent, and he occasionally felt some guilt
that he had turned this new land, this temple of the chosen
people, into one vast countinghouse. But he could salve his
conscience by reflecting that he had left behind a hostage,
not only to fortune, but to all the values which he held so
dear and treated so lightly.... In a society where values
changed frequently, where fortunes rose and fell with fright-
ening rapidity, where social and economic mobility provided instability as well as hope, one thing at least remained
the same—a true woman was a true woman. [6]

Immobility, as rendered by women's sphere serving as the status quo, was perpetuated by the only means to dislodge it: language. When women wrote about their experiences or even those
of the public sphere, the language that was a product and shaper
of this idealistic world was itself as artificial as the idols it described. Examine a typical sermon, treatise, magazine article, poem
of the period. The style is pervasive. Metaphoric, symbolic, full of
hyperbole and elevated word choice, it is a language with blinders
on. A main-line to ideals, it offers not even a peripheral glance at
the drama of dailiness. A.D.T. Whitney might very well claim in
The Other Girls (1873) that "the best and brightest things I've ever
thought have come into my head over the ironing board or the
bread-making," but the reality of such duties is circumvented by
consumptive prose and anaesthetized poetry. What women
learned about themselves and the world through their writing was
exactly what this style was praised for: "an unambitious style and
bland religious spirit." And, of course, this style was but an aping
of models, written by men, and deemed appropriate for their perusal. Note, for instance, the notion of the woman writer and the
style in which she's described in this Whittier poem:

> Foredoomed to song, she seemed to me;
> I queried not with destiny....
> What could I other than I did?
> Could I a singing-bird forbid?
> Deny the wind-stirred leaf? Rebuke
> The music of the forest brook?[7]

Or compare these lines from various sources that merge diverse
subjects with a constant metaphorical style: "The vestal flame of
piety, lighted up by Heaven in the breast of woman" would throw
its beams into the world of men; Lucy "with the seal of innocence

upon her heart, and a rose-leaf on her cheek" came out of her vine-covered cottage. "Purity is the highest beauty—the true polar-star which is to guide humanity aright in its long, varied, and perilous voyage."

The language about women's sphere, then, accomplished the same task the language that was a product of women's sphere (that is, written by women) did: it reinforced the virtues of true Womanhood and cemented its idolic base. But more important, it served, as language and literature always does, as experience. And in this case, "experience" offered no escape from, or alternate view of, the real world. Moreover, language, which may be used to promote understanding, and therefore narrow the gap between the word and the idea, itself became a means for guise in the hands of the genteel writers. Ann D. Wood explains one reason women persisted in writing in the very style that entrapped them:

> If the emergence of a group of feminine writers who threatened to corner the market alarmed men, it alarmed the women as well. The writers themselves wanted to have their cake and eat it too: stay "feminine" and write successful best sellers. On one level, this desire was rooted in shrewd analysis: "feminine" books got better reviews from male reviewers. On another, it genuinely expressed their own ambivalent guilt that they were not leaving the field to the "lords of creation," but taking it over, and enjoying the conquest. As a result of this complex pattern of motives and reactions, most of the women writers of the day like Sarah Hale and Grace Greenwood, subscribed to a rationale, heartily supported by their male reviewers, that attempted to prove how justifiable, innocuous, and even elevating their work was.[8]

Nevertheless, the language that came from women's sphere in the form of literature—for whatever reason—illustrated the gap between the ideal and the real. But more importantly, it illustrated how style may be used to disguise reality and can render language inoperable to explore the hypocrisy implicit in the pretension to certain values Like so much furniture polish, applied until it becomes a veneer, "feminine" literature supplied a gloss that was a coverup for some and a mirror of unrealistic expectations for another. What was needed was a good jibe in the ribs—an alternative to the serious, religious, sentimental literature that existed at the popular and high-brow level. And the jokester need not be a Sut

Luvingood disrupting Sicely Burns' wedding. Better to be a woman, like Marietta Holley or Frances Whitcher, who herself was a product of the literature of woman's sphere, and who could herself create this sentimental heroine, Permilly Ruggles:

> My hair was of that lovely hue that folks calls red and novils calls auburn. Sometimes I suffered it to flow cerlessly over my alagaster sholders, and sometimes I confined it on the tip top of my head with a quill. My face was considered immiently honsome. My figger was uncommon graceful, and I had a gret deal of dignitude. But more'n that. I writ poety of the first order, and I was called the biggest genus in Podunk. I knod I was a touch above the vulgar, as I said afore, and so I kep myself putty scarce.[9]

II

If it takes one to know one, then Whitcher and Holley knew the butts of their jokes very well. That is, of the comic characters they created, three were writers, and two, sentimental poets, precisely a profession both these writers at one time or another worked for. Of course they aimed for the best of this literary level, Holley writing to Longfellow and including with some poems a note: "I want to ask you—is there any *real* poetry in the verses I enclose?" Whitcher, too, confessed this proclivity: "I am heartily sick of Bedotting and Maguiring, and only wish I could be as well paid for more sensible matter."[10]

The conflict in values that seemingly arises when one is both a humorist and a sentimental poet may be explained, in part, by the above implied reasons for writing both humor and poetry. Holley reveals the self-doubts that plagued most humorists of her day: Am I a *real* writer? Can I master serious writing as well? Whitcher indicates a similar dilemma: "sensible" writing doesn't pay. But the resolution to the conflict goes beyond finding a respectable occupation that pays well. Explanation can be made by making two comparisons: one, a comparison of the writer's major characters to themselves; and the other, an examination of why the creators and their characters wrote.

Interestingly, the most notable experiences in the lives of Holley and Whitcher stack up either comparably or as dichotomies.

Indeed, though they were born twenty-five years apart (Whitcher, November 1, 1811–January 4, 1852 and Holley, July 10, 1836–March 1, 1926) and Holley outlived Whitcher by seventy-four years, their lives express both a contemporary feminine sensibility and yet a sense of historical transition.

Frances Whitcher, born Frances Miriam Berry, at a young age was a model for Elizabeth Cady Stanton's favorite essay, "The Solitude of Self." Stanton wrote: "Nothing adds such dignity to character as the recognition of one's self-sovereignty." Whitcher, writing Alice B. Neal, noted personal necessities for her own self-sovereignty:

> I can scarcely remember the time when the neighbors were not afraid that I would make fun of them. For indulging in this propensity, I was scolded at home, and wept over and prayed for by certain well-meaning old maids in the neighborhood, but all to no purpose. The only reward of their labor was frequently their likenesses drawn in charcoal and pinned to the corners of their shawls, with, perhaps, a descriptive verse below. Of course, I had not many friends, even among my playmates. And yet, at the bottom of all this deviltry, there was a warm, affectionate heart—if any were really kind to me, how I loved them.[11]

Her natural "sense of the ridiculous" which first marked an independent spirit thus led to a less desirable social reason for it, and Frances spent a lonely childhood often wandering in the woods. Her imagination gave vent to a strong sense of the supernatural, which probably manifested itself later in life in a religious seriousness, but it also was fed by a quality education, for she was an avid reader of the English classics, Mowatt, Sheridan, and others. No doubt this world of the imagination, along with her precocious expressions of it in parodies, verses, and drawings, assuaged the criticism she received for her satiric gifts as well as enabling her to draw from the very society of teas, social fads, and female gossip her isolation distanced her from.

This natural sense of humor and its consequent experience of independence was somewhat rewarded in her young womanhood, when she was a member in hilarious standing of the Maeonian Society, a literary group in her native Whitesboro, New York. Here she was applauded for such works as her eleven-chapter spoof of the then-popular *Children of the Abbey*, typical of the literature she despised, "filled with the most exalted sentiments, favourable to religion, morality, and virtue." The evidence of Frances Trollope's *Widow Barnaby* and the rustic humor of Seba Smith and Augustus Baldwin Longstreet in her next sketches about the Widow Bedott demonstrates her habit of bringing together her literary background and the observable behavior of her own neighbors.

When she married the Reverend Benjamin W. Whitcher in 1847, she entered into the very society she had, to this point, observed and satirized in her hometown of Whitesboro. Before, she had remained single until the late age of thirty-five, privy to the very active public world of Whitesboro where, in 1823, a new canal brought boatloads of westward bound migrants and a host of fads and reforms, including phrenology, Fourierism, perfectionism, women's rights, Millerism, and the usual religious revivals. Now, as the minister's wife, she moved with her husband to his new pastorate in Elmira, New York, where she continued to draw on the absurdities of village life, and in particular that of church activities, for her humorous sketches.

It seemed, for the first time in her life, she had both the security of an understanding and respected husband, and a career as a writer. She published her sketches primarily in Joseph Neal's *Saturday Gazette,* in Philadelphia, where Neal claimed, "the world is full of Bedott ... our readers talk of nothing else." Certainly, this became an unfortunate truth locally, when, after a local paper ran two of the sketches on the front page, asked "the question now is, about town, who is Captain Smalley?" The question was answered by a threatened lawsuit which resulted in the Whitchers' move back to Whitesboro. In the second set of sketches, most of which appeared in *Godey's Lady's Book,* Frances attempted to vindicate herself in the character of the minister's wife in the sketch "Aunt Maguire Treats of the Contemplated Sewing Society at Scrabble Hill." But her professed literary purpose, "the gift to gie 'em/ to see themsels as others see 'em!," became all too true both for her audience, at least the one in Elmira now critical of her, and for herself. In the accurate dialect of the Down Eastern humor, she had plumbed the materialism and false sophistication characteristic of growing urban centers. In 1850, she turned to an entirely different kind of writing, the result of pious intention perhaps called up by the repercussions of her "close" satire. "Mary Elmer, or Trials and Changes," biographer Thomas F. O'Donnell calls "all but unreadable ... a tale full of the sentimental cliches Mrs. Whitcher had so mercilessly parodied only four years before in the Bedott sketches."[12] She died of tuberculosis at age 41, never having seen her writing in book form, and having married, borne a child, and written most of her work in the last six years of her life.

If Marietta Holley enjoyed a writing career the length of Whitcher's life, never married, never mastered dialect, was forced to quit public school at age fourteen, lived all her life in and around Pierrepont Manor, New York, was never without a receptive audience and a publisher, and saw twenty-one novels published during her lifetime, still she shared important formative experiences with Whitcher. She, too, suffered as a child from the criticism of others about her writing. In her case, she wrote pious verses that when mimicked by her brothers caused her, she claimed, to be not only shy as a child, but to avoid invitations by Susan B. Anthony, Frances Willard, and others to speak when she was an adult. For the same reason, she turned down repeated attempts by publishers to get her to travel abroad to collect material for her books, and she refused Elisha Bliss's offer to bring her to Hartford to meet Mark Twain and Harriet Beecher Stowe. But if she was shy and solitary, she, like Whitcher, cultivated a degree of independence and "self-sovereignty," and a distance which allowed her to meticulously observe life around her. A strong puritan sense marked her family which was poor, unlike Whitcher's family, as evidenced by her sister's comment when she sent away her first dialectical piece for consideration by *Peterson's Magazine.* "You may get the paper back," she said, "but never the postage." Not encouraged by family either in her writing or in her choice of "heroines" (she admired a local school teacher who forsook her job for the more exciting, if "forward," occupation of book agent), she earned part of the family income by teaching music lessons in the Holley home. Later, when her father died, she became in effect a single head of household supporting her mother and sister.

Thus, when Holley wrote her first comic narrative, she was mature (37 years old) and independently established. Though she had no literary clubs or husband to encourage her writing, like Whitcher, she found her religion and voracious reading sustaining. She drew from both, claiming in "How I Wrote My First Books," that often a random turn of the Bible's pages gave her literary direction for the day. She wrote comically about religious questions

(*Samantha Among the Brethren*, 1883), and the appendix of that novel—six arguments for and against admission of women delegates to the General Conference of the Methodist Episcopal Church—testifies to the degree to which her reading materials influenced her choice of subjects. "She was an omnivorous reader," a November 1903 *Ladies' Home Journal* article said. "Her home is studded with books, padded and walled with them ... she always has a book in her hand."

Writing in the tradition of Yankee humor established before the Civil War in the works of Seba Smith, Benjamin Shillaber, and Frances Whitcher, she may be contrasted most dramatically to Whitcher in two areas: her dealings with the "women's question" and her approach to her material. Whitcher dealt with her material from the inside out, we may say. That is, she experienced much of what she satirized. In this way, her satire cuts both ways when she characterizes women; it exposes both the ignorant, pretentious, small-town gossip and the intellectual fool, for instance the "slab-sided critter," Samanthy Hocum, who lectures on women's rights. Holley, on the other hand, wrote from the outside, that is, she wrote "theoretically," often using other sources besides her own for her travel books; Susan B. Anthony and Frances Willard were among those who furnished letters, treatises, and documents for the writing of books on suffrage and temperance. Her guiding literary principle, as compared to Whitcher's reference to Burns, was to "create characters out of principles." Hence, in a very real way, Samantha was "episodin'" and "allegorin.'" Holley bridges the characteristics of the Down Easters and the Literary Comedians. Her characters are universal types, grounded in specific domestic and historical experiences, made more comic with phonetic misspellings like those of Artemis Ward.

When examined alongside their creators, Whitcher's and Holley's main characters (in the works which shared a common time of popularity, *The Widow Bedott Papers* and *My Opinions and Betsey Bobbet's*) represent more than a stylistic transition. The Widow and Samantha are foils; one representing the worst in womankind, the other, the best, that is, "mejumness," as Samantha calls it. The Widow is a gossip who excels in seeing her worst faults in other people, but not herself. In the twenty-one sketches that make up her adventures in Wiggleston, Slabtown, and Scrabble Hill, the widow's main concern is catching a husband since her own (it's rumored she "jawed" him to death) is deceased. The widow's rambling monologues reveal her to be vain, coquettish, vulgar, jealous, two-faced, unattractive—all the shrewish qualities conventionally connected with women. The humor hinges on the cleverness with which she pursues her goal of remarriage, and is grounded in a shrewd Yankee sense which is used to trick any available male. Gossip and "poitry" are her loquacious domains and are similar in the manner in which she uses them to trap her victims. But the men she pursues are just as absurd; though not gossips, they are eloquent, self-righteous, and self-serving. The gap between vernacular language and eloquent nonsense illustrates the hiatus of nature and experience. The Widow is not so much a "born" shrew as she is a victim of the limited experience of women's sphere. Unlike her creator, Whitcher, who knew a degree of individualism and self-reliance and the pleasures of a family, the Widow's dignity depends on catching a man, yet whether married or single, she spends most of her time invading the homes of others rather than sustaining a relationship with her own two children. Jane Curry says: "The center of hypocrisy illustrated by Widow Bedott and others lay in the social and religious pretensions of the middle class, the upkeep of which require much if not most of the time and creative energies of concerned participants."[13] Thus, the Widow's behavior, besides being antithetical to the four cardinal virtues of True Womanhood, questions the viability of those virtues at mid-nineteenth century.

Samantha Allen, on the other hand, or "Josiah Allen's Wife," as she is addressed by most folks in Jonesville, is happily, and realistically married ("If men and women think they're marryin' angels, they better realize they're gonna have to settle down with real critters"). This is crucial, since Samantha singlehandedly wages war on irrationality, sentimentality, artificiality, impracticality—all the foibles oftentimes prescribed to women but in the Samantha books characteristic of both sexes. Like the Widow, she comes from common stock, but she uses these "natural" proclivities to broaden her experiences and the soundness of her judgment, not to limit or to undermine them. In *My Opinions and Betsey Bobbet's*, Samantha's common sense challenges the "tender-headed" notions of spinster-poet Betsey Bobbet, confronts the illogic of Horace Greeley's arguments against women's rights, and exposes the artificial reasoning of husband Josiah's claims about women's inherent weakness.[14] Many times Samantha's actions speak at least as loud as her words, for instance the time Josiah tells her women are too weak to vote and then tells her to bring in two heavy pailsful of milk. Of course Samantha's physique—all 210 pounds of it—fairly squelches the image of a True Woman as a fluttery, helpless being. Samantha would have us believe women can be both tough-minded and loving, rational and caring, politically active and proper wives and mothers. The key, as Samantha advocates, is the ability of women to exist in both the private and public spheres. As she says, "Give a woman as many fields to work in as men, and as good wages, and let it be thought jest as respectable for 'em to earn their livin' as for a man to, and that is enough." The advice she could give the Widow Bedott, in fact, is precisely what she gives Betsey Bobbet: "It stands to reason that a woman wont marry a man she don't love, for a home, if she is capable of makin' one herself. Where's the disgrace of bein' a old maid, only wimmen are kinder dependent on men, kinder waitin' to have him ask her to marry him so as to be supported by him?" Unlike Holley, then, Samantha can have her cake and eat it too. She is happily married, a good wife and mother, a well-respected Christian woman of the town, yet an activist who will travel to New York when principle demands. In contrast to the Widow Bedott, who represents all the evils that precipitate from keeping up appearances of women and men as idols, Samantha is the comic ideal; that is, she exemplifies value made practical by the humorous (and realistic) context. Her "mejumness" is an attempt by Holley to illustrate the need for a transition in women's roles.

A final comparison of what prompts the Widow and Samantha to be writers is a commentary on Whitcher's and Holley's goals as humorist writers. On the simplest level, the Widow writes to catch a husband. This means she writes poems to flatter men and make herself look good. The combination of the two should be good for one husband. In the most telling sketch in the collection, "The Reverend Mrs. Sniffles Abroad," the fruition both of the Widow's second marriage and of her literary career is parodied in a scene of a writers' club. With names reminiscent of Fanny Fern and Grace Greenwood, the lady luminaries—Neil Nox, Kate Kenype, Fenella Fitzallen, and others—convene to read their works. A microcosm of the Widow's back-biting world, the writers pretend to elevated style and sentiments while criticizing each other. Typical of

Whitcher, no one is exempt, even "long-feller," as Priscilla says, "some tall indiwidiwal I s'pose." One of the writers, Priscilla reports, "cut him all to pieces, declaring that he had never writ a line that could be call poitry in all his born days. She said that his Eve Angeline was a perfectly nonsensical humbug." Despite this criticism, Priscilla's vanity gets the best of her and she claims, "She had a dretful severe critisisim on the American poits.... I guess she'll change her sentiments when she hears my piece. She'll think ther is such a thing as poitry in Ameriky then." Having already bagged her a husband, Priscilla is perfectly content to continue her hypocritical ways, this time to elevate herself as an artist. When two local papers battle over whose poems they'll publish, Priscilla remarks: "So I s'pose the tew papers'll be accusin' one another o' stealin' on't, and there'll be a reglar newspaper quarril about it; and I shall be drawn into public notice in a manner very imbarrassin' to my retirin' disposition. But I can't help it. We literary characters must expect to be subjected to a great many more onpleasant things than falls o the lot o' privit indiwidiwals—it's the fate o' genius."

Samantha, who is as bombarded as a sounding board for Betsey Bobbet's poetry as much as any man in *The Widow Bedott Papers*, has one word for Betsey Bobbet who one day is extolling an idol's "tendah verses." "Tender-headed," Samantha says. As for Samantha's reasons for writing, she says in the preface to *My Opinions and Betsey Bobbet's* that a voice instructed her to write a book on "wimmen's rights." With that charge, she gathers her cast-iron "resolution" around her, and addresses the reader on the title page: "Designed as a Beacon Light, to guide women to life, liberty, and the pursuit of happiness, but which may be read by MEMBERS OF THE STERNER SECT, without injury to themselves or the book."

Whitcher's and Holley's personal backgrounds suggest that their ability to debunk the sentimental poet was a way of laughing at themselves, or at least of expressing their doubts as to the quality of their own serious attempts at writing. Remembering Holley's letter to Longfellow quoted earlier, one can understand why Katherine Blyley says that Holley continued to write sentimental verse during her life as a professional humorist because of encouragement by Lydia Sigourney and Whittier. Nevertheless, Samantha confesses again in the preface, "I can't write a book, I don't know how no underground dungeons, I haint acquainted with no haunted houses, I never see a hero suspended over a abyss.... I never beheld a heroine swoon away, I never see a Injun tommy hawked, nor a ghost; I never had any of these advantages; I cant write a book." Yet, Holley published the gothic poem *The Haunted Castle* as one of her first works. Whitcher, too, parodied in the writers' club sketch directly from her own experience in the Maeonian Circle, which boasted as its members two editors of local newspapers who published some of the group's poems.

Perhaps more important was their realization that the language of sentimental poetry, whether excellently written or not, had in some ways lost its effectiveness as well as its aesthetic value because of the number of imitators. Every Tom, Dick, and Harriet—especially Harriet—was answering the call of Fanny Fern, who wrote in the 1867 *New York Ledger*:

> Write ... to lift yourselves out of the dead-level of your lives ... to lessen the number who are yearly added to our lunatic asylum from the ranks of misappreciated, unhappy womanhood, narrowed by lives made up of details. Fight it! Oppose it, for your own sake's and your children's.

Serious verse no longer offered a viable means of expression for writers intent upon exposing human foibles as well as advocating sincere feelings. After all, why did Whitcher and Holley write? They both wrote out of religious traditions, Holley in pious verses and Whitcher in devotional poems. At least initially, each writer's publisher had to convince each of the merits of humorous writing. Holley had to continually be buoyed by Elisha Bliss, who privately sponsored her first book, as it was she, not Josiah, who asked of Bliss: "Who will read the book when it's written?" Whitcher received a letter early in her exchanges with Joseph Neal, himself a humorist, about the value of "the pen of comedy": "It is a theory of mine that those gifted with truly humorous genius, like yourself, are more useful as moralists, philosophers, and teachers, than whole legions of the gravest preachers." If one would read a sermon by a contemporary preacher of the day, J.F. Stearn, one would agree:

> On you, ladies, depends, in a most important degree, the destiny of our country.... Yours it is to decide, under God, whether we shall be a nation of refined and high minded Christians ... or a fierce race of semi-barbarians before whom neither order, no honor, nor chastity can stand.[15]

Thus, in being able to laugh at their own sensibilities as poets, they in effect narrowed the gap between their serious and religious zeal and the secular world. As Jarvis said, it was the first step in enabling a woman to be a humorist. Other gaps created by women's sphere were narrowed too: the ideal and the real; the artificial and the experienced; dialect and polished prose; the serious and the comic. This self-parody, whether directed individually or collectively to women, was an exorcism of "feminine" language; the language of humor became a way of breaking the semantic circle of feminine writing.

III

In 1855, when Hawthorne wrote his publisher William Ticknor his now-famous protest against the "d—-d mob of scribbling women," he exempted one writer, Fanny Fern, of whom he said:

> The woman writes as if the Devil was in her, and that is the only condition under which a woman ever writes anything worth reading. Generally women write like emasculated men, and are only to be distinguished from male authors by greater feebleness and folly; but when they throw off the restraints of decency and come before the public stark naked … then their books are sure to possess character and value.[16]

Not so, said the majority of other critics reviewing the book Fern had just published, *Ruth Hall*, which explored the difficulties of being a woman writer. A *Putnam's* reviewer found it "full of unfemininely bitter wrath and spite"; another reviewer said the author was "not sufficiently endowed with female delicacy." The same commentary was made about Fern's less serious writing, for instance, her racy sketches done for two Boston papers in 1851; her brother Nathaniel Willis, said of them:

> You overstrain the pathetic, and your humor runs into dreadful vulgarity sometimes. I am sorry that any editor knows that a sister of mine wrote some of these which you sent me. In one or two cases they touch very close on indecency. For God's sake, keep clear of that.[17]

Here, indeed, was the plight of the woman writer in the nineteenth century. In earnest, she risked her female delicacy; in jest, she risked her decency. Writing, then, or at least publishing one's writing, became a complex matter of hypocrisy. That is, to gain critical approval, and often to be published at all (Willis recommended "religious papers" for his sister), the woman writer was forced to use what should be the vehicle for truth for just the opposite. By hiding behind a conventional feminine façade in their fiction, they could publish, and to a degree assuage their own doubts and guilt, but the language of this literature functioned as an underhanded means of getting one's way.

Thus, the sentimental poets, primarily the Widow and Betsey Bobbet, take on special significance in Whitcher's and Holley's books. Poetry is not purely the soulful expressions of two soft-headed (if not -hearted) females. It is a means of getting one's way. In fact, poetry from the pens of these two characters functions in a fashion opposite to conventional expectations. In form and tone, it is elevated, dignified, proper, a fit means of expression for a True Woman. But in its expression—that is, in the vulgar or pretentious language in which it is delivered—it is at heart a practical tool, in the case of our characters, for catching a husband. Overall, it is a trick, a hoax, the great American tool of the Yankee character, now linked with feminine guile. Thus, when we laugh at the discrepancy between the poetic form and the language which expresses it, Whitcher and Holley mean to entertain us with two realizations. Certainly, there is the gap between the artificial (values and form) and the real (fact and the vernacular). But there is also the ridiculous image of the woman, caught with her skirt above her ankle, unable to effectively reconcile, at least from the readers' vantage point, the literary heights she pretends to with her own "native" background. If, as Walter Blair says, the popularity of Native American Humor in the nineteenth century may be aligned with democratic ideals, then these sentimental poets demonstrate very well women's need to make this transition.

In examining the two books we are considering, *The Widow Bedott Papers* and *My Opinions and Betsey Bobbet's*, in the thirty sketches of the Whitcher book, twenty-one poems appear to the seventeen in Holley's thirty chapters. The Widow authors all but one of those twenty-one; Betsey Bobbet, all but three of the seventeen. Neither comes to the art with any particular literary background; in fact, each is an example of Fern's call to arms for women writers. Their poetry is both political—that is, in the sense of accomplishing some goal—and personally cathartic. Betsey has a poem called "Desiah" (remember she drops her "r" in the name of perfect grammar, excuse me, grammah) in which she says she will "expiah" for lack of requited love. The Widow delivers one in a conference with Deacon Sniffles, a conquest, in which she warbles a hypothetical epitaph:

> Here sleeps Prissilly P. Bedott
> Late relic of Hezekier,
> How melancholy was her lot;
> How soon she did expire!
>
> She didn't commit self-suicide,
> T'was tribbilation killed her,
> O, what a pity she had n't a' died
> Afore she saw the elder!—

Amateurs though they are, they're no slouches when it comes to poetic competition. Betsey published in the Jonesville *Gimlet*, and later, the *Auger*, because its editor is single, and then, last, in the *Gimlet* again—she changes her "politix," Samantha says, because the eligible editor gets away. And when she does publish, or simply write, she is prolific. Likewise, the Widow publishes in the "Poet's Corner" of the local *Luminary*, and she apologizes to Tim Crane for whom she writes the forty-nine verse "Mr. Crane's Lamentations on the Death of His Companion" that it would have been longer had she not had company. Both boast a wide repertoire of poetic forms. The Widow excels in the elegy, lamentation, occasional, and didactic verse. Betsey writes odes and sonnets along with the occasional and didactic pieces.

Before examining their use of language, it's interesting (and funny) to match the amorous adventures of these women with the poetic forms they use. In the second sketch, the Widow writes an elegy for her departed Deacon Bedott, in which one line reveals the poet's real intent:

> But now he's dead! the thought is killin'
> My grief I can't control—
> He never left a single shillin
> His widder to console.

In "Tim Crane's Lamentations ..." she implies a joy at Crane's singleness, while feigning sadness over his partner's death. After the conquest of Crane falls through (she thought he was courting her, but he was interested in her daughter), she moves to Slabtown where she learns of the widower Elder Sniffles and writes these occasional "stanzys" in honor of his "influenzy":

> O reverend sir, I do declare,
>   It drives me a'most to frenzy,
> To think o' you a lyin' there
>   Down sick with influenzy.
>
>   ...
>
> Both sick and well, you may depend
>   Youle never be forgot,
> By your faithful and affectionate friend
>   Priscilla Pool Bedott.

The "get well" card becomes rather a treatise on Christian forbearance and friendship. The Widow even offers "to your bedside fly ... If't wouldent create surprise." Their own epithalamion the Widow writes and publishes in the paper their wedding day, only to sing the refrains of relieved widowhood:

> Prissilla the fair and Shadrack the wise,
> Have united their fortunes in the tenderest of ties;
> And being mutually joined in the matrimonial connection,
> Have bid adoo to their previous affliction.

Line 2 is particularly pungent since the Widow promulgated a story that she was rich, believing Shadrack also to have ample funds. The penniless elder married the poor widow not for love, but money.

Betsey Bobbet, too, utilizes conventional forms for personal gain. In "Owed to Josiah," we find out not only that Betsey first loved Samantha's husband before they married, but that she indeed "owes" her extended spinsterhood to his marriage of Samantha. She has given the verse to Josiah, not as an exalted lyrical verse, but to make him feel guilty and even imply she wishes him dead:

> I saw thee washing sheep last night,
> On the bridge I stood with marble brow,
> The waters raged, thou clasped it tight,
> I sighed, 'should both be drownded now—'
>   I thought Josiah,
>   Oh happy sheep to thus expiah.

She moves on to her next conquest, the editor of the *Augur*, and in a poem, "It Is Sweet to Forgive," manages to squeeze her old maid values into the last two lines:

> Ah! when twins are sick and hired girls have flown,
> It is sad for a dead man to be alone.

Betsey finally catches Simon Slimpsey with a foot-stomping, rallying poem called "Women's Speah." She literally makes daggers of her words and impales the already sickly Slimpsey with a slip of a line:

> Yes, wedlock is our only hope,
> All o'er this mighly nation;
> Men are brought up to other trades,
> But this is our vocation.
> Oh, not for sense of love, ask we;
> We ask not to be courted,
> Our watchword is to married be,
> That we may be supported.
> Chorus—   Press onward, do not feah, sistehs,
> Press onward, do not feah;
> Remembeh wimmen's speah, sistehs,
> Remembeh wimmen's speah.

Slimpsey accurately whined to Samantha: "It is that spear that is goin' to destroy me."

So similar is this method of these characters—the playing off of underlying purpose with conventional form—that it's obvious Holley had read Whitcher. Many similarities exist: names, situations, word choice. But there is an important difference. The Widow is a wily, if crotchety, fool. The gap between her dialect and the sophisticated poetic forms she uses is one of calculated guile and vanity. Why shouldn't she write poetry? After all, her poetry is a means for competing with two other poets, "Hugelina," and the "widder" Jenkins who also are husband-hunting. Betsey, on the other hand, adopts the pose of the genteel poet out of ignorance. She really believes that good grammar which personifies proper behavior will justly reward her. Betsey is sort of the Horatio Alger of poetry, pulling herself up by her poetic license. Both the Widow and Betsey are climbers. "There aint no use a woman tryin' to be dignified before she's married, cause she can't," Betsey tells Samantha. But they enjoy the "sport" of poetry for two different reasons.

A brief look at their use of language will illustrate. She makes no effort to close the gap between her vulgar tongue and genre. The comic effect of this hiatus is effectively played off against dialogue with the object of her affections, Shadrock Sniffles. When she asks him how his health is—"convalessin', I hope?"—he answers: "It affords me the most unmitigated satisfaction to be able to state that my corporeal system has, to a great measure, recovered its usual tone." The vulgar tongue, with its misspellings, malapropisms, and dialect on one side, the erudite, with its euphemisms and circumlocution on the other, attempt to communicate by understanding the convention in the middle—the poem. The fact that selfish motives prompt this "respect" for convention indicates that these two characters meet, not because this convention is something to be idolized, but because it's serviceable.

The Widow plays a game with the language of the poem, manipulating its appearance for the sport of husband-hunting. In this way, she is a shrewd pragmatist—perhaps a real American—and not at all a sentimentalist. In fact, the Widow contemplates a rather "naturalistic" view of the world as contrasted to the image she must maintain in her public verses. Here's a poem from her diary kept privately on a trip:

> Poor ignorant critters we!
>   To our short-sighted race
> Things futur in life's mystery
> And like enough never'll take place.

The poem shares the philosophy of her first husband's remark, "We're all poor critters." Since he was a minister and Priscilla is married a second time to the elder Sniffles, one wonders at Priscilla's true philosophy when she writes this verse in her diary:

> To-day we're liable to fall,
>   Tomorrow up we climb
> For it ain't our nature to enjoy
> Religion all the time.

In this way, the Widow typifies those female characters who feigned "proper" style in order to achieve the recognition they were seeking. It's possible she doesn't believe in these idols at all—husbands, religion, womanhood, the dignity of writing poetry—but merely genuflects to them because of her sense of practicality.

But Betsey Bobbet is truly the "sweet singer," or at least tries to be. She believes poetry, like marriage, will dignify her. Every poem is exquisitely crafted to reveal the hopelessness of such notions. Fittingly, "sphere" becomes "speah" when Betsey gets through cultivating "proper" language. Here the discrepancy between her ignorance and the tough poetic techniques she attempts illustrates the discrepancy between her inexperience and the philosophy she espouses. Betsey is a sentimental fool. She really believes in the idols of women's sphere: man as strong, independent supporter, woman as a "clingin' vine." "We don't have any rights," she says. "We scorn them." But, whereas Priscilla's savvy at least wins her a husband well-respected in the community and thus solidly reliable, Betsey's undying devotion to her idols wins her this man:

> One week after this I was goin' up to the post office steps and I come face to face with Simon Slimpsey. He had grown 23 years older durin' the past week. But he is a shiftless, harmless critter hurtin' himself more than anyone else. He was naturally a small boned man. In the prime of his manhood he might have come up to Betsey's shoulders, but now withered by age and grief the highest hat was futile to bring him up much above her belt ribbon.... Simon Slimpsey bein' so poor and not bein' no calculator, it makes it hard for 'em to get along.

As Samantha sighs, "And this is woman's only sphere.... I always did mistrust these wimmen that talk so much about not wantin' rights, and clingin' and so forth." Though Betsey writes no poetry after she marries (she's too busy what with Slimpsey's 13 children by his first wife), she reveals her gullibility to the very last in this final poem, "I Am Married Now. A Him of Victory. By Mrs. Betsey Slimpsey's *knee* Bobbet." Here is the first stanza:

> Fate, I defy thee! I have vanquished thee, old maid.
> Dost ask shy thus, this proud triumphant brow?
> I answer thee, old Fate, with loud and joyful burst
> Of blissful laughter, I am married now!

Betsey, then, suggests the other "type" of woman writer who surfaced in the nineteenth century. Poetry is a result of inspiration and an expression of "tendah" feelings, but, moreover, it, like marriage, is a means of expressing principles. Betsey admits to Samantha that she didn't marry for happiness or love but because of women's sphere.

In a scene common to both books, we see just how successful either role of the poet is for Betsey or Priscilla. Each encounters a Yankee peddlar. Each is bested by the peddlar—because of his shrewd Yankee sense and because of her vulnerability to her values. The Widow, who flattered, cajoled, and otherwise tricked her way into the security of marriage, can initially protect herself from the peddlar's assays by confronting him first. "I always tho't I'd like to hev a recknin' with ye about comin' such a trick on me ... dident ye tell me they was fustrate leather ... and dident they bust out at the sides and run down at the heels and split on the instep in less than a week's time—and dident ye *know* they would serve me so when ye sold 'em to me—say?" But soon the peddlar has turned the tables by appealing to the widow's desires and thus tricking her with her own tricks. He confesses compunction over the shoes, based, as he says, on "actiwated religious principles," and proceeds to swap her out of cloth worth twice the amount of his. This he accomplishes for three reasons. He plays on the Widow's lack of experience in the outside world: "Them pocket handkerchers is superior to any thing y'll find this side of New York." He establishes his reputability by feigning good religious character: "I'm glad on't for *your* sake—as I said afore, t' aint no object to me." He cultivates her vanity: "Why a body'd think't was some everlastin' old maid instid of a handsome young widder that had chose such a distressed thing for a weddin' dress.... I tell ye, Widder, you're tew partickler—minister's wives is as dressy as any body." When it's all said and done, the Widow has lost the argument over the shoes, bought handkerchiefs that are thin and inferior which she didn't need, and paid too much for an inferior piece of cloth to the one the peddlar trades her out of. The scene is Whitcher's hilarious, if piercing, vignette of the corruption of women's sphere through language. The Widow is seduced, like the ruined sentimental heroines in the novels of that time, by her inability to see herself for what she really is.

The scene of the peddlar and Betsey Bobbet is less complex. But she, too, suffers from vanity, inexperience, unreal expectations, and her own pretensions to fashions that become a "lady." Consequently, she buys a pair of earrings the peddlar claims "belonged to Hamlet's mother." "Bill bought 'em at old Stratford," he tells her. Betsey's inability to reason prevents her from fathoming the ridiculous embellishments of this tall tale. "Miss Shakespeare wore 'em as long as she lived, and they was kept in the family till I bought 'em. A sister of his brother-in-law's was obleeged to part with 'em to get morpheen." In other words, the values of True Womanhood which she tries to maintain are the very ones incapable of dealing with this rouge from the outside world. Her consequent pride is connected to her lack of common sense, for she is exposed as the fool when the minister tells her his wife traded the useless brass earrings to the peddlar that very day. Yet she stubbornly says "I do not believe it—I cannot believe it," as she hurries off.

To return to Stinson Jarvis' premise about women and their idols, in the characters of Betsey Bedott we can see how accurately he connects the lack of a sense of humor to women's propensity to erect and maintain their idols, that is, their inability to deal with realism. It's no coincidence that Samantha says of Betsey's lack of humor: "You couldn't squeeze a laugh out of her with a cheesepress." To quote Jarvis:

> Women's idols are so much a part of their lives that when these are broken they cannot snap their fingers. They suffer, and their suffering seems to them sacred. To see man's avenue of escape from wretchedness in the *laisser-aller* of mirth would seem, to them, the worst kind of sacrilege. If possible, in time, they seek other idols—perhaps embrace the religion which happens to offer the first consolation, taking care afterward to shut out any truth that might again disillusion them. With them it is always a mere change of idols, never a total giving up of them. They will not face truth which means unhappiness. While man learns that happiness must be confined to quiet and normal limits, woman still seeks ecstasy. She does not love truth—in a masculine way.[18]

Thus, the gap between the values of women's sphere and the hypocrisy, or other despicable traits necessary to maintain them, is actually an abyss that separates women from truth. The language of the sentimental poet illustrates this discrepancy and consequent untruth. But if the "suffering," as Jarvis calls it, can be made the source of a joke, as in Holley's novel and Whitcher's sketches, rather than the cause for the construction of new, vacuous idols, then humor may be substituted for religion. The audience who laughs knows itself and discovers a truth: recognizing absurdity is akin to divinity.

IV

The manner in which Whitcher and Holley let their readers in on this little joke is important since both humorists were tickling their audience's funny bones with some sober truths about themselves. The popularity of their first books can, on one level, be attributed to the traditions in which Holley and Whitcher wrote. Walter Blair, in *Native American Humor*, includes Whitcher in his discussion of Down Easters and Holley, in his section on Literary Comedians. Certainly each type these female characters resembled—the Widow, a shrew, and yet in the tradition of Shillaber's *Mrs. Partington*, and Samantha, a crackerbox, out of the same tradition and that of Franklin's Silence Dogood—struck a familiar note with readers. But on another level, these writers hoaxed their readers by encouraging them to posture themselves in relationship to the characters. This done, the punch line was to be epiphany: the reader was to see himself and his world more realistically.

We might first speculate on just who these readers were. Though, to this point, I have tried to explain the complexities of being a woman/writer/reader in the 19th century and how each affected and was affected by the humorous writer, we may assume the public who enjoyed the Widow and Samantha was made up of men and women. In his "The Popularity of Nineteenth-Century American Humorists," Walter Blair indicates that this popularity attests to a reading public who existed on more than "the sugary fare offered by ladies' books and popular magazines." We might also recall that, though mainly a man's rag, eight women did contribute to *The Spirit of the Times* and B.F. Shillaber claimed in his introduction to the *Life and Sayings of Mrs. Partington* that she was "familiar as a household word." Blair does specify that Holley "most definitely wrote for the great host of feminine readers ... these books evidently lured more dollars out of purses than out of pockets." But with the intent of the American Publishing Company being to reach a rural and city audience and with Holley and Whitcher both publishing in widely read magazines and newspapers, we may assume they reached a diversified audience. This is important since the debunking of the ideal of True Womanhood affected the view of both men and women.

As already discussed, a key to this view is the difference between real experience and literary ideals, selfish intent and professed selfless notions, actions (or thought) and language. But the reader enters into the experience of the fiction in his relationship to the characters, that is, whether he laughs with them or at them. In the framework of the Widow Bedott sketches and in the character of the Widow, Whitcher allows the reader a superior position. The monologues, which allow the reader insight into the Widow's thoughts and her perception of the world, encourage the reader to laugh at the Widow and other characters whose foibles discourage identification. Yet, as the reader laughs, he may find himself committing the same error as the Widow: the sin of presumption. After all, with the array of characters in the sketches, the reader can hardly escape some personal truth. Ministers, wives, bigots, freethinkers, the wealthy, the poor, the liberated man, henpecked husbands, mothers, and children—all are subject to criticism. The satire is double-edged, for the person who recognizes these characters' faults is the reader—the one who himself is ridiculing them.

The same is true of *My Opinions and Betsey Bobbet's* except that, unlike the Widow, Samantha is a character who, supposedly, is passing judgment yet may safely be identified with. As Blair has noted in *Horse Sense in American Humor*, she has that peculiarly American appeal of common sense and, in this way, is admirable— a heroine. Indeed, this is part of Holley's enticement to the reader. Here is someone to both identify with and admire. Samantha is homely, honest, a hard worker. Yet she's smart, accomplished, gutsy. When she discourses in her aphoristic way with the likes of Horace Greeley, Josiah Allen, Mary Walker, and even Betsey Bobbet, we laugh with her, for she can solve problems, douse doubts, and grab the world by the tale. This last word is no malapropism, though that's how Samantha no doubt would spell it. She is a writer, remember, whose "allegorin'" and "episodin'" are ways of dealing with the world.

Indeed, Samantha's rube background—her poor grammar, her obvious lack of formal education, her role as a woman—is another ingredient of Holley's relationship to her reader. As Blair has indicated, Holley is a propagandist for women's rights and as such she cleverly exploits the *woman* Samantha as reasonable, assertive, and of sound judgment despite her background. Moreover, her domestic sphere is as easy for women readers to identify with as her heroic gestures are for men. In fact, she is a clever combination of women's sphere and the public sphere in that she takes her common sense philosophy from the country to the city where she converses on social issues, including women's rights, with Horace Greeley, Victoria Woodhull and others. In this way she accomplished what the feminists of the era failed to do; she capitalizes on the language and experiences of domesticity to champion women's rights. Ellen Dubois indicates that this appeal was the difference in the success of the WCTU and the near failure of the feminist movement:

> The very thing that made suffragism the most radical aspect of nineteenth-century feminism—its focus on the public sphere and on a nonfamilial role for women—was the cause of its failure to establish a mass base. It was not that nineteenth-century women were content, or had no grievances, but that they understood their grievances in the context of the private sphere. The lives of most nineteenth-century women were overwhelmingly limited to the private realities of wifehood and motherhood, and they experienced their discontent in the context of those relations. The enormous success of the Women's Christian Temperance Union, particularly as contrasted with the nineteenth-century suffrage movement, indicates the capacity for protest and activism among nineteenth-century women, and the fact that this mass feminism was based in the private sphere. The WCTU spoke to women in the language of their domestic realities.[19]

Yet, on second look, Samantha's appeal to the reader—her heroics, her "firmly drawn character," as Blair calls her—is a matter of paradox. Certainly, her "mejumness," her Golden Mean philosophy, is appealing as an ideal. It is a result of her possessing the best traits conventionally attributed to men and to women. She dishes out her most memorable truisms while canning peaches or sweating over maple syrup. Her most pungent and piercing remarks are made with cinnamon can in hand. She is both product and prime-mover in her world. That is, the predominant images used to describe her *feelings* ("says I in freezin' tones," "says I in a tone of cold and almost witherin' sarcasm") are those of the domestic sphere, yet they prepare Samantha well for dealing with that world and the public one. Her "mejumness," then, is a blending of background and philosophy, thought and action, womanhood and "heroic" traits, even as it is a blurring of expected male/female behavior. Thus, if the reader identifies with this character, he must admit to something: this "mejumness," far from ensconsing idols, reduces them to a realistic level. If Samantha exercises the traditional "male" characteristics of assertiveness, sound reason, and balanced emotions, then she alters the ideals of submissiveness, piety, and domesticity prescribed to women. If she interacts with men who are sometimes weak, lazy, evasive, overly emotional, and cowardly, then a quite different view of men, rather than the masculine ideal, emerges. What the reader finds he has identified with is not an ideal, but a real character. And one, for all her crackerbox sense, manages to change no one's mind in the course of the novel.

This last fact is important, since to look at Samantha in her milieu we realize she is a transitional figure. That is, she proposes changes, she even illustrates the soundness of her judgment, but those changes still have to come about. Here again the role of writer and reader enter in. *We* are the ones who are to change, or see the "beacon light," as she calls it on the title page. Yet, even in the preface there is the ever-present human response—as evidenced in Josiah—to "truth" in any form:

> "Who will read the book Samantha after you write it?"
> The same question was fillin' me with agonizin' apprehension, but I concealed it and answered with almost marble calm.
> "I don't know Josiah, but I am determined to put my shoulder blades to the wheel and write it."
> Josiah didn't say no more then, but it wore on him—for that night in the ded of night he spoke out of his sleep in a kind of wild way,
> "Who will read the book?"
> I hunched him with my elbo' to wake him up, and he mutters—"I wont pay one cent of my money to hire any body to read it."
> I pitied him, for I was afraid it would end in the Night Mair, and I waked him up, and promised him then and there, that I never would ask him to pay out one cent to hire any body to read it. He has perfect confidence in me and he brightened up and haint never said a word sense against the idea, and that is the way this book come to be wrote.

Samantha's gall is thus matched with her gullibility. She is indeed real.

The best examples, then, of the value of this "real" sense of life come through her use of language as an antidote to illogic and sentimentality. Grounded in rural farm life, she speaks both from her observation with nature and her experiences. These are in direct contrast to the non sequiturs of Horace Greeley, the intellectual haberdashery of Victoria Woodhull, the double-talk of a free-love lecturer, the soppy confessions of Simon Slimpsey, and many others. In the novel, the reader may find a wide scale of linguistic foibles all exposed by Samantha's paring knife mind. Unlike the other speakers, she uses analogies and metaphors not to disguise the truth, but to get to its core. Oftentimes, she takes the verbal tools erroneously used to make a point by another speaker and carries them to their natural conclusion in order to prove the inaccuracy of that character's idea. For instance: "If God had meant wimmen to be men's shadders, we would have made them ghosts and fantoms at once." Or: "If men think that wimmen are obleeged to be vines, they ought to feel obleeged to make trees of themselves for 'em to run up on."

In other words, Samantha purifies ideas as she purifies the language they are couched in. Primarily, she uses the same verbal skills of other characters (for instance, analogy) but makes them accurate by grounding one part of the comparison in visible experience and the other in philosophy. She thus challenges, since she speaks in the vernacular, artificial language and illogical thoughts. The best examples occur with husband Josiah and Betsey Bobbet. And, of course, they share an abuse of the language in common: they unthinkingly repeat conventional notions. In one of the few times she is not opining a sentimental poem, Betsey Bobbet sings the same tune to Samantha: "The study that would be inevitable on a female in ordeh to make her vote intelligably, would it not be too wearing on her?," Betsey asks. Samantha replies:

> No! Not a single bit; s'posin these soft, fashionable wimmen should read a little about the nation she lives in, and the laws that protects her if she keeps 'em, and hangs and imprisons her if she breaks 'em? I don't know but it would be as good for her, as to pore over novels all day long, ... these very wimmen that think the President's bureau is a chest of draws where he keeps his fine shirts, and the tariff is a wild horse the senators keep to ride out on—these very wimmen that can't find time to read the constitution, let 'em get on to

the track of a love-sick hero and a swoonin' heroine, and
they will wade through a half a dozen volumes, but what
they will foller 'em clear to Finis to see 'em married there.
Let there be a young woman hid in a certain hole, guarded
by 100 and 10 pirates, and a young man tryin' to get to her,
though at present layin' heavily chained to a underground
dungeon with his rival settin' on his back, what does a
women care for time or treasure, till she sees the pirates all
killed off with one double revolver, and the young woman
lifted out swoonin' but happy, by the brave hero? If there
had been a woman hid on the Island of Patmos, and Paul's
letters to the churches had been love letters to her, there
wouldn't be such a thick coat of dust on bibles as there is
now.

In a nutshell Samantha had said it all earlier when Betsey asked
her if she had read the "tendah verses" of her favorite poet.
"Tender-headed," Samantha said.

Indeed, Holley connects the emotions of the sentimental poet
with the euphemisms of the anti-feminist. When Betsey Bobbet,
who read Samantha two poems of "Wimmen's Speah," argues the
point with Samantha, Samantha confronts Betsey's high-flown notions with observable reality:

"You may shet a lion up for years, in a room full of cambric
needles and tattin shettles, and you cant get him to do anything but roar at 'em, it haint a lion's nature to do fine
sewin," says I. "And you may tie up a old hen as long as you
please, and cant break her of wantin' to make a nest, and
scratch for her chickens.... And men and wimmen votin' side
by side, would no more alter their natural dispositions than
singin' one of Watts'es hymns together would. One will sing
base, and the other iar, so long as the world stands."

Josiah makes the same mistakes in logic as does the sentimental
poet when he mimes the popular terms of the day to characterize
women. Saying they are weak, delicate, and finally "too good to
vote with us men because they haint much more nor less than angels any way," he gets this answer from Samantha:

Josiah Allen, there is one angel that would be glad to have a
little wood got for her to get dinner with, there is one angel
that cut every stick of wood she burnt yesterday, that same
angel doin' a big washin' at the same time.... I would like a
handful of wood Josiah Allen.

Josiah makes some excuse about his spring's work, and says, "You hint got much to do have you?" The dialog concludes like this:

> "Oh no!" says I in a lofty tone of irony. "Nothin' at all, only a big iroinin', ten pies and six loves of bread to bake, a cheese curd to run up, 3 hens to scald, churnin' and moppin' and dinner to get. Jest an easy mornin's work for an angel."
>
> "Well, then, I guess you'll get along, and to'morrow I'll try to get you some."
>
> I said no more, but with lofty emotions surgin' in my breast, I took my axe and started for the wood-pile.

No wonder Samantha writes no poetry and disdains such. If a woman of many words, at times, she nevertheless is a woman of action. And throughout the novel, Holley connects Samantha's wisdom as much to her words as to the world of the vernacular. It is clear that the reasoning of people like Betsey Bobbet and Josiah may be judged not only by its artificiality but by what little experience founds it. Betsey Bobbet has never been married, yet she can sing praises to women's sphere. Josiah takes little note of what his own wife can do, so he persists in his ideas about women's rights. The reader, speechless to this point except for an occasional giggle, finds his heroine a hero who writes no poetry, but can wield an axe and grind one as convincingly. As Samantha, the realist, says to Betsey, "There might be a chance for sentiment after you've fed a man supper."

V

The years from 1846 to 1872, dates which bracket Whitcher's first publication of a Widow Bedott sketch and Holley's *My Opinions and Betsey Bobbet's*, were ones of transition for women. Barbara Welter in "The Cult of True Womanhood: 1820–1860," notes:

> But even while the women's magazines and related literature encouraged this ideal of the perfect woman, forces were to work in the nineteenth century which impelled woman herself to change, to play a more creative role in society. The movements for social reform, westward migration, missionary activity, utopian communities, industrialism, the Civil War—all called forth responses from woman which differed

from those she was trained to believe were hers by nature
and divine decree.[20]

Certainly, the worst in this nature—the evil of the Widow Bedott
and the ineptitude of Betsey Bobbet—emerged when the Widow
tried to keep up appearances and Betsey aspired to them, that is,
when these types of women could not recognize the necessity of
change. Samantha confronts the whole argument of human
"nature" and the influence of environment (and thus experience),
when she echoes a phrase from Sut Lovingood in explaining the
basis of women's character: She tries to explain her *moderate* opinions to an avid "women's righter":

> "I am a friend to wimmen," says I, "and because I am, I don't
> want her to make a natural born fool of herself. And I say
> agin, I don't wonder sometimes, that men don't think that
> wimmen know enough to vote, when they see 'em go on. If a
> woman don't know enough to make a dress so she can draw
> a long breath in it, how is she goin' to take a deep and broad
> view of public affairs? If she puts 30 yards of calico into a
> dress, besides the trimmin's, how is she goin' to preach ac-
> ceptably on political economy? If her face is covered with
> paint, and her curls and frizzles all danglin' down onto her
> eyes, how can she look straight and keenly into foreign na-
> tions and see our relations there? If a woman don't know
> enough to keep her dress out of the mud, how is she goin' to
> steer the nation through the mud puddle of politics? If a
> woman humps herself out, and makes a camel of herself,
> how is she goin' through the eye of the needle?"

Samantha's logic links the impractical behavior in the private
sphere to women's abilities in the public and in the spiritual
spheres. It's not women's nature that is inferior, but her environment which limits her. In woman's nature, however, are the seeds
of organizational talents, industry, economy, which may be expressed in the construct of the home. Samantha uses the image of
the Queen Bee ("Old Nature herself clapped the crown on to 'em")
and reasons her domain makes her actually an "Executive female":
"You can't impeach *her* administration no how, for no clock work
ever run smoother and honester. In my opinion there has a great
many men set up in their high chairs that would have done well to
pattern after this Executive Female." What Samantha argues, of
course, is a familiar argument of reform movements in the nine-

teenth century. When properly valued and acted upon, training in "women's sphere" prepares a woman for making important contributions to the public sphere. Necessity, as well as experience, dictates the need for an "executive woman," not a robber baron. A new identity for women hinges on the same forces that were making the businessman the new hero of fiction in the late nineteenth century. Yet she would introduce the values and experience of family life into the corrupted public marketplace.

Samantha is thus a throwback to the "natural philosopher," rather than the natural fool. When Horace Greeley asks her opinions of Darwin's theories, however, she is, like the Widow Bedott, ridiculously ignorant due to her lack of formal education. Nevertheless, her innocent pronouncements on Darwin Gowdey, the only Darwin she knows, probably reveal ironically that necessity must meld one's nature to experience. "Darwin Gowdey?," she asks. "I never mistrusted that he had any ideas, he is most a natural fool.... I don't know how it is with you [still talking to Horace Greeley] but I know that I couldn't descend from a monkey, never bein' on one's back in my whole life." Samantha's common sense takes her a long way, but the reader sees even her need for the experience of the public sphere.

Thus, the fact that Frances Whitcher and Marietta Holley identified images, problems, needs in their two very different female characters shows their awareness of the intricately involved role of the writer, the reader, and literature itself. Their humorous pieces certainly mirrored historical reality, and they challenged religious, biological, social and psychological preconceptions. Most of all, they created a new language with which they and their audiences could deal with reality. And, since this was the language of the vernacular, the common man and woman, it offered an important antidote to the contrived language that defined women. In a way, their language suggested an anti-intellectualism that challenged both the myth of progress through materialism as much as tradition. Women who tapped their common sense stretched convention but not for the purpose of corruption of the public sphere. Jarvis' letter to *Century* magazine ends on a very telling note: "Women are not humorists because they never cease to think they know something." The paradox of Whitcher and Holley debunking popular idols, however, is as much men's fault as women's: "For his part, he thinks they suffer too much already; and he is content

that they retain their power for worship—especially for him."
Hence, in the end, these two writers, as *female humorists*, surpassed
their private, religious spheres for the public and secular one. They
leveled the idol of women and thus man.

Notes

1. Stinson Jarvis, "Open Letters," *Century Magazine* (November 1892),
22.

2. Jarvis, 23.

3. Jarvis.

4. See Nancy Walker and Zita Dresner, eds., *Redressing the Balance:
American Women's Literary Humor from the Colonial Times to the 1980s*
(Jackson: University Press of Mississippi, 1988) for a full discussion and
representation of women literary humorists. This collection provides an
important bibliography along with the first complete survey of female
humorists.

5. Dubois, "The Radicalism of the Woman Suffrage Movement: Notes
Toward the Reconstruction of the Nineteenth-Century Feminism," *Feminist Studies* (Fall 1976), 64.

6. "The Cult of True Womanhood," *American Quarterly*, 18 (1966), 154.

7. Quoted in M. Thomas Inge, ed., *A Nineteenth Century American
Reader* (Washington, DC: United States Information Agency, 1988), p. 131.

8. Ann D. Wood, "The Scribbling Women and Fanny Fern," *American
Quarterly* 23, 3–24.

9. Frances Whitcher, The Widow Bedott Papers (New York, 1856). All
further references to Whitcher's character are from this source.

10. Quoted in Morris, Linda Ann Finton, "Women Vernacular Humorists in Nineteenth Century America: Ann Stephens, Frances Whitcher,
and Marietta Holley," Diss. University of California, Berkeley, 1978, p. 85.

11. See Finton, p. 44.

12. Quoted in Finton, p. 82.

13. Jane Curry, "Women as Subjects and Writers of Nineteenth Century American Humor," Diss. University of Michigan, 1975, p. 90.

14. *My Opinions and Betsey Bobbet's* (New York: American Publishing
Co., 1973). All further references in the text are to this novel.

15. Quoted in Curry, p. 54.

16. See Nina Baym, "Melodramas of Beset Manhood: How Theories of American Fiction Exclude Women Authors," *American Quarterly* 33 (Summer 1981), 123–39 for a discussion of Hawthorne and other male writers.

17. Quoted in Finton, p. 39.

18. Jarvis, p. 24.

19. Dubois, p. 68.

20. Welter, p. 170.

POPULAR CULTURE
Vocation and Identity

Frances Bullock Workman:
Early Feminist Mountain Climber

If it's true that a picture is worth a thousand words, then an American Alpine Club photo of two men and a woman—mountaineers—posing cavalierly on a snow mass says a lot about wonder women of Victorian times. Neat in bloomers and mid-calf skirt, the woman, Frances Bullock Workman, opted for pick and rope over the traditional porcelain and lace to become the world's first great woman mountaineer.

In an era when a woman's place was behind a frilly collar in the parlor, primly sipping tea, Fanny's alpine attire was as astounding as the records she set wearing it. In her Himalayan career alone, she walked or climbed 4,000 miles of ice and snow, made 20 first ascents of peaks higher than 16,000 feet, established a new altitude record for women, and drew up the first maps of more than 250 square miles of unexplored territory. All this she managed with a casual dignity (so characteristic of women of her era) which she intriguingly combined with her own spirit of adventure.

This dichotomy was evident from the beginning of her life as daughter of Massachusetts' governor, Alexander Hamilton Bullock. Born in 1859, Fanny's life would seem to have been dominated by governesses, private schools and Continental travel. But under the tutelage of her father, who Fanny says "loved a good walk on a country road," she grew to express a love of the outdoors through her attachment to animals and her penchant for horseback riding. In fact, the ambition of this blue-blooded girl at fourteen was to be a red-blooded American—a blacksmith.

Instead, she met and married a Boston doctor when she was twenty-two. The 34-year-old William Hunter Workman had distinguished himself in studies at Yale and Harvard along with work in Vienna, Heidelberg, and Munich. When he met Fanny, she was fresh from the mountain air of the Alps where she spent many school holidays while studying in France and Germany. The new doctor set up his practice and she, housekeeping, in Worcester, Massachusetts.

At this point, Fanny's past hopes of blacksmithing seemed as remote as her future treks to Mount Nun Kun, considering the couple's antithetical temperaments. While friends of the Appalachian Mountain Club later remembered Fanny as "exuberant" with "a fine sense of adventure," Workman was described as "quiet, thoughtful, and considerate." Yet the differences proved dynamically complementary as the shy Workman found his hobby in geological research and the outspoken Fanny, in writing about their discoveries. Because of these interests, the Workmans made their first ascents of Mount Washington in 1882. These trips were made annually along with jaunts to New Hampshire's White Mountains until 1888 and resulted in Workman publishing articles in geological periodicals. Because of his successful medical practice, the Workmans found they could devote full attention to their hobbies. In 1889, at Fanny's suggestion, they sold their house, left their young daughter with her grandparents and set off with twelve trunks and two bicycles to tour Europe.

Though they had planned to be gone only two years, the Workmans spent the next ten years biking and climbing from Europe to Asia. After they had cycled through Holland, Germany, Switzerland and France, their first important European climb was Mount Blanc. From 1890 to 1895 they listed the Matterhorn, Allinhorn, Breithorn, Willenkupped and Zinal Rothorn among their major ascents.

From Europe they went to North Africa for a year, then to Palestine, Syria, and Turkey and finally to India where they are credited with some 14,000 miles of pedaling alone. At each stop, the Workmans researched the historic past and set records for the future through their exploits. In a search for an obscure temple in the Rajasthan plains of northwest India, heat and exhaustion drove them to the northern mountains where they got their first glimpse of the Himalayas in 1899. It was on the slopes of Nun Kun that, on the heels of a decade of exploring and writing which already had made her famous and honored among scientific societies and mountaineering clubs, the photograph of Fanny with a pick and the ax established her supremacy as a climber.

A world altitude record for women already had been set at 18,660 feet in Miss Annie Peck's ascent of the Orizaba in Mexico in 1897. But in 1906, Fanny broke this record when she reached the 23,000-foot summit of Pinnacle Peak in the Nun Kun region. Though continents apart, a heated competition between the two women ensued. Miss Peck claimed a new record in 1908 in her climb of the north summit of Peru's Mount Huascaran but lacked instruments to prove her estimated 24,000-foot ascent. Fanny determined to disprove it by sending her own 25-man scientific expedition to Peru, which measured the summit and reported it at only 21,812 feet. After six months of name-calling, a committee of geologists appointed by the American Alpine Club confirmed the altitude reported by the Bullock-Workman expedition.

Their 360-mile trek, which composed the first complete circuit of the Nun Kun region, was the most widely-publicized of the Workmans' eight expeditions from 1899 to 1911. Not only did they research and write about regions never seen by Western eyes, but the positively flamboyant flair with which Fanny mastered the world of ice and snow must have caused a cautious smile or two among the prim and proper parlor crowd at home. In a letter to a colleague at the American Alpine Club, Workman writes, "While ... I gasped for breath and the strength to take yet another step, my wife charged ahead to the summit." Some twelve years older than his 47-year-old wife, Workman was overcome by exhaustion and never reached the summit.

Fanny rose to other heights while involved in these Himalayan expeditions. In the book, *The Ice World of the Himalayas*, Fanny indicated she was fully responsible for manning and supplying all the expeditions. Without the modern conveniences of freeze-dried food and lightweight equipment, she had to maneuver a menagerie of 80 coolies to carry some 200 pounds of food, heavy woolen clothing, blankets, canvas tents, paraffin, stoves and firewood, not to mention herding a number of sheep and chickens.

Since such a caravan could only cover seven or eight miles a day, Fanny's plan included leaving coolies and provisions behind at a base camp. On most ascents only the Workmans and their guides ventured above 18,000 feet. But apparently as the Workmans were traditionally toasting their successful ascent with a bumper of champagne atop Mount Koser Gange (21,000 feet), the coolies got cold feet and decamped, leaving to the Workmans a dangerous descent without the necessary supplies of a base camp.

Fanny wrote, "We were all cold and hungry and counted ourselves fortunate that they had, at least, left a bit of wood behind for a fire." It was a two-day journey to the next camp where the Workmans caught up with the coolies and the provisions. Since this was only the first of many such run-ins with their hired porters, Fanny had to resort to bribery to hold them. On the Chago Lungma expedition, she promised every man who completed the expedition a pair of boots comparable to her own. Yet only 32 of the 87 coolies who began the expedition completed it.

Little of Fanny's writing detailed hardships. Conforming to the style of the period's travel and adventure books, there was little of the anticipated graphics of altitude sickness, broken bones, frostbite or threats of death. Instead, the Workmans made meticulous observations on law, customs, music, art, and religion of local peoples and reflections about geology and animal and plant life of the areas.

So popular were the Workmans' expeditions, their books, his scholarly articles and her popular pieces in *Harper's* and *The Woman's Magazine* that, upon returning to the United States, they were much in demand as speakers before scientific societies and mountaineering clubs. Fanny excelled as a witty, self-assured speaker while her husband found his forte in writing more than 30 articles for scientific and geological journals.

Fanny's actions spoke her mind equally well as her words. She flaunted personal preference over entrenched Victorian values which demanded a lady reflect propriety in dress and conduct. As an example of the social expectations ladies faced, in the first expedition to best Mount Olympus' West Peak in 1907, the women were allowed to climb in bloomers only if they wore skirts in camp. Experimentation varied the "proper" dress considerably. Lucy Walker, grandmother of Victorian mountaineering, hiked in pretty print dresses. Some innovative women sewed loops to the hems of their skirts and attached strings which enabled them to raise and lower their hems as they needed. Fanny compromised by wearing an ankle-length skirt over woolen britches. In *Ice Bound Heights of Mustogh*, she tells how she suffered the worst fall of her career as she tripped on her hem and fell neck-deep into a shallow crevasse. Her party spent 30 minutes freeing her from the banks of snow which her heavy wool skirt had toppled in around her. By the time they got her out, she was in shock and it took three days for her to thaw. The result of this fall, made en route to her famous record-setting climb, was a mid-calf-length skirt and a sturdy pair of knickers.

Fanny continued to express her free spirit through those so-called masculine virtues that her era disdained in a woman. With courage, strength, and strong will, she launched two final expeditions to the Himalayas in 1911. The expedition to the seven peaks over 19,000 feet of Rose Glacier, never visited by Western climbers, Fanny had planned to execute by herself, but at the last moment her husband joined her. With the aid of a cartographer, Fanny surveyed and mapped the area, naming many basins, plateaus, and peaks of the area. Even at the age of seventy-four her husband accompanied the 1921 Mount Everest reconnaissance expedition. Unfortunately Fanny was ill then, and so "The Rose" was her last adventure.

Despite Fanny's last major accomplishment on the longest glacier in Asia (50 miles), she found that her actions still often drew male criticism. Her works were criticized for everything from style to content. As one critic put it, "One finds himself unconsciously looking for the legend 'Votes for Women' printed large across the excellently elaborated map of Rose Glacier." The writer had acknowledged her map to be excellent but was chagrined by Fanny's feminist pride. Another critic remarked of her *Two Summers in the Ice Wilds of Eastern Karakorum*, "Instead of receiving stimulant from exhilarating tales of achievement, the reader is wearied by acidulous replies of, and comments upon the author's mountain experience. He is even more pained by the strident assertion and repeated emphasis on the part of the female author to share the enterprise."

For Fanny there was but one reply. She wrote in the *Geographical Journal*: "The object of placing my full name in connection with this expedition ... is not because I wish to in any way, thrust myself forward, but solely that, in the accomplishments of women, now and in the future, it should be known and stated that a woman was the initiator and special leader of this expedition.

"When, later, woman occupies her acknowledged position as an individual worker in all fields, as well as those of exploration, no such emphasis on her work will be needed, but that day has not fully arrived and, at present, it behooves women, for the benefit of their sex, to put what they do at least on record."

Rawhide Heroines:
Perspectives on Popular Culture Heroines

Woman's place in the myth of America may be measured by a simple story. Two Indians are sitting on a fence. One is a big Indian, the other, a little Indian. The little Indian is the big Indian's son, but the big Indian is not the little Indian's father. How can this be? David Potter, who relates the riddle, solves it with this explanation: the big Indian obviously is the little Indian's mother, but we may initially fail to see this since social conditioning often makes us conceive of relationships from a masculine perspective.[1] Potter's story has particular import when we examine the myth of America specifically as the Western or frontier myth in which the qualities of heroism are traditionally masculine ones. Rugged individualism, bravery, nobility, and a love of the wilderness are noted by historians such as Frederick Jackson Turner and writers from Cooper on as traits indigenous to the frontier experience. Turner sees these qualities as part of the national character and evoked by the frontier's challenge to the *civilizing instinct*; yet woman, typically the civilizer, is not typically thought to exhibit them. Our imaginative writers, unlike the historians, view the frontier as *an escape from civilization* and thus seldom treat women heroically. Heroes, like Natty Bumppo, are not the apostles of progress but the antisocial, misanthropic refugees from civilization who bemoan the desecration of the wilderness and wish to defend it from settlement. It follows that such heroes, as William Humphrey observes, avoid the trappings of civilization by avoiding marriage:

> ... if we are to judge by our imaginative literature, we are, beneath all the slogans extolling the democratic social organization and the virtues of family life, a nation of secret

bachelors, hermits of the woods and the plains. In books
about such figures there is no place for any heroine.[2]

If heroines have not emerged from western history and literature, however, a predominant stereotype has—an image perpetuated by writers and historians as appropriate to woman's role in
the Western myth. Emerson Hough describes her thus:

> She is the chief figure of the American West, the figure of all
> the ages. This major figure is not the long-haired, fringed
> legging man riding a raw-boned pony, but the gaunt and
> sad-faced woman sitting on the front seat of the wagon ...
> her face hidden in the same ragged sunbonnet which had
> crossed the Appalachians and the Missouri long before.
> There was America.... There was the seed of America's
> wealth. There was the great romance of all America—the
> woman in the sunbonnet; and not, after all, the hero with the
> rifle across his saddle horn.[3]

This image of the sunbonnet woman is popular for a number of
reasons. On a psychological level, her implied status as mother sat-
isfies the needs of our writers to reconcile their attitudes about
women. Leslie Fiedler says, "Women represent at once the ruined
and redeeming virgin-bride dreamed by Sentimentalism, and the
forgiving mother, necessary to sustain an imaginary American
commonwealth of boy-children.... Both marriage and passion im-
pugn the image of woman as mother and mean the abandonment
of children."[4] The passivity of this creature on the wagon seat further compliments predominant nineteenth-century beliefs about
women's natures and their roles. Emerson noted that civilization
was the power of "good" women. Such a woman remained in the
home and did all that was necessary to maintain that home, even
to following her husband overland from friends, family, culture,
and precious possessions. Any penchant for the wilderness, therefore, was regarded as evil on a woman's part; certainly in literature
"white women who refuse to restrict their behavior to what society
intends for them find the wilderness a natural habitat for forbid-
den sexuality, and for them, separation from the male, and solitary
wandering in the wilderness are considered equivalent to the
fall."[5] Thus, Hough's description of the pioneer woman as "gaunt"
and "sad-faced" is appropriate to her expected sacrificial role. She
was the "seed of America's wealth" in part because she perpetu-
ates its seed. Men who had subdued the wilderness for its great

riches were interested in establishing a "line." Material exploitation and sexual exploitation were closely aligned. This sunbonnet woman is therefore "the great romance of all America" because "she stoically transcended a situation she never would have freely chosen."[6] Long-suffering, pure, persevering, this pioneer woman reaches mythic proportions in her celebration in statues, histories, and literature across the country because she became the symbolic repository of values revered by men but often personally ignored for their own materialistic ventures on the frontier.

The sunbonnet woman thus seldom reaches the status of a true heroine. Unlike the dynamic heroines of European literature, Jane Eyre or Anna Karenina, for instance, her compliance to tedious tasks has none of the heroic cut of her male counterparts in the West—the trappers, miners, cowboys, or soldiers. Characters like Beret Hansa in Rolvaag's *Giants of the Earth* (1926) or Dorothy Scarborough's crazed character in *The Wind* (1925) are not memorable but predictable. Such a woman most often serves as a plot motivator for the more dramatic activities of the hero, making Huck Finn "light out for the territory" or Daniel Boone move West one more time. For the most part, western writers have been content to follow the example of what Judith Fryer notes is a pattern of our major writers:

> Significantly, the women in the novels of Hawthorne, Melville, Oliver Wendell Holmes, Harold Frederic, Henry James, and William Dean Howells are not women at all, but images of women. They are reflections of the prevailing images of women in the nineteenth century, and like the predominantly male creators of utopian schemes, their male creators perceive with cultural blinders the women in the New World Gardens of their imaginations.[7]

Yet the real frontier offered a unique situation for altering these images. Recent historians such as Gerda Lerner suggest the sunbonnet stereotype is far too limiting, for pioneer women often had to be independent and frontier men and women were interdependent.[8] Current efforts to reconstruct history from diaries, letters, and newspapers indicate that historians such as William Sprague and Francis Parkman had not only a narrow but sometimes an erroneous view of women's attitudes, status, roles, and occupations on the frontier. Moreover, one frontier not only necessitated unique behavior by women, but engaged the popular imagination sufficiently to inspire the emergence of perhaps the only true American heroine. That frontier was the cattle frontier, and the "new woman" was the "cowgirl"—the rustler, wrangler, outlaw, or ranch woman whose occupation depended on her mastery of the horse. In real life, she had to exercise the masculine traits revered by historians such as Turner and by western writers. She attracted no attention from major American writers—perhaps because her character was particularly antithetical to their image of the American woman—but her character as it evolves in popular culture from the dime novel to films comes close to resolving the dilemma of the woman in American fiction as Fiedler and others see it.[9] She was neither mother nor virgin-bride. At times she was a full-fledged partner of the hero; at times she was the hero herself.

The particular manner in which the cattle frontier effected a heroic role for women may be attributed to its distinct nature. Unlike the other moving frontiers in which progress depended on settlement, the cattle frontier thrived on its own uncivilized expanses. In such a vast country as even the smaller ranches of New Mexico, Arizona, Texas, Montana, Wyoming, and other states encompassed, a rancher's wife was part of a self-sufficient unit and often had to take a nontraditional view of the home, division of labor, the land, and even the law. Thus Mrs. Charlie Hart of New Mexico was the only hand her husband had and when the first baby came, she placed him in a tomato box in front of the pommel of her saddle and took him with her to ride fence.[10] At least eight women are known to have gone up the trail with their husbands, and one, Lizzie Williams, drove her own herd up the Chisholm Trail from 1879 to 1889, even though she was married.[11] When the husband of Mrs. William Mannix was struck with polio, the care of thirteen children and their ranch fell to Mrs. Mannix. She drove a stage for fifteen years to supplement the family's income while she ran the ranch.[12] Mrs. Cassie Redwine of the Texas Panhandle was left with a ranch after her husband's death; when cattle rustlers began terrorizing the upper Red and Canadian Rivers, she lost five hundred head of cattle and decided to take the law into her own hands. She and her cowboys captured a few of the rustlers in their camp, changed into their clothes, and ambushed the remainder of the gang when they rode into camp. Mrs. Redwine shot the leader herself when he rode into camp, and the next day the rest were hanged.[13] Thus, the isolation of ranch life not only demanded an adjustment in the traditional roles of women, but fostered a new independence as well. Though most women married into ranching or were second-generation ranch women, a few women bought their own spread and herd. In the 1880s Fanny Seabride of Chicago went to Texas as a governess, learned to ride and do ranch work, became a bounty hunter, and after bagging "531 coyotes, forty-nine lobos, thirty-nine wildcats, two bear cubs, and a Mexican leopard," established her own ranch with her $1,261 of bounty money.[14]

The results of this new independence were attitudinal as well as occupational. Alice Marriott in her book, *Hell on Horses and Women*, says: "Never once ... did I hear a woman acknowledge the truth of the statement that 'The cow business is ... hell on horses and women.' ... I have come to the conclusion that that oft-quoted statement originated with a man and, manlike, they said the words and attributed them to women, without asking women how they really felt."[15] Agnes Smedley identifies herself positively with the land which women supposedly fear and abhor: "The deserts were indeed gray and sinister wastes ... but ... lay there, calling to you to come on and on.... The Arizona desert came closer to my spirit than has any place I have ever known."[16] The main reason for Smedley's lyricism is that of other cowgirls: she rode a horse almost everywhere she went and says "it was a land where women were strong."[17] The two go together, for as J. Frank Dobie explains in *The Mustangs*: "No man by taking thought can add to his stature, but by taking a horse he can."[18] The same was true of women, perhaps even more so, since the horse not only added status for women but was an equalizer. Unlike other frontier women who were practically prisoners of their homes, cowgirls were mobile, and therefore not only could master ranch chores and be full partners to their husbands, but also could achieve a new identity. Folklorist Joyce Roach observes: "If you spend all your days in a field, behind a plow, looking at the rump of a horse, trying hard not to step in something, it affects your attitude. But if you get on that horse, ride him, then the world's a completely different place."[19] With the mastery of a horse often came a new mode of dress. Skirts gave way to split skirts or pants. Women learned to shoot guns and carried them both for protection when out on the range and for shooting coyotes and other threats to cattle. An example of this altered identity due to necessity, occupation, dress, and habit is

Mrs. E.J. Guerin who was widowed at age fifteen and worked as a river pilot, a miner, a bartender, and a rancher:

> I would say from the fact of my being so long thrown among strangers and all along accustomed to depend on myself, I had attained a strength of character, a firmness, and self-reliance, that amounted to almost masculine force. In addition to this, I was impetuous, self-willed—traits induced by the peculiarities of my surroundings, and whose existence will account for much of my subsequent career.[20]

Though certainly not all ranch women rode the range, carried a gun, and assisted with branding and wrangling, even the more traditional wives like Mrs. Charles Goodnight found their roles expanded from those usually expected. Mrs. Goodnight's nearest neighbor in the Texas Panhandle was 200 miles away and she was doctor, nurse, homemaker, and spiritual adviser to innumerable cowboys, hunters, trappers, and traders. She also ministered to orphaned baby buffalo.[21] On the other end of the spectrum was Sally Skull, a hard-nosed business woman on the southern border of Texas who was a horse trader and freight wagon driver across the Mexican border during the Civil War. She had a reputation as a sharpshooter, landed in Mexican jails several times thanks to her bargaining, and was a veteran cardsharp and "cusser."[22] Some other women who had experience with guns and horses violated the law. Seventeen-year-old Annie McDoulet and sixteen-year-old Jennie Stevens—Cattle Annie and Little Britches—were delinquent teenagers who rode with the Doolin gang in 1894.[23] Thus, whether as partners of their husbands or widows, daughters, or independent women, to some degree these cowgirls shared in the violence, various activities, and values of the range and, in proportion to the independence this life allowed, were able to shape their lives.

During the height of the cattle industry, the dime novel, which had popularized western characters and action since 1860, transformed heroines from crinoline objects to active participants in the plots. First came the use of Indian girls who could ride and shoot. Then writers disguised women in men's clothing and explained their acts of violence and aggression in terms of revenge. But by 1878, in Edward L. Wheeler's *Bob Woolf, the Border Ruffian; or the Girl Dead-Shot*, Hurricane Nell assumed all the skills and functions of a Western hero. There may be several explanations for this

transition of the heroine's role, and each indicates that real cowgirls could to some degree capture the popular imagination.
First, there were the requirements of Erastus Beadle, head of
the firm of Beadle and Adams, who had been to the frontier twice.
Beadle recognized the impact of good storytelling that had dramatized the opening of the Eastern states, the Revolutionary War, and
the War of 1812, and he expected his writers to achieve verisimilitude through adequate research or, even better, first hand knowledge of the West. Thus, at least some of his stable of writers—
Joseph E. Badger, Prentiss Ingraham, Sam Hall, Mayne Reid, and
E.L. Wheeler—were not only familiar with the West but had lived
there. Certainly, they would have had opportunities to observe
real cowgirls, and several examples illustrate a direct connection
between real women and the characters in dime novels. For instance, Rowdy Kate of *Apollo Bill, The Trail Tornado; or Rowdy Kate
from Right Bower* (1882) boasts in a typical Southwestern style: "I'm
a regular old double-distilled typhoon, you bet." There was a
Rowdy Kate in the 1870s who was a dance-hall girl, among other
things, and possibly could pass as a double-distilled typhoon.[24] In
The Jaguar Queen, or, the Outlaws of the Sierra Madre (1872), Katrina
Hartstein goes about with seven pet jaguars on a leash and is the
leader of a gang. Anne Sokalski, who accompanied her soldier-
husband to his duty post in the mid-1860s, took along her thirteen
trained hunting dogs which she kept on a leash. She wore a riding
habit made of wolfskin and trimmed with wolf tails, topped with a
fur hat. She spent hours at target practice, was a deadly shot, and
could outride some of the cavalry.[25] The author of *The Jaguar
Queen*, Frederick Whittaker, who had served in the army, would
have found Anne inspiration for his character. Even Hurricane
Nell has authentic roots. Mountain Charley (Mrs. E.J. Guerin)
joined miners at Pike's Peak in 1859. She was dressed like, and
passed for, a man.[26] In 1861, she published her autobiography—
ample time for the dime novel author to have heard of her.
    With the availability of real models—women, we must re-
member, who were at home with horses, guns, and even violence—the addition of the "Amazon" character in the dime novel
was an effort to reconcile reality with certain social predilections of
an Eastern audience. Erastus Beadle's list of rules for writers ended
with "We require unquestioned originality," but it began with "We
prohibit all things offensive to good taste in expression and inci-

dent."[27] Though critics of the dime novel are quite right to note the disintegration of the novels due to overt sensationalism after about 1880, the development of two types of Amazon characters dramatized the cowgirl folk heroine and indicated a growth in the Western myth since Cooper. Dime novels, of course, were fashioned after Cooper's Leatherstocking adventures with a backwoods hero—comic, dialectical, unsuited for marriage—contrasted to his Eastern sidekick who, by virtue of his aristocratic breeding, always got the girl. As the writers refined the bifurcated plot—one part adventure, and one, love interest—into the activities of a single, cultivated protagonist, the two new heroines emerged. One, the "Sport," was usually a beautiful woman dressed in a mannish fashion, who performed manly feats with gun, whip, and knife, drank liquor straight, and swore expertly. She might save the hero from danger, but she almost never got his romantic attention. In this way, she replaced the noble backwoodsman, since she was strong, brave, capable of action. Moreover, since there was no love interest, she in no way threatened the hero with her strength; she was his equal, his friend. A classic example of the "Sport," and probably the most famous, is E.L. Wheeler's Calamity Jane. In *Deadwood Dick on Deck; or Calamity Jane, The Heroine of Whoop-Up*, she has a pretty, but hard face, wears buckskin pants, "met at the knee by fancifully beaded leggins," dainty slippers, a velvet vest, a velvet jacket, and a Spanish broad-brimmed hat "slouched upon one side of a regally beautiful head." Wearing one revolver on her waist and a rifle on her back, she rides a black pony fitted out Mexican style. When asked why she dresses like a man, she replies: "I don't allow ye ken beat men's togs much for handy locomotion and so forth, an' then, ye see, I'm as big a gun among men as any of 'em."[28] In *Deadwood Dick in Leadville; or A Strange Stroke for Liberty* (1881), she saves a man's life and calls ammunition "condensed death."

The "Pard" character, on the other hand, often won the hero. She was also masculine in her skills, but did not try to pass for a man like the rougher "Sport." Rather she was a partner to the hero, capable of doing what he did, sharing equally in danger and daring with occasional concessions to femininity. Probably she is one of the few egalitarian female creations. Two classic "Pards" ran in dime novel series from 1900 to the 1920s—Arietta Murdock, created by Cornelius Shea for *Wild West Weekly*, and Ned Taylor's

Stella, the cowgirl heroine of *Rough Rider Weekly*. Arietta, displayed on about 80 percent of the *Wild West Weekly* covers, regularly rescued the hero by hurling dynamite, leaping chasms, shooting her gun, riding for a posse, and stealing guns or horses from outlaws. Like Arietta, Stella was a blonde, known in her native Texas as "Queen of the Range." She sidekicks with ex-Rough Rider Ted Stong and cuts a dashing figure in her white stetson, bolero jacket, white leggings, and red skirt, with her gun strapped to her hip. Thus, unlike the earlier pale heroines of Cooper's novels, these western women, whether friends or lovers, were strong, independent, brave, athletic, and full partners to the hero. Like their historic sisters, the ranch women, they fill a unique literary role.

An indication of this uniqueness, outside the fact that these heroines are fully "heroic" and share in the Western myth, is that they are called "Amazons." The use of this classical character for reference indicates the lack of any American literary predecessor. Unlike the dime novel hero, who has as his native reference the backwoodsman, the mythical forerunner of the cowgirl character is rooted in a legendary female culture where strength and athletic prowess were aspects of female heroism. The reference also indicates the difficulty of perpetuating a myth that runs so counter to nineteenth-century sensibilities about women. Perhaps only in popular culture, where myth making is intricately involved with entertainment, could such a heroine evolve. Nevertheless, in the pattern described by Richard Slotkin, the character of the cowgirl moves through the primary, romantic, and consummatory stages of myth development. That is, the character is identified in the repetition of formulas (as in the dime novel); the character is adapted to specific social and literary requirements by artists, thus obscuring the original meaning of the myth (as in the Wild West Shows, some literature, and films); and, finally, an attempt is made to recapture the real meaning of the myth by providing new visions (as in some recent novels and films). Moreover, as Slotkin points out, the effective use of myth depends on the development of traditional metaphors in the narrative that indicate change.[29] Crucial to this acculturation is the medium; in the case of the cowgirl character the narrative is told through literature, sport, and film.

Along with the dime novel, the evolution of the "Pard" or "Sport" characters continued in western literature dating from the turn of the century. Unlike the dime novels which emphasized action to the exclusion of character development, the evolution of the cowgirl in this Western popular literature establishes a workable metaphor for this character. As Slotkin notes, "The success of the myth in answering questions of human existence depends upon the creation of a distinct cultural tradition in the selection and use of metaphor.[30] Thus, the dime novel established the formula for the myth—action, dress, character type. Other writers adopted the formula but discarded the Amazon reference for an American metaphor: the natural woman.

In 1908, Lester Shepherd Parkman wrote a story in verse introducing this natural woman. *Nancy MacIntyre*, though strictly inferior poetry suitable perhaps for recitation, is about cowboy Billy, owner of eighty acres in Kansas and his love for Nancy, a cowgirl "Pard" who dresses in long skirt with a gun and cartridge belt. Nancy possesses all the attributes of a hero: she saves Billy from an ambush, stands off a possee in behalf of her father, and shoots Jim Johnson who steals Billy's eighty acres. But Billy admires her lack of artificiality:

> Now, those women that you read of
> In these story picture books,
> They can't ride in roping distance
> Of that girl in style and looks.
> They have waists more like an insect,
> Corset shaped and double cinched,
> Feet just right to make a watch charm,
> Small, of course, because they're pinched,
> This here Nancy's like God made her—
> She don't wear no saddle girth,
> But she's supple as a willow
> And the prettiest thing on earth.

Though Billy speaks in part of natural beauty, the poem connects scenes of the western landscape, and of her ability to deal with the harsh life of the prairie, with her authenticity.

Thus, like the pastoral hero, the natural woman as cowgirl is at one with nature. In the works of Eugene Manlove Rhodes, for instance, love of the land is connected to the heroine's capabilities. Eva Scales in "Maid Most Dear" (1930) says this about the desert country of New Mexico:

> "I've lived here all my life. Except for a few trips to Silver City and El Paso. I've never been out of these hills." Her

head lifted, her eyes lingered on the long horizons, lovingly. "If it is any better outside, I'm willing to be cheated."

Eva is the brave and daring heroine of the story who shoots it out with a lynch mob in order to save Eddie and Skip, the heroes of the story. Other Rhodes stories reiterate the same idea. In "The Desire of the Moth" (1902), "Beyond the Desert" (1914), and "Bird in the Bush" (1917), the heroines derive their strength from nature.

Thus the "Pard's" ability to take full responsibility for her life depends on her capacity to enjoy harmony with man and nature. In the novels of Bertha "Muzzy" Sinclair, the cowgirl heroines often choose this harmonious relationship at the cost of approval by townspeople. Though Sinclair's novels often are humorous and avoid historical themes, she often juxtaposes the heroine's character, formed and sustained by the range land, against the expectations of society. In *Rim O' the World* (1919) Belle Lorrigan is a tough, athletic heroine. She races across the prairie in a buckboard pulled by two pinto ponies, Rosa and Subrosa. A sure shot, she teaches her three sons manners by plugging a hole in one boy's hat when he forgets to remove it. When the sheriff arrives to check the brands on some green hides, she threatens to put a bullet "about six inches above the knee," if he doesn't leave. He continues to talk and she determines to shoot his front tooth out. Needless to say, the women in town dislike Belle, but the author clearly illustrates that the "natural" woman maintains integrity by answering to the laws of the land, not the conscience of snooty town women.

The reconciliation of the strong woman with her role in the family further is handled by William Sydney Porter in his story "Hearts and Crosses" (1907). After Santa inherits a ranch from her father, she runs it so expertly that her husband leaves to become foreman of another ranch. When he orders a shipment of cattle from her, she sends a pure white steer with the brand—a cross in the center of a heart—which she and Webb had used before their marriage to denote a secret meeting. Webb returns to find he is father of a son, and he and Santa continue to share equally in the running of the ranch. Santa's acumen as a "Pard" is memorably described in the night scene when she ropes, ties, and brands the white steer single-handed.

The early literature of the cowgirl heroine, therefore, seized on the distinctive "active" behavior of the heroine—the skills necessary to survival and to heroism—and added to the one-dimen-

sional dime novel authentic frontier situations. Character thus was
a matter of independence, ingenuity, and physical skill fostered by
the demands of the environment. The heroine typically coped with
so-called female concerns—love, marriage, family, societal expectations—by exhibiting "masculine" traits. The metaphor of the
"natural" woman was a statement of her ability to cultivate these
traits, yet still be a woman, and to achieve equal status with the
hero or even be the center of the work herself. Other writers such
as Owen Wister in *The Virginian* (1902) used this metaphor to test
the fitness of Eastern values. In the westerning of Molly Wingate,
Wister indicates that her acquisition of the skills of the cowgirl favorably influence her character. But in the novels of Zane Grey, the
cowgirl character changed and the metaphor of the natural woman
was diverted to an earthiness that suggested sexuality rather than
heroic dimension. In novels such as *Hash Knife Outfit* (1920), Grey,
like Wister, tested the Eastern girl against the land or against
Western values, but, like his heroes, he essentially domesticated
the heroines' love of independence and sense of freedom. The later
novels of Luke Short, Max Brand, Nelson Nye, and Louis L'Amour
continue this trend, returning to the pat stereotype of the woman
as either "good" but inert, or active and assertive but sexual. Gone
is the girl "Pard" who can coexist with the hero because of her androgynous abilities. The myth, therefore, is diverted from its original sources and content to a reflection of social or literary obligations—the second stage of mythogenesis Slotkin speaks of when
the nature of reality is less important than the social requirements
of the artist. Grey, for example, uses the Western myth to work out
his own peccadillos. John Cawelti notes:

> In a period where ... traditional American values were under
> attack, Grey and other contemporary novelists ... trans-
> formed the western formula into a vehicle for reaffirming a
> traditional view of American life.... In contrast to contempo-
> rary American society where women were increasingly chal-
> lenging their traditional roles, the West of Grey ... was,
> above all, a land where men were men and women were
> women. In novel after novel, Grey created strong, proud,
> and daring women and then made them realize their true
> role in life as the adoring lovers of still stronger, more virtu-
> ous, more heroic men.[31]

Another explanation for the loss of the original thrust of the cow-girl character was the historic or personal distance writers such as Grey had from the West. By contrast, many of the dime novelists and other writers such as Parkman, Sinclair, Rhodes, and O. Henry had either grown up in the West or spent time there. Their interest, though the works often were melodramatic, was in recording real Western characters and experiences. As an example, Joe B. Frantz and Julian Choate write of "Muzzy" Sinclair: "She had what so many cowboy writers lack, a real background of life among the bowlegged brethren.... She was reared in Montana where she rode the range and fraternized with men on horseback. She did not try to pontificate about the epic role of the cowboy, and she had no pretense to history as such, but she was faithful to the Western his-torical milieu which she knew first hand."[32]

This same matter of historical distance affected the cowgirl's portrayal in another medium, the movies. Initially, the movies were affected by real cowgirls, women who had ridden in Wild West Shows and who originally were from ranches. Therefore, early silent films treated fairly authentically the cowgirl's skills and costume. Rodeo star Bertha Blanchett was an early stunt rider; Mildred Douglas and Dorothy Morrell did bit parts after the Miller Brothers' 101 Wild West Show folded in 1991 in Venice, California; Helen Gibson of the Miller Brothers' show played the heroine in the serial *The Hazards of Helen* (1914). Early celluloid cowgirls were cast in action-packed parts of the dime novel variety: in *Frontier Day in the Early West* (1910) a woman dresses like a man and rides her horse in a race; sisters in *Western Girls* also dress in cowboy clothes, capture stage robbers at gunpoint, and bring them to the sheriff; in *The Border Region* (1918) Blanch Bates rides wildly across the country and shoots a man during a struggle. Most of these parts were adjunct to that of the hero, however, and reminiscent of the popular events of the Wild West Show and rodeos. *Trail Dust* and parts of *North of 36* were filmed at the Miller Brothers' 101 Ranch. Occasionally, character development was attempted as in *The Prairie Pirate* with Ruth Delaney. Cornered after a valiant fight to escape a bandit and his gang, the heroine picks off the gang members, but, when the leader traps her in a cellar, she saves the last bullet for herself. During the 1930s just following the peak years of women's star performances in the rodeo, the cowgirl movie heroine was "more self-reliant, more athletic, and even sexier," but seldom the central figure of the film.[33] One exception was *The Singing Cowgirl*, starring Dorothy Page, where the heroine's role was more important than the hero's. By the 1940s and 1950s, the age-old dichotomy of the heroine as good girl or sexual temptress was the staple of Westerns; even the authenticity of dress, behavior, and riding and roping acumen was gone. The role of the "Pard" survived only in the Saturday afternoon kid show, played by the cowgirl who could rope, ride, and sing—Dale Evans. As in some western literature, film converted the cowgirl myth from its primary characteristics by using it as a means of perpetuating social expectations. The raw action of the early cowgirls was a necessary element for the visual media, but the metaphor of the natural woman or "Pard," as in the case of Grey's novels was lost. Moreover, the medium of expression was itself determining. Later actresses who had no notion of how to ride a horse, costume designers who glamorized female characters, and directors, such as John Ford, who depicted the West not as it was but as it should have been ignored the original character of the cowgirl.

Movies most conveniently illustrate probably the primary reason for the adaptation of the cowgirl's characteristics into other stereotypes of women. The delicate balance between hero and heroine seemingly precludes the heroine being too strong, capable, and independent. In *Giant*, for instance, Lutie, the hardened, outspoken, and capable ranchwoman, is killed off so that the true heroine, Virginia-born, can flourish. The dependency of the heroine is essential, if we trace the evolution of the Western. In fact, with few modern exceptions, the formula of the Western demands that the hero work within a masculine code that excludes, for the most part, civilization and women. Will Wright, in *Six Guns in Society*, names only three films in which the hero and heroine are partners, and one of these involves a child—Kim Darby in *True Grit*.[34] However, despite the lack of primary attention to cowgirls as central characters, films have managed to dramatize the various aspects of the cowgirl mystique. The early films characterized the cowgirl in terms of raw action. Later films, such as *The Big Country* (1958), coupled the realistic action of tending cattle and overseeing a ranch with attention to the heroine's thoughts, concerns, and motivations.

The final link in the evolution of the cowgirl—the Wild West Show and the rodeo—illustrate yet another manner in which the cowgirl heroine reached the public. These events are unique, for they may be said to be metaphors for the cowgirl without the context of narrative. As we have seen, the cowgirl was associated in various ways metaphorically in the changing Western of the dime novel, western literature, and film. But the Wild West Show and the rodeo centered on the *event* and, as such, allowed the cowgirl to function as part of the iconography of the old West. In fact, the name "cowgirl" was first applied to second-generation ranch women who demonstrated their skills at the Cheyenne Frontier Days in 1897 where the term appeared on the rodeo program. Personalities as well as gutsy performance of events made these early cowgirls popular. Teddy Roosevelt saw thirteen-year-old Lucille Mulhall perform in 1889 at a Cowboy Tournament at the Rough Riders' Reunion in Oklahoma City. As a child, Lucille had exhibited the daring that would make her a championship cowgirl. Her father told her she could have her own herd when she could brand her own cattle, and she went out and branded all the strays she could find—with her saddle cinch! After seeing her roping performance in Oklahoma City, Roosevelt told her she could ride in his inaugural parade if she could rope a wolf, and three hours later she returned from the range with the creature dragging behind. She was known during her career as a top roper, trick rider, and steer tier. An old cowhand reports:

> They had a big steer tying show, Zack Mulhall and his bunch at our fairgrounds, and his daughter, Lucille. She looked about eighteen and wore a divided skirt. First woman I'd ever seen that wasn't on a side saddle. And she was a fine steer tier. She could rope those steers, drag 'em down and tie 'em just like a man.[35]

Other famous cowgirls included Ruth Roach, Tad Lucas, and Florence Randolph, who, during the golden age of the rodeo in the 1920s, participated in all-male events such as bronc riding and bull dogging. These women were big drawing cards for the traveling shows and rodeos in different parts of the country. For example, one year at the Fort Worth rodeo Florence Randolph performed her trick riding on a grass mat in the lobby of a downtown hotel to publicize the local rodeo. Randolph was a great beauty and, as with the other rodeo cowgirls, the combination of her looks, her prowess on horseback, and her dashing costume cut a memorable figure in the public imagination. The rodeo today is a bland reminder of the remarkable feats of these earlier performers. Today women participate in their own events, primarily barrel racing, as trained athletes in a highly competitive business. Unlike their earlier sisters who at least suggested a historical affinity with the West, today's cowgirls, like the rodeo cowboy, are images of sports heroines rather than part of a metaphor of them.

The athletic ability of the cowgirl, however, is her unique and sustaining attribute. From the deeds that distinguished her in real life throughout the physical escapades in the dime novel, western literature, the Wild West Show, rodeo, and film, her identity is grounded in physical capability. Studies show that athletically oriented people identify themselves with athletic traits associated with success—aggressiveness, tough-mindedness, dominance, self-confidence, and risk taking.[36] These traits, of course, are antithetical to those usually attributed to women. Hence, the cowgirl who can ride and rope and run her ranch as well as a man is able to carve out a portion of the Western myth for herself by means of her athletic bearing. Such talents not only put her on equal footing with the hero, but they allow her the very traits our writers attribute to the Western hero. Thus, if the behavior and attitudes of the hero are of interest because he exhibits these characteristics as a trapper or cowboy or soldier, the cowgirl also commands this interest. Indeed, one of the complaints of novelists such as Wallace Stegner is that women's lives on the frontier constituted a view "from the inside," that is, only from the home.[37] Such drama of dailiness has proved uninteresting to our novelists. No doubt the cowgirl had special appeal because she exhibited behavior thought to be unusual for women. She was, in fact, the "New Woman" of the frontier, and her popularity parallels new freedoms women were experiencing toward the end of the nineteenth century and during the 1920s. In this sense, however, her athletic inclinations presented as much of a problem as they did a unique status. Because she did contradict the typical female role, writers tended to refine her by centering her in melodrama or even making her exploits so sensational, they bordered on comedy. Audiences, no doubt, found this treatment of her entertaining and therefore acceptable. Later, of course, writers and filmmakers converted the qualities of the athletic heroine to sexual energy, so that she became the "dark" heroine.

But the athletic "Pard" offered an opportunity for writers to resolve their dilemma over the "masculine wilderness of the American novel," as Carolyn Heilbrun calls it.[38] Rather than pose a sexual threat to the hero by representing the marriage and civilization that inimitably followed association with a woman, the girl "Pard" functioned as a buddy would: she was friend, sidekick, and, if she became a wife, at least she could rescue the hero from a jam. If this cowgirl character was an "Amazon" she nevertheless was described by the dime novelists as a "honey-throated" Amazon; her androgyny made her a companion of the hero. The alternative—more prevalent in our literature—fits this description of Texas by J.B. Priestley in 1956:

> I am convinced that good talk cannot flourish where there is a wide gulf between the sexes, where the men are altogether too masculine, too hearty and bluff and booming, where the women are too feminine, at once both too arch and too anxious. Where men are leavened by a feminine element, where women are not without some tempering by the masculine spirit, there is a chance of good talk.... But here was a society entirely dominated by the masculine principle. Why were so many of these women at once so arch and anxious?... Even here in these circles, where millionaires apparently indulged and spoilt them, they were haunted by a feeling of inferiority, resented but never properly examined and challenged. They lived in a world so contemptuous and destructive of real feminine values that they had to be heavily bribed to remain in it. All those shops, like the famous Neiman-Marcus store in Dallas, were part of the bribe. They were still girls in a mining camp. And to increase their bewilderment, perhaps their despair, they are told they are living in a matriarchy.[39]

Priestley not only gives good reason for a balance of male and female elements, but he fingers the reason for the dearth of heroines in western literature: heroic stature is conceived in purely masculine terms. Unlike the Greek goddesses and British, French, Russian, or Spanish women who assumed leading roles in mythology, literature, and history, American heroines are a pale lot—except for the cowgirl, whose evolution from the lives of real women on the frontier makes her embodiment of masculine and feminine traits unique.

Notes

1. David Potter, "American Woman and the American Character," *Stetson University Bulletin* 17 (January 1962): 58.

2. William Humphrey, *Ah Wilderness: The Frontier in American Literature* (El Paso, 1977), p. 15.

3. Emerson Hough, *The Passing of the Frontier* (New Haven, 1921), pp. 93–94.

4. Leslie A. Fiedler, "Evasion of Love," in *Theories of American Literature*, ed. Donald M. Kartiganer and Malcolm A. Griffith (New York, 1972), p. 246.

5. Dawn Lander, *Women and the Wilderness: Tabus in American Literature*, University of Michigan Papers in Women's Studies, 1976, no. 11, p. 66.

6. Ibid., p. 64.

7. Judith Fryer, *The Faces of Eve* (New York, 1976), p. 23.

8. Gerda Lerner, *The Woman in American History* (Berkeley and Los Angeles, 1972), p. 45.

9. Along with Fiedler's *Love and Death in the American Novel*, see Carolyn Heilbrun, "The Masculine Wilderness of the American Novel," *Saturday Review* 55 (January 1972), Lander, *Women and the Wilderness*, and Fryer, *Faces of Eve*.

10. "From Cowboy to Owner and Operator of Vast Domain Marked Life of Charlie Hart," *Clovis News Journal*, May 29, 1938.

11. Emily Jones Shelton, "Lizzie E. Johnson: A Cattle Queen of Texas," *Southwest Historical Quarterly* 50 (January 1947): 351.

12. T.J. Tertula, "There Was No Christmas," *True West* 2 (November–December 1963): 20–21.

13. "Frontier Sketches," *The Denver Field and Farm*, April 29, 1911, p. 8.

14. "A Daring Western Woman," *Denver Times*, February 7, 1910.

15. Alice Marriott, *Hell on Horses and Women* (Norman, OK, 1953), p. 10.

16. Agnes Smedley, *Daughter of Earth* (New York, 1935), p. 56.

17. Ibid., p. 110.

18. J. Frank Dobie, *The Mustangs* (London, 1955), p. 32.

19. Interview with Joyce Roach, May 1978.

20. Mrs. E.J. Guerin, *Mountain Charley or The Adventures of Mrs. E.J. Guerin, Who Was Thirteen Years in Male Attire,* ed. Fred Mazzula and William Kostka (New York, 1971), pp. 13–14.

21. J. Evetts Haley, *Charles Goodnight, Cowman and Plainsman* (New York, 1936), p. 262.

22. Hobart Huson, *A History of Refugio County* (Austin, TX, 1955), p. 203.

23. Evett Dumas Nix, *Oklahombres* (Norman, OK, 1929), p. 147.

24. Henry Nash Smith, *Virgin Land* (New York, 1950), p. 129.

25. Dee Brown, *The Gentle Tamers* (Lincoln, NE, 1968), p. 59.

26. See Guerin, *Mountain Charley.*

27. Albert Johannsen, *The House of Beadle and Adams* (Norman, OK, 1950), p. 204.

28. E.L. Wheeler, *Deadwood Dick on Deck: or, Calamity Jane, The Heroine of Whoop-up* (New York, 1899), p. 24.

29. Richard Slotkin, *Regeneration Through Violence: The Mythology of the American Frontier, 1600–1860* (Middletown, CT, 1973), p. 12.

30. Ibid., p. 14.

31. John Cawelti, *Adventure, Mystery and Romance* (Chicago, 1976), p. 240.

32. Joe B. Frantz and Julian Earnest Choate, *The American Cowboy* (Norman, OK, 1955), p. 175.

33. George Fenin and William Everson, *The Westerns: From Silents to Cinerama* (New York, 1962), p. 40.

34. See Will Wright, *Sixguns and Society* (New York, 1975).

35. Typed interview from a tape recording made by Mody Boatright, December 27, 1952.

36. I. Broverman, D. Broverman, F. Clarkson, P. Rosenkrantz, and S. Vogel, "Sex Role Stereotypes and Clinical Judgments of Mental Health," *Journal of Consulting Psychology* 34 (February 1970): 5.

37. Wallace Stegner, "On the Writing of History," in *Western Writing,* ed. Gerald W. Halsam (Albuquerque, 1974), p. 26.

38. See Heilbrun, "The Masculine Wilderness of the American Novel."

39. Quoted ibid., p. 44.

The Lady as Jock:
Evolution of the Woman Athlete

Since the advent of Title IX, legislating "equal" opportunity and funding for women in sports, public awareness of the meaning of female athleticism has declined as a political concern. Understandably, in times which headline sibling murders of parents and parental abuse of children, let alone gang warfare and weapon-toting in schools, the lady as jock seems less than a burning cause. After all, women's sports history seems to have been written, if not comprehensively by the press or academic analysts, at least by the very acts of the women themselves. Yet history recounted exemplifies the credibility, identity, and accessibility women athletes worked for. Moreover, despite generally favorable opportunities and social tolerance, women athletes, especially in certain sporting arenas, remain on the margins today, sidelined in the public eye, still conditioned according to largely male expectations for athletic prowess, importance, and celebrity and commercial appeal. For every Mary Carillo who is considered astute enough to work as a television analyst of both men's and women's professional tennis, there is a nation full of male sportscasters on local news shows, primarily attending to men's sports. For every Ann Miller who excelled as a basketball player and also has worked as a professional athlete in men's basketball and as an analyst of the sport, most women athletes have no "second career" to go on. Even Martina Navratilova, contemplating her retirement, admits to the continued "discrimination" against her in terms of her sexual preference. She may have a post-professional tennis player's job as occasional commentator at Wimbledon; she has yet to have any major commercial endorsements made available to her.

Part of this continuing dilemma for women who may or may not wish to be "ladies" and "jocks," popularity and thus social sanction historically and even currently rest on a cultural reading of the heroic mode. Women may be heroines, playing second fiddle to the superior athleticism of the male body, or even heroes among themselves, but in contemporary society the heroic has blended with the celebrity, making style, fashion, and marketability a necessary aspect of popularity and sanction. In the past a stigma to hero-making for women in sports has been both a lack of media coverage and the historically controversial image of woman as athlete. Yet within the confines of acceptable femininity, and thus respectability, women athletes have fashioned themselves by negotiating between self-determination and physical excellence and commercial appeal which has allowed them to market a positive image. Despite the tremendous inroads made in opportunities for women athletes in the last twenty years in America, feminine appeal remains crucial to this opportunity. The history of women's sports argues, ironically, for a reclaiming of women's bodies and identities through the very commercial and social constraints—the femininity game—that many women have felt limiting.

That women have always been on the losing end of status is an historical reality not only of the body politic but of the body personal. Because of cultural and psychological conditioning, women long have been in touch with their bodies from without. Throughout history, with the possible exception of attitudes about childbirth, the female body has been regarded as a repository of evil, unfit to darken the door of important institutions such as churches or exclusively-male status organizations.[1] One of the most common explanations for recurrent negative attitudes is the belief, common to many cultures, that the female is a castrated male, indeed, half a person, or, at best, second best. Though her fertility has constituted some status, even so her menstruation is a sign of impurity, weakness, and even insanity. Yet her attempts to become a whole person and thus to operate exclusive of roles that reaffirm her femaleness, which is said to be passive, weak, and inept, have resulted in rebukes from her peers ranging from scathing looks of disapproval at her dress in a supermarket to more obvious ramifications like a single life of loneliness without man and marriage.[2] The gap between ideal behavior befitting a male and female is reinforced by such theories as Jung's archetypal analysis, which demonstrates the secondary position the image of "heroine" plays to the image of the "hero." Though Jung's types of Earthmother and Platonic Ideal are not wholly negative, even they suggest that women exist for men physically and intellectually. Only perhaps in the near stasis of the utterly laconic and whalebone-bound Victorian lady did Western womankind approach the perfection befitting Adam's rib, and then only when to sweat was to perspire and when piano legs were called piano limbs. In literature, heroines outside the Victorian cut are not "heroic," but in their physical expression are seen as sexually capricious. Modern heroines like the persona in Anne Sexton's poems and the protagonist in Sylvia Plath's *The Bell Jar* are psychologically convulsive because they exhibit the frustrations of centuries of women who are out of touch with their physical selves. When Sexton says in "Those Times" that "I was spread out daily/ and examined for flaws," she capsules the anthropological, cultural, and psychological attitudes that permit her to see herself as others see her. Or in more succinct and empirical terms, analyzing attitudes about body image and physical prowess, Eleanor Metheny says of the connotations of movement in sports that the greatest likelihood of role conflict occurs in physical activities of body contact, application of force to a heavy object, projecting the body through space over long distances, and face-to-face competition. We might then guess that Metheny finds these physical activities most acceptable: presenting the body in aesthetically pleasing patterns, use of a manufactured device to facilitate bodily movement, utilization of a light implement, and maintenance of a spatial barrier with the opponent.[3]

Thus, when modern women do act physically to "come out on top," it is in the very sporting arena where they may profit from being the inert, passive and helpless creatures we know them to be and where body contact, application of force to a heavy object, and face-to-face competition may be guised by the dark. For, as we are told by articles like "How to Become Sexually Active Over 35," the bedroom is the one field where pros like happy hookers and amateurs alike may secure a place in the world by conforming to those physical attributes that supposedly attract men. So, winning for women has become a coquettish game of losing to men. And the only game in town is the femininity game.

Given such cultural conditioning and image-making, how then have women's competitive athletics ever attracted females? Basically, the means of popularization has come in three areas: educational necessity, feminist efforts, and advertising.

The need for physical proficiency first was necessitated by the stress of attending college. Believed to lack the physical stamina necessary to withstand the rugged schedules at college, women were conditioned through physical education programs instituted by Vassar, for example, in 1862, and Wellesley in 1875. After the addition of facilities for tennis, skating and swimming at Wellesley, and regular exercise classes directed by a woman physician at Smith College, the U.S. Commissioner of Education in 1884 gave a favorable report on women's health in the schools and attributed the improvements to physical education programs. As a result, by 1890, most schools had gyms for women and special sports programs.

Perhaps as significant as these education inroads is the fact that, once allowed to condition their bodies, women began to prefer competitive sports. With the introduction of basketball in 1891, volleyball in 1893, and field hockey in 1897, there was a qualitative change in women's physical education. What had been education for health and beauty became sports for competition. By 1900, a controversial attitude that has since proved insightful was advanced by Gertrude Dudley of the University of Chicago, who suggested that athletics might be valuable as a means of later social and professional success.[4]

To early feminists, Dudley's idea was far from what her name suggests. Freeing the mind must entail freeing the body. What physical education programs had done for educational opportunities of younger women, feminists' efforts would do for older women. The first vehicle of such change was a piece of technology: the bicycle. Though early publicity went to women like Lillian Russell, friend of Diamond Jim Brady, who rode a fancy machine (handlebars of diamonds and rubies) on the side-streets of New York, Frances Willard and Gladys, as she called her plain, black bike, were the dynamic duo. As head of the Women's Christian Temperance Union, Willard wrote *How I Learned to Ride the Bicycle: A Wheel Within a Wheel*. No doubt Willard's text made an interesting companion piece with other "how-to" manuals of the times which were almost exclusively concerned with the "perfect home."

For health, Willard advocated getting out of the home. Reportedly, one young lady took her seriously enough to mount her newly-bought bike and ride away, forever leaving husband and perfect home behind.

According to Willard, the bike gave incredible freedom to women. As a cure-all for societal ills and lack of co-ordination, it was also a salve for nerve wear for the 53-year-old Willard who said, "I found a whole new philosophy of life in the wooing and the winning of my bicycle, through the learning of every screw and spring...." Moreover, she prophesied the possible effects this "sport" would have on women:

> The old fables, myths, and follies, associated with the idea of women's incompetence to handle bat and oar, bridle and rein, and at last the crossbar of the bicycle are passing into contempt in the presence of the nimbleness, ability, and skill of "that boy's sister." Indeed, if she continues to improve after the fashion of the last decade, her physical achievement will be such that it will become the pride of many a ruddy youth to be known as "that girl's brother."[5]

The optimism and presumption of Willard's statement is perhaps nowhere better documented than in the historically changing sports arena where "that ruddy youth" was rarely known as "that girl's brother," but rather as a "freak" like Frances Willard. Willard's modern successor, at least in the area of cycling, Sheila Young, proved the point most dramatically in 1973 in the World Cycling Championships in San Sebastian, Spain. Fouled by her Czech rival in the last race, at a speed of about forty miles an hour, she crashed into the track. After opting for doctors to staple the wound rather than have numbing stitches taken, bandaged and bloody, Sheila captured the gold medal. It was a stoic performance worthy of an Olympic medal and a world-wide audience. Obvious in this isolated example, which is like so many others (that no doubt we have not heard of due to lack of coverage), is that popularity of women's sports hinges not only on brave performances or on dreams of women like Frances Willard, but on media exposure.

Historically, advertising media cleverly has lent this kind of buoyancy to women's sports in times of stress. For example, in the thirties, the influence of Mrs. Herbert Hoover, who headed up the Women's Division of the NAAF and the committee on Women's

Athletics, found that girls were performing on the basketball courts with men rather than remaining in their expected roles as spectators. Apparently, what bloomers had done for cycling, women's gym clothes were doing for competitive athletics—exposing the female body. So, even though Mrs. Hoover's harangues led to a drop in the number of colleges sponsoring varsity competition for women from 22 percent to 12 percent in 1930, the image of women athletes in revealing clothes was seized as a selling point by advertisers. At the same time that bloomers were criticized for prompting more than passing looks from males, the Pan Handle Scrap tobacco company included with its product a series of cards picturing women athletes in bathing suits along with body specifications and records.[6] Bike posters of the same period displayed attractive young women in bloomers at the side of the company's bikes.

In retrospect, we can recognize the unwritten rule of these advertisements is that the buyer will be enticed by attractive displays of the female body, athlete or not, and not by the likes of a Frances Willard (described by one newsman as "a fat boy who was blessed with neat ankles") or the bloodied Sheila Young. An example of this necessary selling point was the situation of jockey Mary Bacon who did several advertisements for Revlon cosmetics. Despite the fact that the pretty blonde made her name as one of the first successful female jockeys, Revlon rejected an early take for an advertisement of Mary in the stables and at the side of a thoroughbred. In fact, the final ad shows Mary, in a close-up that could be of any good-looking model in habit and make-up, away from the barn and the horses. Advertising will sell the idea of physical astuteness only inadvertently when it is a means of capitalizing on what the public accepts as traditionally "beautiful" and "feminine."

Behind the effort to cover stable odors with perfume is the underlying major obstacle in the popularization of women's sports: the contradictory role expectations of women and athletes. Physical education coach Peggy Burke admits that this conflict and resulting fear of being tagged "masculine," has influenced her recruitment: "I encouraged attractive girls to become physical education majors regardless of their skill levels and discouraged the highly skilled, motivated girls from being majors because they did not meet any standards for appearance and behavior."[7] Though there are inconsistencies in attitudes expressed by women athletes about the effect that sports has on their feminine image, generally there exists a dichotomy between behavior that is traditionally feminine and behavior that is traditionally regarded as athletic. I. Broverman along with several colleagues reports the following behavioral traits which a group of clinical psychologists characterize as those of an adult female—dependent, emotional, intuitive, and passive. Conversely, traits usually associated with males, and with being athletic, include aggressiveness, tough-mindedness, dominance, self-confidence, and risk-taking.[8] No wonder that in her studies, M. Hart points out that "the woman who desires to participate in sports and remain 'womanly' faces great stress. By choosing sport she usually forces herself out of the social mainstream."[9]

Swimming against the mainstream is undoubtedly as difficult as violating the historical precedent of rhythmic dancing being the sport offered for early sportswomen. In lieu of this difficulty is the traditional alternative which enforces traditional role expectations of women and rewards them as well—the femininity game, so called in the book of the same name by Dr. Thomas Boslooper and Marcia Hayes.[10] The prime goal of the game is the woman's interest in getting a man and in getting married. The sporting equipment includes charm, guile, social shrewdness, cosmetics, clothes, and hopefully a sufficiently enticing physical apparatus. Since the victory pay-off is love and security, all of a woman's competitive and aggressive skills are rechanneled into this game. The major rule of the game is that a woman must be ready to lose at all other games. Because men don't love women who win, girls learn early to lose rather than to be rejected.

Of course, as a result, girls at puberty are conditioned socially to pursue what attracts boys rather than their own special interests. Any contrary activity, though it may bring success, often results in anxiety. Boslooper and Hayes cite a basic study conducted by Matina Horner, past president of Radcliffe College, where sixty-five percent of a group of women at the University of Michigan expressed anxiety over feminine success figures, equating the success of a hypothetical medical student with a loss of femininity.[11]

Sociologists John Roberts and Brian Sutton-Smith explore the conditioning that dictates such attitudes in a study that establishes a correlation between choice of games and the roles expected of boys and girls. Competitive gym sports involving the displays of power and physical skill were game models mostly for boys whose parents encouraged achievement and success. Games of strategy—chess and backgammon—were found to mirror childhood training in responsibility. As models for social responsibility and for power, games, like football, which combine physical skill and strategy, were chosen. However, games of chance and fortune—bingo and fish—were the choice of two groups, children who had been strictly disciplined in obedience, and girls. Because they were discouraged from initiative and achievement, these children dreamed their desires could become real through chance alone.[12] Follow-up research revealed in polls of 7,000 adults that business executives, politicians, and other men in positions of power overwhelmingly favored games that combined strategy and physical skill. Men having blue-collar jobs enjoyed games of pure skill, whereas women (and members of ghettoized minority groups) showed a preference for games of pure chance, or for those providing strategy, like bridge.[13]

Obviously both strategy and chance are needed to play the femininity game and these, in turn, are tools of every second-class citizen who sees his chance for success as determined by his fortunate or shrewd connection with those first-class citizens who attain success. Women have learned in their auxiliary roles to use this same guile and chance to approach success indirectly, through marrying a man who himself has the drive, ambition, and assertiveness to directly attain success. However, strategy is less and less effective as one's chances fade with age and women whose identity is based on the rewards of good looks become correspondingly unhappy with age. Boslooper believes that these women are happiest who "are physically active and feel feminine, no matter what they do." He adds that "all mature, intellectually creative women were tomboys when they were young," and he concludes that "what's important for women is to have a positive and realistic attitude about their strength and physical abilities, about aggressiveness, about competition."[14]

A most positive and lasting identity, then, seems to be related to the degree to which one may control his fate through honing the bodies and pitting oneself competitively against others via set rules and regulations. Thus, learning to be in touch with oneself has increased the popularity of women's sports for participants. A most vociferous proponent of this popularity, Billie Jean King, indicated in her magazine *WomenSports*: "I know from experience that athletes, or athletically-minded people, tend to be independent, sure of themselves, and their bodies, and tend to think for themselves."[15] In this editorial King supports this personal view with data collected from her own readers.

Other data that are supportive of King's general attitude include a study by Eldon E. Snyder and Joseph E. Kivlin of the Department of Sociology at Bowling Green State University. Using the variable of psychological well-being and body image to analyze degrees of athletic participation by women, Snyder and Kivlin collected data through self-administered questionnaires from respondents consisting of women athletes who participated in Women's National Intercollegiate Championships in basketball, gymnastics, swimming and diving, a second sample of American college women who were enrolled in general sociology classes at Bowling Green State University, and two additional groups of university women in Australia and India.

Acknowledging that if role conflict exists for the woman athlete or the woman who is a high participant in sports that the result would be attitudinal ambiguity, confusion, and anxiety, Snyder and Kivlin focused on aspects of self-identity that have been expressed in the stereotyped view of women athletes in our society as Amazons, masculine, and therefore, unfeminine. But, contrary to the usual stereotype, they found that athletic women did not differ appreciably in height and weight from non-athletic women and, hence, could not qualify physically as Amazons. Moreover, they found that in terms of psychological well-being, the athletes and high participants shared a similar outlook on life, that being a very positive one. In fact the group of athletes and high-participants exhibited more positive attitudes than the low participant sub-group. In the measurement of attitudes toward various processes of the body, the general pattern revealed that athletic participation is positively associated with body image. A contrast in the percentage of positive responses given by athletes and low participants interestingly supports this statement:

	Women Athletes	American Students
	All	Low Participants
Health	97	77
Body Build	72	47

| Posture | 69 | 35 |
| Energy Level | 91 | 43 |

Most revealing is that concerning areas of the body that could be considered imperative for femininity, the bust, face, back, legs, hips, the women athletes recorded an average of 23 percentage points higher ratings of themselves that the American non-participants. Though Snyder and Kivlin hasten to add that their study is "exploratory," they do conclude that serious doubts may be raised about the usual stereotypes of women athletes. They conclude that there are two reasons for these findings: "Apparently, even though women athletes have frequently received negative sanctions, their participation in sports has been sufficiently rewarding to counter the social costs and tensions associated with conflicting roles.... Another possible explanation is that many female athletes are sufficiently secure in their femininity and they can participate in a socially defined "unfeminine" activity without suffering an identity crisis."[16]

Future popularity of women's sports depends on the projection of positive and respected images of participants by the media as encouragement for more women to get hooked on the rewards of the flesh. Small, subliminal tributes have been made through such ads as Peggy Fleming's endorsement of ballpoint pens, Billie Jean King's winning Colgate smile, and more television spots on sporting events that involve women such as the Super Stars competition and women's pro football. However, it is doubtful that any sportswoman can match the Joe Namath breakthrough. What Broadway Joe is to pantyhose, it is doubtful that even Billie Jean King will become to jockey underwear. Yet, that Namath flair for "show-biz" is another necessity for the popularization of women's sports. A major turning point for women's sports was the King-Bobby Riggs match, gimmicks and all. Beneath the huckster techniques of Bobby's Sugar Daddy image was a seriousness that King drove home in front of a television audience of 40 million, 6–4, 6–3, 6–3.

This publicity should start young, and one manner in which young women can be influenced to pursue athletics is to have before them, on television, on cereal boxes, on bubblegum cards, the image of a sportswoman. Both fiction and non-fiction books are beginning to fill this area. Works include *Delilah* by Carole Hart (about a liberated ten-year-old who plays drums and basketball),

Zanballer by R.R. Knudson (about a 13-year-old who persuades her friends to leave a dance class for the football field), and *Not Bad for a Girl* (which is about a girl's attempt to play Little League Baseball and has been adapted for television) and non-fiction like *Karate for Young People* by Russell Kozuki and *Swimming the Shane Gould Way.*

Legislated opportunities may include Title IX, the controversial bill which affirms the right of women to participate equally in all phases of athletics. Though the final draft of the regulations of Title IX by the HEW is especially vague in the area of what a "basic equality" of funding is, the law has made possible publicity for the negligible attitudes of schools toward women's sports. Since 1972, when it was passed by Congress, Title IX is credited with improvements in budgets, scholarships, and audiences for women's sports. One example of this change is at Michigan State University where the women's budget jumped from $34,000 to $84,000 between the '72–'73 and '73–'74 academic years. The new budget included services men have always received such as tutoring, medical treatment, a modern dressing room, and the movement of women administrators to the traditionally all-male field house. Of course, huge discrepancies still exist nationwide as exemplified by the budget at Ohio State where women receive $43,000 compared the the men's $6 million a year. There women swimmers are allowed to use the pool from 6:30 a.m. to 9 a.m. and at dinnertime when the men are not using it. Other laws which have been newly discovered by coaches and participants alike in their fight for equality include the Title VII of the 1964 Civil Rights Act, the Equal Pay Act, the Equal Protection Clause of the Fourteenth Amendment to the Constitution (used by high school basketball player Rachel Lavin to win the right to play on a boys' team) and the Equal Rights Amendment.[17]

While these battles ensue in the trenches for amateurs, the desirability (and profitable nature) of being a woman athlete are enhanced by emerging real life heroines, the pros. Women like Billie Jean King offered an alternate lifestyle to that which girls have been reared to anticipate. As a symbol of the "lady jock," King offers a healthy alternative to the cultural protoype of femininity. Spectacled and muscular, she is as robust physically as she is aggressive athletically. Yet she, like Mary Joe Peppler, the winner of the 1975 Women's Super Stars, appears comfortable in her long gown in an interview on the *Tonight Show*. In fact, King may seem enigmatic to those who still express femininity through fluttering false eyelashes and prescribed morality. Though in her extravaganza with Bobby Riggs, King was carried high in her Queen's chair, she still embodies the values of the old hero type. She disciplines herself. While Riggs was popping an undetermined number of vitamins a day for the match, King was lifting weights and working on her serve. She disdains the partying and pampering so many athletes demand. But even as she says that discipline "is the secret of champions." and "means of giving things up,"[18] so her abortion, her feminist sympathies, and her magazine *WomenSports*, represent a liberal self-indulgence which characterizes the modern heroine.

King, and other women stars (like Carol Mann in golf, Olga Korbut in gymnastics, Mickey King in coaching) have in hand what seems to be the ultimate proof of success (and, therefore, "right reason") in America: they have been what they are, women athletes, and have made money doing it. But, hopefully, the ultimate result of this popularity will not be in measurable materialism but in attitudes. The ultimate influence of women's sports is as a vehicle of cultural change. As Judith Bardwick says in *Psychology of Women*, "Those women who have developed an independent sense of self and positive self-esteem will be able to elect their roles and enjoy their freedom of choice."[19] Boslooper indicates another advantage in this new-found liberation: "One of the reasons men put women down professionally is that they are accustomed to putting them down physically. Men can keep women in a secondary position by keeping them weak and the best way to keep them weak is to keep them physically inactive."[20] So, as the "firsts" include women reporters covering locker rooms, women trainers being admitted to Professional Trainers Association,[21] and Super Stars getting Sunday prime time coverage, new advances are being made to broaden the concept of femininity. By being successful in sports, traditionally a high-status occupation, women may up their status, which historically has been auxiliary and low compared to men. "Female-bonding" (and I am playing on Lionel Tiger's term "male bonding," though I don't advocate the segregation he deems necessary), once escaping the level of a "hen-party," may realign the old pecking order so that women may feel they can socialize without stigma.

The resulting blurring of sex roles would free not only women but men as well. "Woman winning" would not mean "men losing" but rather the de-stereotyping of roles for each. As Carolyn Heilbrun says in her essay "The Masculine Wilderness of the American Novel":

> The idea of androgyny, which does not address itself to the particular sexuality of individuals, desires for them many choices along the whole spectrum of experience. Seeking to free men from the compulsion to violence and women from the compulsion to submission, the androgynous ideal images for each human being the fulfillment of this unique destiny and also a less violent future for the world.[22]

So with all the hoopla about women's sports, we can hope that women athletes will accomplish more than just create new markets for clothes, cosmetics, and exercise salons. After all, it is a little insulting that *Vogue* magazine in its May 1975 issue capitalized on the new vogue of sports by putting its same models in sports clothes and calling them sportswomen. Ideally, women's invasion of the masculine territory of sport will help erase its modern cosmetic quality and return to it some of the patience, perseverance, and sacrifice that are traditionally called feminine qualities. Actually, whether sports are seen in their original etymological context, as "diversion," or in their post-World War I transformation as a masculinity rite, somewhere there is an aesthetic aspect of sport that has been lost in all the poop sheets on individual scoring, total yardage, r.b.i.'s, and other so-called measurements of skill. It would be encouraging if the popularization of the woman athlete could be the popularization of "feminine" attributes in sport which have been forgotten by the male majority of athletes and spectators.

Coming "a long way, baby" certainly is a reality in women's sports. Yet the continued pressure to market appearance, and a socially acceptable appearance at that, continues a degree of cultural constraint over women athletes. The recent rumored prevalence of lesbian athletes and coaching staff at the University of Texas led to an outcry among Texan schoolgirl coaches and players and a scramble apparently to discourage certain behavior and recoup recruiting losses in Austin. Interviews with Martina Navratilova reveal that recently the women's tennis association required that top stars such as Navratilova go through a cosmetic remake session in order to pose, model-like, for promotional materials for women's tennis. In a world where blurring of sexual identity occurs from the bedroom to the fashion world, there seems to be a propensity for subtle control of the image of the super-star women, perhaps to safely define the masculine and feminine in our culture. Even before the full brunt of the Tonya Harding scandal broke, the press and public had taken sides on the Kerrigan/Harding "image" of the American female athlete. Navratilova has remarked that she wonders about her legacy in women's tennis. Though even her coach confesses she hasn't been up to speed in recent years (by this he means sheer power by younger ground-strokers has surpassed her own), Navratilova refers to the style of play she alone brought to the female tennis world. Though she seems ready to metamorphose back into the more shapely and softer (more body fat) Martina we knew as the young Czech who fell for American fast foods, she also is talking about having a baby (albeit by artificial insemination). Is she feeling the pressure of that very tangible legacy, that solely sanctioned physical act of women, birthing a baby? The legacy in tennis she referred to was muscular, grunting, yet fabulously adroit and graceful net play. To come to the net, to rush the net—that was Navratilova's answer to the safety and femininity of baseline play. "Obviously I didn't change the game, because everybody is staying at the baseline now," she says. But for some of us, our lifetimes as women and athletes have been marked by at least three women athletes who not only came to net, but pushed the margins of athletic women's play to unforgettable heights. As a child, I had only two models of the lady as jock: Babe Zaharias, who appeared in one schoolbook, and Wilma Rudolph, whom I watched on television. Though both disappeared from view, until recently with the moving memorials to Rudolph as an athletic ambassador, the metaphor of overcoming disabilities—physical, racial, social, international—were not lost. On the eve of Navratilova's retirement, I savor the moments she gave us in her ups and downs, her private and public struggles, basking in her audiences but not wilting when commercial endorsements were not forthcoming. Somehow we fundamentally know that once having been underdog, one's sense of self is challenged significantly. As the Title IX debates now enter a new arena, we can only hope that heroic glory and celebrity can continue to mean not popularity, but a liberation of body and mind in the actions of a

Wilma Rudolph who greeted her own retirement and even obscurity from the public youth-embracing eye by enabling others to run.

Even in the light of such personal observations, it is striking how prevailing the cultural constructions of female exceptionalness—super-heroine stature—are. Though the evolution of the woman athlete through time suggests some changes, still degrees of what society views as femininity apply in degree to different sports. As we have seen, women have worked within such conventions by external means, wearing appropriate costumes for example while possibly altering behavior. Yet women dedicated to the sporting life still justifiably feel themselves exceptional, isolated, and perhaps lone. In this way, sportswomen share the isolation American women have historically felt because of their outstanding or unique achievement. In an endeavor where both the individual and the team may star, depending on the sport, women still occupy secondary status. As individuals they are likely to feel they are isolated cases, rather than shining celebrities, whereas the heroic mode for the male in our society nearly always translates into the positive image of cultural hero. Even if a woman is famous, she may feel that she is the exception to the rule, therefore unusual. As a teammate, conversely, she is not equally sanctioned as a male is in a similar situation. Male bonding, which may partake of a kind of tribalism and exclusivity even into late adulthood, and may even carry aspects of same sex alliances, is not the same as female bonding. Though women have historically functioned communally, in groups, the "team" as communal experience is viewed primarily as adolescent or pubescent, safe for young women before the age of their primary attachments to men. When enjoyed late in life, the athletic team for women nearly always carries the specter of lesbian associations. Why else would women prefer to be with women in physical settings? So in both the individual and the group sporting experience, women sports and sports figures represent a status quite different than men.

What is important, then, about women's sports history is its parallel to other histories of women's perceived and perpetuated role in society. Recent studies of African-American women's writing, even beginning in the eighteenth century, demonstrate that, though the perception has been that there were no "literary" or personal histories of these women, in fact many exist. However, these women did not know or know about each other. The same may be said for women athletes. Historically, we are beginning to realize how many athletes there were and how challenging to stereotypes of the ideal women they were through time. Even if the ladies who were jocks did not know or know about each other, we do. And knowing this, even in the contemporary experience of secondary worth, sanction, or isolation, we can know intellectually at least they play on.

Notes

1. Though many good discussions of female evil exist, one interesting and fresh approach occurs in Andrea Dworkin's *Woman Hating*, publishing by E.P. Dutton in 1974.

2. Great theorization about sex differentiation and cultural expectations and pressures to maintain sex-related behavior for women generally has been said to hinge on the dependent variables of psychological well-being and body image.

3. Eleanor Metheny, "Symbolic Forms of Movement: The Feminine Image in Sports," in *Connotations of Movement in Sports and Dance* (Dubuque, IA: William C. Brown Co., 1956), pp. 43–56.

4. *WomenSports*, Sept. 1974, p. 59.

5. Maury Z. Levy and Barbara Jane Walder, "Frances Willard and Amelia Bloomer," *WomenSports*, July 1974, p. 24.

6. One of these cards, as each did, very graphically details the female body in numbers: "Annette Kellerman, No. 40, is the most famous swimmer and diver of her sex, in the world. She began swimming at the age of nine, and although known in the United States chiefly for her fancy, graceful diving, it was in distance contests that she first attracted attention. She is 25 years of age, and weights 137. He height is 5 feet 3 3/4 inches; neck, 12.6 inches; chest, 33.1 inches; chest, expanded, 35.2 inches; waist, 26.2 inches; hips, 37.8 inches; thigh, 22.2 inches; calf, 14 inches; ankle, 7.7 inches; upper arm, 12 inches; stretch of arms, 65 inches."

7. "Letters," *WomenSports*, Sept. 1974, p. 6.

8. I Broverman, D. Broverman, F. Clarkson, P. Rosenkrantz, and S. Vogel, "Sex Role Stereotypes and Clinical Judgments of Mental Health," *Journal of Consulting and Clinical Psychology*, XXXIV (February 1970), p. 5.

9. M. Hart, "Women Sit in the Back of the Bus," *Psychology Today*, V (October 1971), 64.

10. Thomas Boslooper and Marcia Hayes, *The Femininity Game* (New York: Stein and Day, 1973).

11. Thomas Boslooper and Marcia Hayes, "Why Women Lose," *WomenSports*, July 1974, p. 40.

12. John M. Roberts and Brian Sutton-Smith, "Child Training and Game Involvement," in *Sport, Culture and Society* (New York: The Macmillan Company, 1969), p. 126.

13. Brian Sutton-Smith with John M. Roberts and Robert Kozelda, "Game Involvement in Adults," in *Sport, Culture, and Society* (New York: The Macmillan Company, 1969), p. 253.

14. Boslooper, "Why Women Lose," p. 78.

15. Billie Jean King, "Publisher's Letter," *WomenSports*, September 1975, p. 3.

16. Eldon E. Snyder and Joseph E. Kivlin, "Women in Sports: Cross-National Comparisons of Psychological Well-Being and Body Image," a paper presented at the National College Physical Education Association for Men, Phoenix, Arizona, 1975.

17. "Revolution in Women's Sports," *WomenSports*, September 1974, p. 38.

18. Billie Jean King, "How to Win," *WomenSports*, June 1974, p. 34.

19. Judith Bardwick, *Psychology of Women* (New York: Harper and Row, 1971), p. 205.

20. Boslooper, "Why Women Lose," p. 79.

21. Joan Gillette, a 27-year-old trainer, was the first woman to be admitted to the elite Professional Trainers Association after she broke the sex barrier in Texas by becoming a high school trainer for football and baseball at Paschal High School in Fort Worth.

22. Carolyn Heilbrun, "The Masculine Wilderness of the American Novel," *Saturday Review*, September 23, 1972, p. 45.

Violence as Liberation:
Belle Starr, Bandit Heroine

To thumb through the Western dime novels of the 1860s and 1870s is to notice the stereotypes of women that were being penned during the period in Western fiction. Titles like "The Frontier Angel," "The White Squaw," and "The Woman Trapper" each typify the three major female roles that existed in the literature of the Western movement. Women were a civilizing force, influencing the West with Eastern values and culture. Their femininity provided dramatic tension and thematic material as they were contrasted to the masculine mystique. As pioneer women they often filled a wide range of expectations in the wilderness from rifle-toting to mothering in the unsettled territories. All three of these roles is combined in the characterization of the Southwestern woman, Belle Starr, in the most popular *Belle Starr, The Bandit Queen or the Female Jesse James*, published by Richard K. Fix in the *National Police Gazette* in 1889. Though the accounts read as yellow journalism of the most tarnished degree, Fox unwittingly reveals truisms about the American Dream through the life of his "dashing female highwayman." In her he subverts the ideals of Eastern civility and femininity for the self-reliance and individuality she expresses through violence. As wife, mother, widow, forger, bandit, and murderer, Belle finds violence to be the most expedient liberation.

What was considered fitting behavior and popular fodder for fiction of her day was Belle Starr's as she moved from Missouri to Texas in the 1860s. Her family's social prominence in Carthage, Missouri, along with her own liberal education, which provided her with literary and musical tastes, made her, at sixteen, the epitome of the genteel heroine. Until she met the outlaw Jim Read, there is every indication that she was destined for the role of a leatherstocking woman: the early Western prototype who was delicate in thought, speech, and action. Fox records Belle's first aggressiveness in her defiance of her father: "I'd marry Jim if I knew that all h_ll was concentrated in his makeup."[1] Her first act of violence was perpetrated by the murder of her 17-year-old brother by a sheriff's posse at Spring Creek. She married Jim and murdered the posse member explaining her deviance in this way in her journal:

> My life is a wreck. A great necessity is within me. I must either drift high upon the waves of notoriety, or sink into the level of common life. This latter I can never do. Should I fail to gain a positive reputation for virtue and talent, I shall seek a superlatively bad one, through the channels of vice—dreadful and reckless daring. I must rise above the reach of my sex that men shall tremble at the mere mention of my name. Oh! God! That I could content myself with being simply good and leave greatness for others to achieve.[2]

The logic of Belle's chosen lifestyle is apparent. To be good is not always to be great. To be a woman is not to be powerful. In fact, to be notorious is to be dreadfully and recklessly daring. Belle had, after all, achieved the reputation for virtue and talent in Dallas high society and had announced to friends that civilization was not only a failure, but an outrage to human happiness. The traditional roles of women were the very antithesis of the competitive natures that were forging greatness and notoriety in the West. The truth is, underneath the lacy bodices of her upbringing was a tomboy who itched to shed frilly dress with tradition for the possibilities of being free-riding and female. The tomboy was one of admirable capabilities in a land that, sooner or later, demanded physical labor over fastidiousness. In fact, the name "tomboy" was coined in the West to exonerate a woman who could do a man's work. But few channels for the expression of this quality were open to women. After all, while tomboys worked their fingers to the bone, the ladies of the evening were rising to social prominence as matriarchs in California society. And those primitive values of leatherstocking had been replaced by a craving for progress and industry even as the Western hero, with six-shooters, had replaced the peaceful Cooper hero. If she was to enjoy a "man's" reputation, and rise above the "reach of her sex," then Belle would have to funnel her creative and independent instincts into a "man's work" which increasingly demanded violence. She would become a desperado.

While the overt motivations for her deeds were to achieve fame, the use of violence to realize her independent nature vented two other highly respected qualities of American character— shrewdness and aggression. In what other occupations reserved for women could Belle have earned $150,000 as she cleverly did in the Flood and O'Brien forgery and $17,000 as she did in the Grayson mail robbery? Traditionally, women had acquired power through feminine wiles. They might sleep with men to murder them or perform the deed indirectly through their manipulation of other men. But Belle's behavior may be typified in the incident in which she avenged her husband's imprisonment by riding in full daylight through the streets of Dallas to shoot Sheriff Nicols at point blank between the eyes. Though she had been forced, as she was disguised as a man the night before, to double up with the sheriff in the overcrowded Planter's hotel, she was not only chaste but sat up all night plotting the death of her bed partner. The reward for her direct and "masculine" approach to such issues was not only successful revenge but instant wealth and excitement that would shame "women's work."

In fact, Belle found the exercise of violence so successful in the Southwest that it was a vehicle necessary to her performance of traditional feminine roles. While a woman whose brother and husband were killed must wait out the actions of a pursuing posse, Belle tracked the men herself. As the mother of the adopted May Flower, she avenged her daughter's deflowering by a rich and rakish Californian by following the young man, fitting into his social group, leading him astray from his companions on a hunting trip, and finally stabbing him as the two lay camped that night away from the party. Even in marriage she resorted to violence. When Bruce Younger, a commonlaw husband, ran off one night, Belle could have lapsed, helpless and lachrymose, into a stupor. Instead, she rode mercilessly to Baxter Springs, Oklahoma, beat Younger to the hotel where she knew he would stay, and had a wedding party complete with twenty witnesses awaiting his arrival. When he walked in, she, with pearl-handled pistols, initiated the "I do's" after which they both parted, never to meet again. No papa's shotgun marriage could have been more expedient in making Younger face up to his cowardice.

With all the embellishments of "masculine" behavior that Fox provides, he forever reminds us in his narrative that Belle, nevertheless, is a lady. In fact, many of her mannish pranks are performed in male disguise. However, this indicates nothing about her concern with propriety, but merely that she must even look like a man to enforce her woman's will. She successfully poses as a preacher (and, forgetting the Bible, she reads from Mark Twain) and gets the sick minister the collection money, passes as a Spanish trick rider and wins the all-male event in California, and parades with cigar in teeth as a gentleman on trains from California to Missouri to escape forgery charges. However, when dressed as a woman, she is naturally admired and pursued for her womanly qualities as she elopes twice, is twice proposed to, and marries three times. Though Fox reconciles these two extremes by justifying each murder as revenge and making her out to be a Robin Hood figure who robs only the rich, he also indicates that she is at home in her androgynous makeup.

At first glance, Belle Starr may seem like nothing more than a reprint of many other Amazon athletic heroines who populated the dime novels. Like them she possesses great athletic ability, could out-shoot and out-ride most men. Like them, too, she resorts to violence, is aggressive, and is sexually liberated. However, in her character the reasons for an arch-villain qualifying as a heroine are more clearly defined. It must be remembered that little separated the gunslinger lawbreaker and the law-enforcing sheriff, for both craved power through violence. But what would seem to be a similar situation for women was vastly inequitable. *Much* separated the life of the aggressive and dominant woman from the weak and submissive woman of virtue. That Belle must exercise her innate qualities through violence in order to achieve fame and reputation proves to be ironic. It indicates that the so-called masculine and American traits of self-reliance and independence, carried to their extremes, can result in the destructive end of power, greed, and ego. Yet it shows that violence is needed for women to express their whole natures in a man's world. Furthermore, it indicates the dynamic tension between the civilizing forces that would make Belle's lifestyle, and thus her integration of the male and female roles, less possible, and the sparsely populated frontier that would allow her free rein. Her popularization among a largely Eastern readership must indicate the appeal this androgynous person had for those who could never experience the hazards and latitudes of the Southwest. Fittingly, these ruffians of the Southwest found their haven in a land which Frederick Whitaker called "The Hidden Valley," a new Garden of Eden where the Chain of Being could be altered. For as Burton Rascoe says of Parrington's omission of Fox's *Belle Starr* from *Main Currents in American Thought*: "That sprightly, well-edited, highly moral and romantically imaginative, illustrated news weekly had a much more profound influence upon national culture of its period than had all the work of all the romantic writers discussed by Parrington put together." Since Belle Starr was a real woman, the point is doubly made. In her motivation for her deeds were the guts women were going to need to turn the century.

Notes

1. *Belle Starr, The Bandit Queen, or the Female Jesse James* (New York: Richard K. Fox, 1889), p. 6.

2. *Ibid.*, p. 7.

LETTERS AND AUTOBIOGRAPHY
The Nature of Nature

Mary Austin: Writing Nature

I

When Mary Hunter Austin died in August of 1934, 135 jars of jams and jellies were found in storage in her Camino del Monte Sol residence in Santa Fe, New Mexico. This domestic expression of the essential country woman in Austin was often overlooked by those who knew her. Most people, even friends, chiefly noticed her domineering nature—the "I-Mary" some believed signified the egoist or at least the outspoken author of more than thirty books and some one hundred articles. Mabel Dodge Luhan most astutely located the storyteller in the domestic sphere:

> She was one of the best companions in the world in a house or on a trip. She loved to put on a big apron and go into our big old kitchen and toss a couple of pumpkin pies together. She loved to hob-nob, to sit and spin out reasons for strange happenings, to hear and tell about all the daily occurrences in both our lives. She was a romantic and loved the romance of the mystical and occult and often induced in herself peculiar symptoms. She could see and hear and truly experience more than the rest of us, so when she least knew it she really became fascinatingly delphic and sibylline.[1]

In an article entitled "Greatness in Women," Austin linked the domestic or homemaking quality—"givingness to others," she called it—with the intellectual, prophetic, and intuitive qualities in women that make their acts or arts contributory. Thus, the great woman who is a storyteller realizes her intellectual and intuitive gifts, as they are centered, unlike those of men, says Austin, "on the recipient rather than on the act."[2] Moreover, as Austin observed in her autobiography *Earth Horizon*, the writer herself is a recipient—a vessel through which the story is told:

273

> From the time I was thirteen there has been nothing new in my life. What I should do later was pretty clear to me then. I realized that I should be interested in people, for I was then. I liked the place where I lived and the people with whom I lived, though there was nothing dramatic about my life, and no contacts which could be called literary.
>
> What I did in the way of study of people, of cities, of the Indians in their villages, of literary folk in art communities has been directed by some design in my life for which I am not responsible. I knew when I was very young that I should have a good deal of mystical experience, but I have always felt that I was not doing it, that something outside me was responsible, that I was not the shaper but the shaped.[3]

Confronting the issues of women's sphere, the equation of art with masculinity, and her era's culturally imposed contradictions between femininity and creativity, Austin discovered a self and a voice that argued for certain artistic qualities particular to women. She noted too that creativity could be inspired by daily life, which itself is revelatory. Her life and work signify what Eudora Welty notes as the connection between autobiography and art: "The events of our lives happen in a sequence in time, but in their significance to ourselves they find their own order, a timetable not necessarily—perhaps not possibly—chronological. The time as we know it subjectively is often the chronology that stories and novels follow: it is the continuous thread of revelation."[4] The story of this revelation, implicit in all of Austin's works, is that of the woman writer's struggle for self, a voice, and a contributory relationship to society.

Just why Austin found this essential relationship with society so conflicting may be first seen in her youthful struggles to recognize, faithfully pursue, and share her creative life. She noted that the most serious deterrent to the success of women greatly and originally endowed was society's incapacity to recognize original genius when it occurred in a characteristic womanly fashion. In her interior life as a child, she often found herself at odds with the very "womanly" attributes she later championed as key to the creative life.

Austin was born in 1868 to a Midwest family in which the father was an invalid and the mother an ardent Methodist, activist in the Women's Christian Temperance Union (WCTU), and later taxed supporter of four children. She recalled her childhood as deprived, her early creative and mystical experiences ignored. This sense of loneliness and isolation she related to being the middle child, unwanted, as she believed, because of physical and financial stress in the family. Further, she was unusual in that she early preferred intellectual interests, announcing her plans to become a writer. Also, she lacked conventional attractiveness, which the family feared would preclude her marrying. In her inner-directed alienation from typical American extroversion, she was enraptured from childhood with the solitary cosmological experience—and one not bound to religious creed or formal practice. By the age of ten, the major losses of a father who had shared her love of books and nature and her sister Jenny ("the only one who loved me") had intensified Austin's isolation and reliance on her inner resources.

Austin's account of her discovery of "I-Mary"—the independent and imaginative self, which as an identity crucially countered "Mary-by-herself," the socially dictated Mary, meeting the expectations of the external world—centers on two experiences through which this inner self made itself known. While she was learning her letters at her older brother's elbow in the kitchen one day, when she was around two and a half years of age, they came to the "i" in the vowels and Austin pointed to her eye. Her mother explained, "No, I, myself, *I* want a drink, I-Mary," and pointed to the girl. For the first time, Austin perceived herself as existing significantly separately in the adult-ordered world. She had a self; moreover, a self connected to letters, words, and reading. Later when she relied on the inner knowledge of this self to describe events as she imagined they had happened, her mother accused her of lying—"storying," as she called it. Also, when Austin truthfully claimed to be able to read when she first attended public school, the teacher, too, accused her of lying. Her important and precocious gift for "stories" apparently signified to the outer world willful, independent behavior inappropriate in a girl.

Austin further confirmed the authenticity of this developing inner voice when she found that her storytelling thrilled her playmates in the woods near her Carlinville, Illinois, home. Away from the stifling conventions of home, community, and school, Austin became a kind of pagan priestess. Here the "totem" friends in the woods were paid homage through the properly told story and acts of daring and occasional pranks of rebellion against the adult world. Moreover, nature was a sanctuary for this newly discovered self. The "little bird on the tongue," which at home leaped out with sometimes ill-mannered truths to her mother's displeasure, in the woods enjoyed a clear, uncaged cry. And—someone answered. In her account of the mystical experience under the walnut tree, Austin experienced a confirming response not found in any of her other "outside" experiences in Carlinville. Of the "presence" under the walnut tree she asked "God? God?" and felt a reply to her inward spirit. Austin's mystical experiences in the woods clearly confirmed her writer's vocation and the story's authenticity. Further, the story became a bridge between this precocious, prophetic, and isolated child and the outside world.

Later, at Blackburn College in Carlinville, Austin again felt her identity and purpose sanctioned, this time in an intellectual community that, unlike the milieu of her family and Carlinville society, offered opportunities to both young men and women to develop their gifts. Yet here, perhaps because she was anxious to prove herself intellectually equal to men and also to gain her family's approval, she chose to major in science rather than in English. She may also have turned to the objective study of nature as a way of factualizing her awe. Through this intellectual approach to her feelings, she sought to reconcile her inner life with the outer—to validate her genius while assuaging a lack of fundamental attention. In the study of botany, she could re-create the kind of emotionally charted life she had found in her girlhood reading of Hugh Miller's *The Old Red Sandstone*, a scientific yet philosophical and poetic work centered on natural history study.

In the essay "Woman Alone," Austin writes:

> Long before I came to the intellectual understanding of the situation I had accepted as fact that I was not liked and could not expect the normal concessions of affection.... I had learned that it was only by pushing aside all considerations of liking and insisting on whatever fundamental rightness inhered in a particular situation, that I could secure a kind of factual substitute for family feeling and fair play.... Out of this I developed very early an uncanny penetration into the fundamental ethics of personal situations which my mother was too just to refuse and not always clever enough to evade. By the time I was old enough to discuss our relationships with my mother the disposition to seek for logical rather than emotional elements had become so fixed that I

had even made myself believe that being liked was not important. I had, at least, learned to do without it.[5]

At Blackburn College, there was justice or "rightness" in Austin's success as assistant editor and contributor to the literary magazine, *The Blackburnian*, where her intellectual gifts were praised.

When removed against her will to a homestead claim in the Southern California desert immediately upon her graduation from college, Austin at once felt exiled both from the garden of her childhood, the Carlinville woods, and from her sanctioned success and intellectual stimulation at Blackburn. Initially, she felt the rigors and bleakness of the desert denied her a vocabulary and her mysticism: This was a "wordless wilderness" for which her reading of Hugh Miller, Emerson, Tennyson, and the Romantic poets hardly prepared her. At first she was spiritless and voiceless as the desert erased her familiar ways of seeing, but slowly, forced into a psychic pioneering not unlike the resourceful "mother-wit" she admiringly championed in her female forebears, she interpreted for this setting a longing that matched her own deep self, a "beauty-in-the-wild, yearning to be made human."[6] Much as she had discovered the magic of words as a child, here as a young woman she discovered the magic of the desert and its people, which would frighten, temper, and inspire her.

Austin recognized in the ancient rhythms of the land and indigenous lives a primordial truth akin to her initial inner awareness of the "presence" in the Carlinville woods. The discovery of "self behind the self," as she later called it, allowed her to finally "begin to write in my own character." Seeing a kinship between the feminine principles she recognized and the ancient patterns of life in the desert, Austin experienced this landscape as both test and confirmation. "The friend in the wood" returned to companion her in her maturing life, not as faun or fairy but as the "ultimate Pan,"[7] "the voiceless passion of spirit toward form."[8] In her new world of Paiute and Shoshone, sheepherders and homesteaders, she further learned the difference between knowing something and knowing *about* it. Direct experience of what she had previously sensed imaginatively activated her creativity as a voice for ancient wisdom.

As her creative life took new energy from the environment, her marriage to Stafford Wallace Austin and the birth of their mentally disabled child made writing a practical necessity as well. From

1884 to 1912, the years Austin lived in California, she was displaced a number of times due to her husband's failures or restlessness. On a trip to San Francisco, she was befriended by Ina Coolbrith, a former editor of the *Overland Monthly*, whose habit it was to encourage young writers. Austin's first work to be published, a story entitled "The Mother of Felipe," subsequently appeared in the *Overland Monthly* in November 1892.

During 1898–1899, the family homesteaded at Tejon Pass on the Beale Ranch, where Austin learned much lore from Wallace and the Mexican sheepherders. Then she and Wallace took up a claim on a series of rocky ridges near Owens Lake called the Alabama Hills. Here Austin explored the mysteries of the arroyos and befriended the local miners, enjoying their folksongs, card tricks, and country dances.

In 1899, she was invited to teach at the Los Angeles Normal School by Dr. Edward T. Pierce, head of the school and a friend of Charles Fletcher Lummis. Lummis at that time had published nearly a dozen books and was editor of *Out West* magazine. Through him, Austin met local writers Sharlott Hall, Edwin Markham, anthropologist Frederick Webb Hodge, Charlotte Perkins Stetson (later Gilman), and Grace Ellery Channing, among others. Lummis advanced the opinion that Austin had talent but no genius. Nevertheless, in July of 1900 she published a story, "Shepherd of the Sierras," in the *Atlantic Monthly*. A number of her early writings appeared in various publications in the period between 1897 and 1904 before her success with her nonfiction work *The Land of Little Rain* in 1904. Austin sold poems and stories to *Munsey's Magazine*, *Cosmopolitan*, *St. Nicholas*, and the *Atlantic* while Lummis continued to publish her stories in *Out West*, along with the writings of Eugene Manlove Rhodes, Emerson Hough, and Ernest Thompson Seton. Lummis no doubt influenced her interest in Native American and Hispanic culture, while with David Starr Jordan, a scientist and later first president of Stanford and a member of the Lummis circle, she shared the belief that nature shaped human societies.

Though her creative efforts provided needed funds for them, her family still rejected the idea that she could be a writer. True, her mother had once ferreted one of her discarded poems out of the trash and given it to Frances Willard for publication in the WCTU newsletter. Still, this gesture seemed to the girl solely in her mother's own interest. Austin claimed that though she always sensed she would be a writer, was indeed "endowed" for it, the family's attitude was "What makes you think *you* can write?" She confesses:

> In truth, I did not know. Looking back on the idea of a literary career which prevailed in the Middle West of that period, it was probably well for me that nobody knew. I won a college degree by dint of insisting on it, and by crowding its four years into two and a half. My brother had a full four years. That I got so much was partly a concession to the necessity of my earning a living. With a college education I could teach, and teaching was regarded then as a liberal profession, eminently suited for women. Being "plain," and a little "queer," it was hoped rather than expected that I would marry. My queerness consisted, at that time, in ... stoutly maintaining against all contrary opinion that I would some day write, and in the—to my family—wholly inexplicable habit of resting my case on its inherent rightness rather than upon emotional reactions it gave rise to.[9]

The conflict between writing, marriage, and the mothering came to seem overwhelming at such times as after the birth of her mentally disabled child Ruth, when Susanna Hunter remarked: "I don't know what you've done, daughter, to have such a judgment upon you." Ironically, Susanna Hunter thought marriage and childbirth would settle Austin down—cure, in fact, the ill health from which she suffered throughout her life. Austin herself believed marriage and writing totally compatible—under normal circumstances: "I thought two intelligent young people could do about as they liked with life."[10] Later she claimed to have realized this freedom only through tragedy. In 1905, she committed her child to an institution, where Ruth remained until her death at twenty-two. Austin wrote in 1927, "In a way this tragic end to my most feminine adventure brought the fulfillment of my creative desire, which had begun to be an added torment by repression. Caring for a hopelessly invalid child is an expensive business. I had to write to make money."[11]

The failure in this personal arena, while thrusting Austin into a writing career, encouraging her radicalism, and creating a practical necessity for the expression of her imaginative abilities, also encouraged her to translate the feminine principle into "man's sphere," the professional world outside the home. Here, certainly through her intellectual and intuitive faculties and often with tenderness, she addressed nature, religion, feminism, and folklore.

The last cause Austin and her husband shared was that of the Owens River water issue in which water promised to develop the Owens Valley was diverted, through political maneuvering, to Los Angeles. The Austins were heartbroken over the turn of events, and Mary saw the outcome as a blow to her faith in cultural evolution—the growth of people in harmony with natural resources. The couple separated during part of this time and later divorced. Austin sought once again, as she had with Lummis, a larger family unit, this time in the artist colony of Carmel.

The power of the desert life of Southern California and its people emerged in her successful first books, *The Land of Little Rain, The Flock, Isidro, Santa Lucia,* and *Lost Borders.* With the proceeds from these books, she built a house at Carmel in 1905 where she could share her creative life with Jack London, Harry Leon Wilson, Charles Warren Stoddard, and later George Sterling. For an outdoor study, she built a wickiup in the fashion of the Paiutes and there began to experience the "larger life":

> Released thus to the larger life which opened to me with literary success, I found plenty of reasons for being a feminist in the injustices and impositions endured by women under the general idea of their intellectual inferiority to men.... I thought much that was said at that time about Home and Mother sentimental tosh; I thought it penalized married love too much to constitute the man she loved the woman's whole horizon, intellectual, moral, and economic. I thought women should be free to make their contribution to society by any talent with which they found themselves endowed, and be paid for it at rates equal to the pay of men. I thought everything worth experiencing was worth talking about; I inquired freely into all sorts of subjects.... I talked freely of art as though it had a vital connection with living.[12]

Austin was to participate in this larger life as one of the leading American women writers of her time, living in writers' colonies in Carmel, New York, and later Santa Fe, traveling abroad as a speaker and gaining an enviable reputation as a lecturer in the United States, and, toward the end of her life, recognized for her many creative contributions.

In 1908, she became the first prominent woman writer from the American West to tour England. She traveled to Italy as a guest of the Herbert Hoovers, meeting the Joseph Conrads and H.G. Wells, and attended the meetings of the Fabian Summer School, where she conversed with George Bernard Shaw. When she returned from Europe, Austin established residence in New York City to produce her play *The Arrow-Maker* and publish the works *Fire* and *Outland*, based on life in the Carmel colony.

Her New York period, which lasted from 1912 to 1924, is distinguished as her most productive. There she was occupied with the feminist movement, largely reflected in her books during this time, the war effort, and a furthering of her interests in Indian myths and poetry. *Love and the Soul Maker*, a lengthy philosophical dialogue between the author and Valda McNath, expresses the idea that true love is a creative force governed by influences outside of man. Austin notes in this work that the structure of married love can be a creative force governing the great artist, shaping something beautiful, honest, and permanent. This force she calls the Soul Maker and at other times Wakonda, the Friend of the Soul of Man, Everyman's Genius, and the Sacred Middle. Speaking of these same ideas earlier at the New York Legislative League in 1912, Austin advocated the instruction of women in the psychology of the sex relationship, organization of marriage on an equitable financial basis, and investigation into the ancestors of each member in the relationship. Her pragmaticism as well as the personal experience of her failed marriage emerge in this plea.

Never solely a theorist, Austin involved herself in the war effort by working on the Mayor's Committee for National Defense, disbursing food to the needy. She also sponsored a war garden that provided fresh vegetables. Her novels during this period, *A Woman of Genius*, *The Lovely Lady*, *The Ford*, and *No. 26 Jayne Street*, reflect her contribution to the feminist movement of the time. *The Man Jesus* (which she preferred to be titled *A Small Town Man*), a psychological biography of Christ based on her experiences in Italy, indicates her continued interest in religion and mysticism. *The Trail Book*, a collection of animal stories, and *The American Rhythm*, translations of Indian songs, illustrate her work with Amerindian materials and her role as popularizer and interpreter of this folklore.

A trip to New Mexico at the invitation of Mabel Dodge Luhan, whom she had met in Greenwich Village earlier, and a lecture tour of the Plains states in 1921 reconfirmed Austin's belief in the vitality of regional America. She noted the importance of musical instruments, festivals, local art exhibits, and community theaters in the cultural life of each region. In New York City she had found that "I was bothered by the rage for success; the idea that an immediate success was the sign of capacity; that the little whorls of success that kept appearing on the surface of affairs were final and invincible."[13] New Mexico now succeeded New York as her essential creative environment. Serving as a surveyor of Taos County Hispanic cultural institutions for the Carnegie Institution's Americanization program in 1917–1918, she toured northern New Mexico and, the next summer, traveled with the Gerald Cassidys down the Rio Grande and into southern Arizona, sketching and writing, collecting materials for what would become *The Land of Journeys' Ending*.

Austin decided New Mexico would be her permanent residence and built "The Beloved House" in Santa Fe in 1924. In the decade that she lived there, though she was accused of being uncommunicative, preoccupied, and unfriendly, she pursued relationships with those who shared her interest in indigenous cultures, the preservation of arts and the land, and the regeneration of American literature through regional roots. At Mabel Dodge Luhan's house, she met the D.H. Lawrences. Lawrence satirized both her and Mabel's attitudes in his unpublished play, *Altitude*, but Austin shared with Lawrence a deep faith in the power of the collective unconscious, the meaning of primitivism to modern man, and a love of the New Mexico landscape's beauty and creative force.

Largely through her efforts, there was a revival of interest in their music and drama among the Hispanics of Santa Fe. She had collected Penitente hymns during her visit in 1919 and argued that they were "authentically as American as the Negro Spirituals." In her leadership to preserve both Hispanic and Indian art and culture, Austin was instrumental in the restoration of the Santuário at Chimayó, joining Frank Applegate and architect John Gaw Meem, then-president of the Society for the Preservation and Restoration of New Mexico Mission Churches. She and Applegate established and nurtured the Spanish Colonial Arts Fund to preserve and promote the creation of these native works.

Along with other Santa Fe and Taos colony members, Austin helped rally national support for the defeat of the Bursum Bill that would have deprived the Pueblos of vast tracts of agricultural and grazing lands. Reacting to Commissioner of Indian Affairs Charles H. Burke's order to ban dances among the Pueblos, Austin fired a strong letter to Burke accusing him of depicting the Pueblos as "half animals" and interfering with their religious freedom. She and other members of the community brought enough pressure on Burke so that he relaxed his order. Austin further argued that Congress should adopt laws guarding Native American rights. She worked for federal legislation to emphasize Indian arts and crafts in the federal Indian-school curriculum. So well known was her reputation as an advocate of Indian culture and welfare that the Mexican government in 1930 appointed her a consultant to assist in that country's effort to restore its own Indian arts and culture.

Working with Witter Bynner on language experiments affecting Hispanics in an Anglo-dominated school curriculum, Austin strongly advocated bilingual education in New Mexico's public schools. She also promoted the local library and community theater and for several years urged federal officials to establish a national department of arts and letters (the forerunner to the present National Endowment for the Arts and Humanities) so that creative people could turn from "struggling for place and honor among themselves" to "developing art of the people."[14] As an environmentalist, Austin was appointed in 1927 to the Seven State Conference on Colorado River Basin Development, during which she lobbied for recognition of the river as both a national asset and of international importance to Mexico.

As a professional public speaker during this period, she was booked by L.J. Alber World Celebrities Lecture Bureau and other agencies. Austin lectured on college and university campuses, was a particular favorite at Yale University, and for years lectured annually to the Women's University Club in Los Angeles. In 1926, she spoke at Clark University as a guest of the Department of Psychology's "Symposium on Psychical Research." Some of her topics were "Southwestern Literature and the Common Life," "Primitive Drama," "Genius and the Subconscious Mind," and "American Fiction and the Pattern of American Life." In 1930, she addressed the Seminar on Latin American Cultural Relations in Mexico and, while there, lectured at the National University on "American Indian Art."

The tremendous productivity of this period centered on Austin's protective attitude toward Santa Fe and issues affecting the Southwest and its native elements. Her poetry of a regional emphasis appeared in *Poetry, Saturday Review of Literature, Literary Digest*, and several anthologies; articles, both interpretative and popular, were featured in *Ladies Home Journal, Art and Archaeology, New Republic*, the *Nation, Collier's*, and the *Saturday Evening Post*. In her ten years in Santa Fe, Austin published eight books, including her acclaimed autobiography *Earth Horizon* ("A profoundly original interpretation of the American spirit," one reviewer applauded) and the highly acclaimed *Starry Adventure* and *One Smoke Stories*.

Austin's tremendous accomplishments were acclaimed by critics in her lifetime and upon her death in 1934 T.M. Pearce noted her ability to write of one locale yet create universal stories of lasting import. Henry Seidel Canby, the founder and first editor of *Saturday Review of Literature*, memorialized Austin as "one of the greatest American women of letters of our time," deserving a "prominent place in American literature."[15] Despite her primarily southwestern identification, she was compared with Tolstoy in her ability to utilize regional materials to express the universal. Some critics recognized her insightful and mystic influences while others still saw these tendencies as dubious. In answering one such critic who challenged her to produce her research in developing her theory of the American rhythm, Austin had retorted:

> I recognize no such objection as you lay upon me to demonstrate an American Rhythm "by means of vast documentation, special reference, and detailed analysis." This is a matter I had out with myself many years ago, after I discovered myself in possession of a field of scholarly research that had not been entered by many of my contemporaries. I see myself, primarily, as a creative thinker—a creative writer, whichever term suits you best—which I feel to entail a higher obligation than that of stodgy and meticulous demonstration for the uninitiated of what has come to me through regular channels of scholarly experience. I felt that I couldn't be faithful to my primary obligation if I must go

dragging after me all the fructifying sources, as a queen bee trails the entrails of her mate.[16]

Thus, Austin asserted that her intuitive certainty had a fundamental rightness—that feeling could be argued in the outer world as fact. As critic Carl Van Doren expressed after he death: "She was the master of the American environment ... whose books were wells that drive into America to bring up water for her countrymen, though they might not have realized their thirst."[17]

Austin claimed an ability to "read patterns," through which, as storyteller, she could anticipate life patterns and meanings, the significance of "man turning his insides out"—the manifestation of universal archetypes, coming from the subjective unconscious in behavior and beliefs. Though her claim to these intuitive powers often seemed egotistical, Austin argued as a storyteller of place and universal elemental experiences the value of these primary resources for the psyche of mankind. For her fellow Americans, she said that she wrote not of survival but of a life, lived harmoniously upon the land, which conveyed "elemental truths which are antidotes to those provided in industrial slums where minds are torn and bodies worn."[18] Moreover, the wells she drove deep, which her countrymen often ignored, held antidotes to the characteristic criticism of Americans as Babbitts. Shouldering her mantle of intuitive power as surely as a medicine woman her manta, Austin ultimately created a new image of the American woman writer as seer, sayer, and healer—a role expressing the feminine principles she advocated. This "calling," her sacrifice for it, and the heroic stature she thereby won, she explained during the celebration of the publication of her *Earth Horizon* in 1932. Noting that she had been lonely most of her life, she said she nevertheless joyously paid the price for the intuitive and intellectual gifts with which she served society: "I knew that I had lived symbolically, that I had done what any woman perhaps could have done, but which for some reason or other most of them do not. I was the medium, the tool of forces I could not control."[19]

II

The American Southwest landscape and its people contributed to Mary Austin's sibylline voice and her identity of woman writer as a kind of prophetess. Nature also offered external proof of what she claimed intuitively: that people were significantly tied to environment and those people who had lost this basic contact could revivify themselves through close observation of lives still harmoniously part of the land. Art—in Austin's case, "writing" nature—could reunite nature and human nature. The subconscious common ground for what Austin called the "Sacred Middle," the "middle ground between art and knowledge"—distinctively Mary's own—was the source of a "feeling-knowledge" Austin believed could heal by restoring a psychic wholeness. Art, as it emerged from the rhythms of landscape, contained the imprint nature made on individuals and societies and the imprint the subconscious made, in customs, ritual, and ceremony, on the land. In that microcosm of her thoughts on this subject, *The Friend in the Wood*, Austin says this interpenetration calls "the grass to be man." She also shows in her nature-centered fiction and nonfiction writing that this interpenetration of "Life on lives" also calls the writer to respond to "the ever living and as yet uncreated Life, pressing to be shaped as tree and shrub"[20]; or to, as she says elsewhere, "the voiceless passion of spirit toward form."[21] Giving form in her writing to this spirit was Austin's ultimate declaration of the meaning of nature, chronicled in her work from an essentially romantic, transcendental view to a political, social, and finally aesthetic and feminine one. As a tongue for the wilderness, Austin relates most of her mystical, critical, literary, and cultural theories through nature's meaning.

Her initial identification of the nature essay with religious and philosophical matters came through her reading of Emerson, Thoreau, John Muir, and Hugh Miller, whose *Old Red Sandstone*, a philosophical natural history, was the first book Austin purchased with her own money as a young girl. Charles Robertson, her biology teacher at Blackburn College, inspired her study of natural adaptation; with her husband, Stafford Wallace Austin, something of a botanist as Registrar of the United States Land Office in Inyo County, she shared field trips in which they studied the flora and fauna of the desert and the Sierras. Years of observing the Shoshone and Paiute Indians in Owens Valley acquainted Austin with a primitive faith analogous to that of Emerson's faith in Spirit. The animal stories of Ernest Thompson Seton, with which she was familiar, incorporated philosophical and botanical observations

and exemplified the fruitful combination of the factual and the
mystical and their relationship to the primitive mind. But as Dudley Wynn has observed, perhaps the most crucial matter of
Austin's early "membership" among American nature writers is
that she took transcendentalism to the desert: a land bereft of the
conventionally sublime or picturesque. Unlike Emerson or Muir,
Austin claimed that no part of nature—even the desert—lacks
beauty or the power to inform the spiritually perceptive. No doubt
her own hard experiences pioneering in Southern California desert
areas, which altered forever her girlhood conception of the
"friend" in the woods, awakened her sensitivity to a unique and
primarily ignored aspect of American landscape.

In her first book, *The Land of Little Rain*, Austin, though working in the romantic, transcendental tradition, noted the beautiful
and the redemptive qualities of the Southwest desert, creating
from it a new way of seeing. She attends to the adaptive facts of
flora and fauna, people, places that speak of the ancient definition
of beauty based on harmony. As she sets the geological and botanical background—the wind and water trails, the habits of buz-
zards, the rare gorges, mountains, and forests with their particularized plants—she also emphasizes that life is naturally religious
when lived in proper adjustment to nature. Linking natural
rhythms and human rhythms, she speaks of the relation of people
and place—the significant connection between the individual (such
as the carefully drawn Basket Woman or the old prospector) and
the communal. The specific details emphasize uniqueness yet suggest that these elements of man and land represent larger primordial "history" or truth. Describing the grand in the commonplace,
the beautiful in the average, she suggests a democratic way of seeing that nevertheless reaches epic proportions.

Within the minute observation, which Austin articulated loy-
ally through local place names, Spanish and Indian words not
known to the larger American public, is the transcendental rapture
that suggests this new American epic is both ancient and ongoing,
both a storied landscape and real. Even in this Muir-like passage,
Austin communicates the awe she feels in a distinctly direct, personal, yet magnificent way:

> The shape of a new mountain is roughly pyramidal, running
> out into long shark-finned ridges that interfere and merge
> into other thunder-splitted sierras. You get the saw-tooth ef-

fect from a distance, but the near-by granite bulk glitters with the terrible keen polish of old glacial ages. It is terrible; so it seems. When those glossy domes swim into the alpenglow, wet after rain, you conceive how long and imperturbable are the purposes of God.[22]

Austin's tone is often that of a friendly travelogue, yet her resonances are those of poetry as she utilizes the conversational in the service of the spiritual. Her method in experiencing the landscape, aside from her rich direct situations, involves a use of poetry to clarify the images and thoughts of prose. She once told Charles Minton, a young acquaintance in Santa Fe, that direct perception, rendered in poetry then realized in prose, came closest to the revelatory event. "There's a figure of speech, for example," she remarked to Minton one day as they passed some goats on a road outside of Santa Fe: "Brown goats like the sunny sides of winter hills."[23] In her book, *The Flock*, she practiced this approach, ably demonstrating that the history of sheep raising in California contained certain mimetic elements. This book is at once an account of her history of sheep raising and the effect of the rhythm of the returning flocks, the ways of the shearings, festivities, and hireling shepherds. To effect the rhythmical significance of this historical and political event on the greatest meaning of the rightness of harmonious adjustment to the natural environment, Austin sometimes employs an archaic language, suggesting the ancient, even everlasting, quality of the present activity:

> Here I heard at intervals the flute, sweet single notes as if the lucid air had dripped in sound. Awhile I heard it, and between, the slumberous roll of bells and the whistling whisper of the pines, the long note of the pines like falling water and water falling like the windy tones of pines; then the warble of the flute out of the flock-murmur as I came over the back of the slip where it hollowed to let in a little meadow fresh and flowered....[24]

Ambrose Bierce, favorably reviewing the book, noted the important connection between Austin's power of observation and her style. "The best of her reading is her style," he said. "What a knack of observation she has! Nothing escapes her eye."[25] Thus, Austin created a style that both recorded and elevated; she suggested in it the landscape as activator, the writer and reader as discoverers, the artistic American plain as connected to the primordial.

In her next book, *California, the Land of the Sun*, the rhapsodic voice is placed in service of the prophetic as she argues for the recognition and preservation of the beauty she discovered in California. The sweep is broad as it is deep, indicating through the encompassing horizons of California geography the ancient truths (vertical, subconscious, primordial) lost on what she called "the most impotent—culturally and spiritually impotent"[26] American society of her time. Seeking to awaken this society to truths visible in its own landscape, yet ignored, commercialized, or managed without stewardship for profits, she often characterizes the land as feminine, applying the Native American concept of Mother Earth. Such chapters as "Mothering Mountains" exemplify Austin's belief of the feminine principle of the land also expressed in some of her fiction, for example "Lone Tree" and "The Last Antelope." The land is nurturing, spiritual, and resilient. Austin believed that despite the (largely) Anglo destroyers, "the land would have its way."[27] She connects the feminine aspects of the land with the aesthetic—the feminine with the beautiful and the perseverance of the landscape with art and culture. "With their low and flat pitched roofs they [modern houses] present a certain likeness to the aboriginal dwellings which the Franciscans found scattered like wasps' nests among the chaparral along the river, which is only another way of saying that the spirit of the land shapes the art that is produced here."[28] Not only do these shapes survive in future revivals, but the very patterns of art and civilization are manifestations of the shapes, rhythms, essence of this life force. Austin sees this outer world bringing influence to bear on the "patterns of the mind of man which existed before they were ever extroverted in carved bones or reduced to painted figures on bits of pasteboard."[29] In this book, Austin prophesies an ongoing battle within man to retain this inner awareness, what she calls his "genius," and hence his art and culture. In *The Trail Book*, a later book designed for juveniles but with similar themes, Austin traces ancient trails, and ancient stories told there of the rapport of prehistoric men and animals, with the hope that such stories might lead modern man to subtle spiritual perceptions lost in contemporary sophisticated society.

Thus, in the face of the lost or altered landscape, the storied landscape becomes crucial: story, style, and teller are the guides for the lost genius of humankind. In two of her plays, *The Arrow-Maker*

(1911) and *Fire* (1913), Austin anticipated her psychological and philosophical ideas on the subject that were substantially developed in *Everyman's Genius* and *Experiences Facing Death*. She remained concerned with the searching for the "soul" of man through the concepts of racial memory and Jung's notion of collective unconscious. Like *The Arrow-Maker*, *Fire* is an allegory of the artist's relationship to society. In relating the story of Coyote, the fire-bringer, and his connection to the tribe, Austin addresses the idea that the artist's power and ability to benefit society depend on his or her intuitive feeling of kinship with the whole world. Evind, the fire-bringer who is told by brother Coyote how to seize fire from the mountains for the tribe, comments to his wife, Laela, about the significance of the tribe's demand that he reject Coyote, his fellow creature:

> Sometimes, Laela, I have thought—
> If I could find my brother beast again
> And with him follow
> The viewless track which leads
> The moth of moonless nights to honeyed hollows;
> To windy pastures where the wild sheep are;
> Where the keen eagles wheeling high
> Seek for their meat afar—
> If I could feel that rock and tree again,
> And every creeping thing were sib to me
> I should be more unto my fellow man.[30]

The play suggests that in order for modern man to get inside the Amerindian's psychic processes he must cultivate his relatedness to animals. The necessity of this intuitive effort to engender kinship and creativity is vital. Austin insists that Evind's (Prometheus's) gift is a deep, implicit sense of connectedness, and her experience and literal acceptance of Indian lore shape her notion of the storyteller as guide, capable of *relating* man to nature through the telling of the story.

In a speech delivered before the Unitarian Church in New York City, Austin said that the primary value of mystical experience—the instinctive ability to perceive subconscious truths—was the relatedness it enabled one to feel. "The average man wants not so much an explanation of ultimate reality as some sort of relation to it which will 'work,'" she explained—not a new doctrine, a new definition, but a "freedom of experience." She went on to say that the mystical faculty had been rendered impotent by modern education, psychoanalysis, and intellectuality. This "studied release," as she termed it, of the creative faculty, she argued, denied the significance of the inner act and often shifted what happened to one in search for God to simply how one thought about it. As a practical equivalent of these ideas, Austin argued for the settling of the Colorado Basin according to the village pattern of small-scale communalism, local integrity, self-sufficiency, and "aesthetics as a mode of life behavior."[31] These aesthetics, in her sense, included the search for relatedness of one individual to another, of culture to culture, of human nature to nature.

In Austin's literary theories—her methods for translating Native American poetry, the idea of the American rhythm, the landscape line, and the value of regionalism to American literature—background, environment, the land were basic. Her theory of the landscape line established a direct relationship between what people look at daily and their art. Austin claimed that she could listen to any poem, chant, or song and trace its origin by connecting its rhythms to the landscape source. This theory also influenced her method of translating Native American materials, as in the poems in *The American Rhythm* and *The Children Sing in the Far West*. She maintained that to accurately translate from the original linguistic sources, interpreters must be used, but also one must achieve a prayerlike mood so that she may absorb the correct rhythm into which the poems are translated. Her book, *The American Rhythm* (1923), antedates William Carlos Williams's *In the American Grain* and anticipates Williams's and other American writers' reclaiming of vital local, regional, and indigenous elements. In her poem "Western Magic," she says there "are no fairy folk in our Southwest," then proceeds to make a case for the powerful native sources of folklore, myth, and legend. Out of a distinct environment, therefore, comes particular lore and literature. In a 1922 forum on the novel, Austin expressed the idea that the pattern of a story and the arrangement of its elements must occur in true relationship to the social structure by which they are displayed—"a revelation of place, relationships, solidarity."[32] American writing would be authentic, she said, only when it revivified these elements; in fact, American writing could be a "democratic" art to the degree to which it tapped into the patterns available through the collective unconscious. The loss of the meaning of landscape was for Austin the loss of culture as well.

In her final nonfiction nature book, *The Land of Journeys' Ending*, Austin convincingly connects the significance of nature, the individual's intuitive self, and culture, as represented by the larger social group and its art—ceremony, stories, writing. In the section entitled "The Left Hand of God," she writes of the model of the Indian's wholeness, his "unselfconscious translation of first-hand contacts with the environment into rhythm of color and design, "his keeping of cultural interests in one pattern, his group-mindedness running "higher than the individual can reach":

> Behind this cultural wholeness, making it possible, is a psychic unity, so foreign to our sort of society that we have not yet a name for it. Sometimes in intervals of the Corn Dance, when the wind comes up and blurs the long, rhythmic line in the dust of its own dancing, or waiting outside the governor's house in Taos, where the sky over Pueblo Mountain holds on blue until long after midnight, while the council deliberates within and the young men are singing to the moon between the North House and the South, the word swims up and circles, flips its bright tail, and vanishes. It is a word woven out of the belief that there is god-stuff in man, and the sense of the flow of life continuously from the Right Hand to the Left Hand. But why seek for a word defining the state of the Whole, who have not achieved wholeness? Somewhere at the edge of the experience the word lingers, intuitively felt, and still to be brought to consciousness by some happy observer if the Pueblos live long enough.[33]

How well Mary Austin must have understood this eternal search of the woman aware—the writer! Her line, "beauty-in-the-wild, yearning to be made human," is another expression of this search for the word that would encapsulate the cultural wholeness of the Pueblos; or, as anthropologist and curator Peter Sutton said recently at the exhibition of aboriginal Australian art in New York City, "The land is already a narrative—an artifact of intellect—before people represent it. There is no wilderness."[34]

III

Within the pattern of Mary Austin's life and works is the development of the familiar "American Self"—the myth of the self as connected to the American romantic story of self-discovery and self-transformation. Yet what is unique about Austin is that she applied this story to the woman writer, thus including her in what Carolyn Heilbrun calls "the masculine wilderness of the American novel"[35]—that almost solely masculine arena of questing, self-reliance, and individuality that typifies the predominantly male experience with nature in our literature. Austin, who lived and wrote about the necessity for individuality and lone heroism, knew that individuality and individuation, in the Jungian sense, are not the same. The fully integrated individual searches for the shared myth, the universal language represented by the collective unconscious, thus accomplishing in her inner awareness a tribal connection. Despite the sometimes lonely, isolated, renegade, or outcast conditions of her characters, Austin advocates the eternal wholeness of the family of man and the conscious actions that bespeak this integration.

Her image of the woman writer as vessel for the creative spirit is a significant twist both to the American ideal of the created self and the nineteenth-century idea of the woman as vessel—and vassal—for the dominant male culture. As Austin listened to the narrative of the landscape and came to represent it, she activated the myth of the continual pilgrimage in search for the word, the alchemy that could call back to life the spirit of the closed, tribal world.

Austin's belief in the power of the image or the word was similar to that of the Imagists, some of whom lived or lectured in Santa Fe during Austin's tenure there. Like the Imagists, she sought to restore a direct relation between the concrete and the emotional, discarding abstract verbosity. As her friend, Alice Corbin Henderson, said of Imagism:

> In looking at the concrete object or environment, it [this poetry] seeks to give more precisely the emotion rising from them.... Great poetry has always been written in the language of contemporary speech, and its theme, though leg-

endary, has always breadth and direct relation to contemporary thought, contemporary imaginative and spiritual life.[36]

Since Austin believed the past to be ever-active, ever-present in the
person of genius whose intuition could recall or activate it, she believed also that the revitalized word encapsulated and delivered
this past to the present. With Pound, who believed that the reverberating image mirrors the moment, making the language and the
thing one, Austin thought that the intellectual and emotional energies generated by capturing the moment implied a complex of desires and memories. In her essay, "The Walking Woman," she explains:

> All building is out of the deep self; in whatever name the
> Friend is called upon it answers. To me it answers most
> completely out of the back of beyond sleep, from which also
> our Lost Others drew their wisdom. Times when I wake
> seeing all our ancient life falling into perspective behind me
> in the swiftly vanishing illumination of sleep, I know where I
> have been and what doing. I have been walking in the Wild
> Hills with the beast figures of ancient wisdom, which will
> little by little clarify in my intelligence, according to its ca-
> pacity. Then I know that the recovery of lost wisdom does
> arrive not at finality in the figure of the suffering Man-God
> and more than it did the Animal Helper; but in the continu-
> ing recovery and reapplication of that wisdom to the way of
> life. That is why I call the friendly presence masked as beast
> or god, Never-Was and Never-to-Be. It is my own lost self I
> run with as the Coyote Brother, my own unrecovered self
> that beckons in the Wild Hills.[37]

This Walking Woman is the eternal quester, who, in searching for
the word as wisdom, is continually "pressing toward life adventure." Austin conceived of this articulation—physical movement
and word—in terms of the life, death, rebirth cycle, as is implicit in
this passage from her poem, "Going West":

> Lay me where some contented oak can prove
> How much of me is nurture for a tree;
> Sage thoughts of mine
> Be acorn clusters for the deer to browse.
> My loving whimsies—will you chide again
> When they come up as lantern flowers?[38]

In her poem, "When I Am Dead," she repeats this theme of vegetal consciousness when her "happy ghost/Walk(s) with the flocks again ... and is one with his thought at last/And the Wish prevails."[39] Thus, the cycle of the story is in its process the ongoing pilgrimage itself.

Developing this central mythic idea, Austin demonstrates that myth can enter the work as a dominant theme existing below the surface, or as an allusion to or incorporation of specific myths of a culture, either shared or borrowed, or by the invention of new fictions that attain mythic stature in the work, perhaps because they offer new versions of old patterns. Certainly, Austin accomplished the first two of these, often implying the theme of the inward journey either comparatively, say to the Paiute, Shoshone, Pueblo, or Mexican cultures, or stylistically through a narrative voice that expresses a journeying experienced by the writer. Austin also created new fictions out of old myths, reviving archetypal stories.

In her early novel, *Isidro*, she utilizes the prosaic setting of a dime novel, with a conventional hero, to suggest a new twist: the male character is a woman in disguise who accomplishes heroic feats and, in the tradition of the pard ("chum") character in the later dime novels, "saves" the hero and establishes herself as noble, resourceful, and independent. In *The Lovely Lady*, she attempted a juvenile treatment of *A Woman of Genius*, trying to popularize a serious feminist theme of the intellectual, talented, and successful new woman. Most notably in the creation of male-female relationships, she rewrites the conventional and, to her mind, failed interplay of men's and women's expected roles and behavior. Many of her male characters are child-men, innocent, naive, molded into soul mates by the strong mother or woman figure. In these stories, if men reject women as equals and refuse to adopt broad liberal attitudes as standards for personal relationships, they fail to successfully adjust to life. Women fall short of fulfillment when they do not develop intellectually and do not assert independence from masculine domination. Sex is a satisfying experience in these novels only if it reflects a democratic and spiritual alliance.

Many of Austin's women characters reflect her ideas on the satisfactory realization of their own genius or talents. In *The Basket Woman*, Olivia in *A Woman of Genius*, and the Chisera in *The Arrow-Maker*, we see the culture hero realized as a strong, intuitively wise, and healing woman. Yet in some of these fictions, the price for exceptional ability and action is ultimately the sacrifice of the individual to the larger society. The medicine woman in *The Arrow-Maker*, after losing her mystic abilities and asking to live as a normal woman, is shot and killed with her own poison arrow by the man she professes to love.

Though the price of the woman protagonist often is sacrifice of the self, Austin makes clear this sacrifice is not to society's inequities but for the ultimate change of societal patterns. It is almost impossible not to read her reworking of these conventional and archetypal aspects in her stories biographically, since she knew the price of "genius" and the sacrifice to be an artist. Also, these new fictions, ultimately creating new roles for men and women who, valuing both their respective "male" and "female" sides could be whole, functioning, creative individuals, reflects Austin's own continuing inner conflict. Calling this inner division her Siamese twin selves (the conflict between the publicist and the poet), she struggled between the dictates of the rational, external world of knowledge and the inner world of myth and story. Restoration, she argued in "Woman Alone," could come through a strengthening of character from sources other than the superficial role definitions of modern American society:

> As for not being under the necessity of being liked which began as a defense, it has become part of my life philosophy. I see now that too many of the impositions of society upon women have come of their fear of not being liked.... It is in this weakness of women displayed toward their sons which has fostered the demanding attitude of men toward them. It puts women as a class forever at the mercy of an infantile expectation grown into adult convention.... But it is women I am aiming at, women and their need for detachment from the personal issue. At present the price for refusing to "manage" men is high, but not too high for a self-respecting woman to pay.[40]

Just how prophetic Mary Austin was may be noted in the timeliness of her considerations of ethnicity, class, and gender, the role of the woman artist, and the consequence of landscape. Her timelessness—the universality of her themes, the primary myths forming her work—lies in more than her historical work as naturist, folklorist, mystic, or feminist. In fact, the reader, observing that neither Southern California, the lives of Native Americans, nor the role of women are exactly the same as during her lifetime, may justifiably ask what the "value" of Austin is today. Perhaps it is the world within the word that speaks to us so resonantly, for in many cases, it is the word, the style of the work, that still exists to make magic for us in the way in which experienced nature did for Austin. In the unfolding pattern of her life realized in her various works is a special meaning of the pilgrimage, the search. In her own continual expulsion from gardens that harbored her imagination, she had to travel the journey to yet another phase or state, and in so doing discover that one is always in the midst of the pilgrimage—writing—because one does not know the whole story.

"The true emergence of self," Austin wrote, "is dependent upon discipline, upon the *doing* of effective acts rather than the acceptance of dogmas or the practice of selected emotions."[41] As she said of the "friend" in the woods, it is neither form nor symbol but the substance of experience that in its illumination sets in motion the search for words, the pressing toward life adventure. For readers largely estranged from the mysterious and awesome world Austin knew—from the association, say, of the seasons with festival—such universals touch them only when a writer can provoke a deep recognition, a sense of personal relevance in them. Because these events happened to Austin and live in her works, the reader may experience a sense of the sacred though he or she has had no direct contact with the event. As Denise Levertov observes: "Man is the animal that perceives analogies. Even when cut off from tradition, the correspondences that, if he holds open the doors of his understanding, he cannot but perceive, will form images that are myth. The intellect, if not distorted by divorce from the other capacities, is not obstructive to the experience of the mysterious."[42] Renewal and inspiration may be found, if not directly through a set of conscious beliefs or in dream, vision, or archetypal revelation then in the events and intuitions of daily life as re-created in the story. Therefore, style—the process of the story with its recognizable analogies—is itself the journey toward understanding.

Mallarmé observed that convictions that do not find their proper language are not poetry, for poetry is made not of ideas but of words. If Mary Austin's words speak to us today, it is not solely through her polemics on women, creativity, art, or the environment. It is because, at her best, the myths still speak as the words do: Having discovered "Pegasus among the cockleburs," she reveals to us what we forgot we knew.

Notes

1. *Mary Austin, a Memorial*, ed. Willard Houghland (Santa Fe, NM: Laboratory of Anthropology, 1947), p. 22.

2. Mary Austin, "Greatness in Women," *North American Review* (February 1923): 200.

3. T.M. Pearce, *The Beloved House* (Caldwell, ID: Caxton Printers, 1940), p. 17. Pearce retells the observation that Austin made in *Earth Horizon*.

4. Eudora Welty, *One Writer's Beginnings* (New York: Warner Books, 1983), p. 75.

5. "These Modern Women, Woman Alone," *Nation* 124 (March 1927): 228.

6. Mary Austin, *Earth Horizon* (Boston and New York: Houghton Mifflin, 1932), p. 187.

7. Ibid., p. 187.

8. Mary Austin, *The Friend in the Wood*, Mary Austin Collection, Henry E. Huntington Library, San Marcos, CA, p. 20.

9. "Woman Alone," p. 229.

10. Ibid.

11. Ibid.

12. Ibid., p. 230.

13. Austin, *Earth Horizon*, p. 330.

14. Letter from Mary Austin to Alfred Kidder, Mary Austin Collection, Huntington Library.

15. *Mary Austin, a Memorial*, p. 126.

16. Letter to Arthur Ficke, March 27, 1930, quoted in James Rupert, "Mary Austin's Landscape Line in Native American Literature," *Southwest Review* (Autumn 1983): 389.

17. Carl Van Doren, "Mary Austin," *Scholastic Magazine* 21 (September 29, 1934): 23.

18. Austin, quoted in Pearce, *The Beloved House*, p. 86.

19. Mary Austin, quoted in T.M. Pearce, *Mary Hunter Austin* (New York: Twayne Publishers, 1965), p. 63.

20. *The Friend in the Wood*, p. 21.

21. Ibid., p. 20.

22. Mary Austin, *The Land of Little Rain* (Boston and New York: Houghton Mifflin, 1903), p. 186.

23. Letter from Charles Minton to Peggy Pond Church, April 15, 1968, Peggy Pond Church Papers, Albuquerque, NM, n.p.

24. Mary Austin, *The Flock* (Boston and New York: Houghton Mifflin, 1906), p. 106.

25. Letter of Ambrose Bierce to George Sterling, February 3, 1906, quoted in Dudley Wynn, *A Critical Study of the Writings of Mary Hunter Austin*, New York University, 1941, p. 22.

26. Mary Austin, *The Lands of the Sun* (Boston and New York: Houghton Mifflin, 1927), p. viii. This was a reissue, with slight changes, of *California, the Land of the Sun*.

27. Ibid., p. viii.

28. Ibid., p. 34.

29. Mary Austin, "Walking Woman," Mary Austin Collection, Huntington Library, p. 13.

30. Mary Austin, "Fire, a Drama in Three Acts," *The Play-book* (Wisconsin Dramatic Society) 2, no. 6 (November 1914): 19–20.

31. Mary Austin, *The Land of Journeys' Ending* (New York and London: Century, 1924), p. 40.

32. "The American Forum of the Novel," *New Republic* 30 (April 12, 1922): 6.

33. Austin, *The Land of Journeys' Ending*, p. 264.

34. Quoted in *Time Magazine*, October 14, 1988, p. 32.

35. Carolyn Heilbrun, "The Masculine Wilderness of the American Novel," *Saturday Review of Literature* (November 22, 1974): 46.

36. Harriet Monroe, introduction to *The New Poetry*, eds. Harriet Monroe and Alice Corbin Henderson (New York: Macmillan, 1917), p. iv.

37. Austin, "Walking Woman," p. 4.

38. "Going West," in *The American Rhythm, Studies and Re-expressions of American Songs* (New York: Harcourt, Brace, 1923), p. 35.

39. "When I Am Dead," *New Mexico Quarterly* 4 (August 1934): 234–35.

40. Austin, "Woman Alone," p. 230.

41. *Notes on the Validity of Modern Mysticism*, Mary Austin Collection, Huntington Library, p. 4.

42. Denise Levertov, *The Poet in the World* (New York: New Directions, 1973), p. 69.

The Correspondence of May Sarton
and Peggy Pond Church

On December 16, 1984, two years before her death, southwest poet and writer Peggy Pond Church composed a poem for May Sarton. Entitled "For You, May," it reads:

> For you, May, the muse has been everything,
> a goddess in human form
> many times worshipped and embraced
> flesh to warm human flesh—
> the hand of a goddess that
> wakens your inner music
> so that flowers bloom
> and wild beasts become still.
> Even the briar that draws blood
> also comes toward you singing.
>
> My muse
> has been only Narcissus in the pool,
> never to be approached,
> a speechless image
> mirrored for me to gaze at
> and interpret,
> which sometimes shows me a Medusa's face
> and the wild longing in Medusa's heart
> to see herself human in my eyes.

Besides the evident contrast in creative transformation the muse takes, in Church's estimation, in the lives of each of these poets, the poem speaks to a number of concerns the women shared through four decades of correspondence. In fact, Church sent the poem in one of the two letters she wrote to Sarton in 1985, after moving to the retirement village El Castillo, in Santa Fe. As a part of the overall exchange of letters—some forty-eight beginning in

1948 and concluding with Church's last letter October 12, 1986—
these words chart a continual conversation on matters of aging,
death, women's creativity, identity, family, nature, place, poetry.
Spontaneous, yet graceful, the language of these letters heightens
what as a result became a warm friendship through the years—and
a belief in poetry as a truth beyond fact.

What initially brought these two poets together was a common
friend, a common theme, and a common landscape. In the visits to
the West in the 1940s when the Southwest in particular revivified
her imagination and energies, May Sarton met a number of remarkable people, including the poets Peggy Pond Church and her
mentor Haniel Long, and Edith Warner, whose manner of living
and dying in her modest house on the Rio Grande, companioned
by local friends from San Ildefonso and Los Alamos, continued to
inspire even her acquaintances. Warner had come to the Southwest
for her health in the early 1900s, stayed to run a freight station for
the Chili line, the narrow gauge railroad along the Rio Grande, and
in her quiet and spiritual ways deeply exhibited the holistic and
centered patterns of her neighbors, the San Ildefonso Indians. She
kept journals, wrote letters, which, in their simple yet profound
insight like her modest life created a bridge between the modern
world of the atomic scientists newly come to Los Alamos and the
ancient world of her neighbors. Though Church later wrote a
memoir, *The House at Otowi Bridge*, about Edith Warner, it was
Warner's process of facing death—from cancer—that led Church to
write Sarton on April 23, 1951: "She showed us how to live. Now
she is showing us all how to die." Church referred to Edith
Warner's conscious withdrawal from food when the time came
and her choice not to be hospitalized. Sarton responded: "Of
course, I have been thinking of her—my mother too died of starva-
tion, but it takes longer than one could imagine. The mysterious
thread will not break even when the person is at peace with herself.... But when finally my mother did die it happened so peace-
fully and suddenly and simply—and so it will.... I do think people
must have their own deaths and a hospital death is no one's
death." Sarton concluded this May 1, 1951, letter by remarking:
"The ripples of Edith's life, so still and secret like a source or well,
did touch the very rim of the world." She also longed for the silence and space of the southwest landscape.

Though the letters sometimes were prompted through the years by the regular exchange of Christmas poems, this theme of death is connected psychologically to transformations in even their own work. On May 8, 1951, in the context of telling Sarton of Edith's death, Church writes "I am mute as a stone," one of the many references each poet makes to writer's block through the years. Yet they both knew stones were not really mute, simply remnants of a source temporarily dry or dormant. "Poetry is an underground river we cannot reach," Church writes in the same letter, and describes the dry periods she assesses to be part of middle age. The letters read chronologically give a real sense not only of the commonality of certain topics but of the process of aging and its effects on each woman's private and creative life.

In fact, it is the element of the stages of one's life and the metaphorical articulation of each that propels the letters through the years. At the beginning of their correspondence in 1948, Church was 44 and Sarton 32. Each had been writing since childhood. Each desired, even at that juncture, to be best known as a poet while gaining reputations for other kinds of writing. Church was, and remains, by critical standards the more minor talent, in some ways largely due to her own shyness and commitment to a marriage and children. However, she was the youngest of the group of Santa Fe artists and writers of the 1920s and 30s who included Witter Bynner, Haniel Long, Alice Corbin Henderson and others. Educated at Smith, a resident in Berkeley, her father and husband educated at Harvard, she possessed considerable literary and intellectual skills which were deepened and sophisticated by her pervasive love of the southwest landscape and people. But she recognized early an affinity for May Sarton as a "sister in poetry," as she called it. Certainly this relationship is true as each companioned the other through years of successes, depression, exuberance, and loss. In her May 20, 1951, response, Sarton writes:

> I was very much moved by how the time is here that poetry seems an underground river.... I really believe that middle age is a very difficult time, a time of transition in which patience and the power to endure seem the only things to cling to. I have never been as depressed and empty as I am this year.... But I do believe that the underground river finds its way out again and also that the dry periods are really grow-

ing times, though one does not feel it happening and perhaps
in the end without them, we would not be poets at all.

It seems natural that both women would return to nature imagery through which to describe their own seasons, for in the most
profound ways both were shaped by their environments. During
the 1950s, as each discussed her struggle with middle age, they
also debated the issues of war and peace facing the country.
Church chose the pacifist beliefs of the Quakers as an answer to
her own depression over the Manhattan Project and its lineage of
violence, for the building of the bomb had dispossessed her of her
own childhood landscape on the Pajarito Plateau near what became Los Alamos labs. In one letter she concluded by choosing the
baking of bread as the essential religious activity during the times.
The more outspoken and pragmatic Sarton wrote passionately
back about the hunger of the world, the insensitive role of the U.S.,
and the futility of the pacifist's life without direct action and commitment. Ironically, Church had identified the limits Sarton's ardor
could achieve when she complimented Sarton after reading the
Phoenix, but added: "I felt, somehow, how much you had had to
live up to, with what devotion you have served the creative
spirit—so much so that I could not help wondering if that Genius
has not lived at the expense of your human life?"

These kinds of gentle but firm disagreements indicate the
foundation of this friendship rested intriguingly on fundamental
differences as well as shared experiences. In the same letters where
intellectual celebrations of Colette, Ruth Pitter, and current readings went on, so did the creative tension between the Jungian
Church, whose mistrust of the overweening animus made her fear
the prospect of an ego-driven career and the artist Sarton, who
viewed the creative spirit as the well from which other life experiences could flow. In their discussion of women's creativity and the
identity of the muse, these differences are most evident.

While Church's own droughts on occasion ended when she
traveled or interrupted the demands of the domestic scene, as in
the case when in 1951 she excitedly wrote Sarton about poetry
coming again after a trip west to Yellowstone, Sarton continued
her search for a sense of home in the American landscape. When
she finally acquired the Nelson house in New Hampshire, she
wrote Church, "the house and all it stands for makes me feel
American for the first time." The sense of place both felt necessary

for writing and their own identities and even relationships was in a way the source for their own political concerns for the environment, the world. When Sarton vacationed in Hawaii in 1952, she wrote the landscape too lush despite her enjoyment of the palm fronds and the soft trade breezes. The stark southwest landscape, the rigorous New England coastline and hard winters of the interior strengthened both women and translated into a rhythm and rigor they could physically as well as spiritually participate in.

Finding a place which would also accommodate a room of one's own both writers agreed was another of the challenges of middle age. For Church, her family's history in Santa Fe, as well as her reputation as a writer, now cut into the privacy that had been restored somewhat once her three sons were grown. At one point she writes Sarton, she had rented an old, stone chickenhouse, certainly as a disguise far from the madding crowd. Sarton, who was teaching at a number of institutions through these years, bemoaned the demands of teaching which "scatters me into little pieces." In the Nelson house, she attempted to "marry solitude," to which Church later replied that "reading each other's poems is sharing each other's solitude." Both continued to identify their poetry with their own sacred space. Sarton dutifully felt she must finish her nonfiction and fiction so then she could write the poems; Church, having achieved some measure of public success in the publication of the memoir of Edith Warner, delayed her own poetry to begin research on a book about Mary Austin.

No wonder several of the letters exchanged in the 1960s treated the sources of women's creativity and the identity of the muse, for both writers at this point were finding freedom an elusive claim. Church had temporarily felt the headiness of independence in her travel alone to England—one of the rare trips made without her husband or friends. As Sarton's reputation grew during these years, freedom from accompanying obligations—lectures, letters, teaching—was rare. On April 26, 1959, on the eve of yet another lecture tour to Illinois, she says, "the woman artist becomes one at her own peril, if one wants to put it that way." She resumed the dialogue in her next letter:

> But about the most important thing, the constant struggle between art and life. I do not believe any woman whether married or not, can go through life without suffering from this conflict excruciatingly. There are always the human claims

which one either takes on (even writing a letter) and then feels guilt because the work is undone, or the work, and then one feels ruthless in regard to people.

She continues:

I think where it is harder to be a woman is when the woman is also an artist and thus is torn apart between life and art in a way men simply are not. A young man goes to college and goes into a career and marries right on the trajectory he has designed in college. The young woman who wants to write, say, and goes to college and then marries, if she has children, for about ten years or more suddenly is thrown back into a life of domesticity where most of her energy must go into the home. The artist is buried.... Personal relations do not eat at men in the same way, it seems to me. They are not primarily nurturers and women, even single women, are.

As the topic continues in the next three letters exchanged, Church rejoins by concurring that despite the split that women creative artists feel, that the muse is feminine, found in projections in another woman or in "the woman in a man." Yet for herself, a married woman, she saw the female elements of herself which necessitated her finding a way to at once be creatively independent and yet a woman to her husband.

As each woman moved into the 1970s and into yet another portion of their lives, there is at least some shared regrets about the new decade. Though Sarton often mentions the peace and tranquility she experienced when in Santa Fe, Church chronicles the Aspenizing of the capital and even more broadly the lack of continuity she sometimes feels in the modern world.

I find as I grow older and older that my heart is wrung more often than touched. The world is so marred—shattered shard on shard. There are moments when one manages to go up somehow onto the mount of transfiguration. We went to the May Day dance at San Felipe Thursday, by a road on the west side of the Rio Grande, and ate by the river before we got to the crowd around the Pueblo—strong and muscular that water, and there were more dancers than I ever had seen, many small children dancing and through half of one dance a boy who couldn't have been more than 15 accompanying that wonderful drums of old men. Can you imagine one of our fifteen year olds conducting the Philharmonic?

But the bulk of the letters during this period concern the primary relationships of both women. Church's husband, Fermor, died of a brain tumor in 1978 at the same time Sarton faced the end of 35 years of love and companionship of Judy Madlock.

Significantly, both women had solidified a view of themselves by this most demanding period, due to their notions of women's creativity and commitment. These sisters in poetry, while experiencing many things in a patterned way, seemed to have blocks at different times and be able to offer support to each other. At 53, Sarton had looked ahead to what she wanted to do with the next twenty years, increasingly seeing her poems as her opus. Church likewise talked of the meaning of the ancestors, who guide and sustain us in slack times. In her March 28, 1968, letter, Sarton responded to the image again, noting more cheerfully by the end of the letter, despite her block: "You must come back to these very old mountains sometime, so old they are worn down, and maybe you will find some little pull towards the ancestors.... I certainly do when I get back to the lowlands of Europe." Both needed this feeling, for when Church's husband of fifty years died, she wrote to Sarton about how she survived through an intuitive knowledge of another sisterhood of women—those who shared death and dying, outliving their families and spouses. Church wondered, almost soliloquied in the letter, about "how the spirit can survive this time"—a time of aging that she, so many years older than Sarton, felt.

Yet Sarton, too, had begun signing her letters "ever your old raccoon," and the handling of the years passing, with the death of loved ones as the deepest reminder, is a constant subject in the letters at the end of the 1970s. The two letters exchanged in 1978 are an intense dialogue about this loss, with both women pointing the way for the other through encouragements about writing. Sarton, who always worried that Church spent too much time researching and writing nonfiction when she was first a poet, suggested she write her own life through the poetry, "for the women who struggle on." She of course was intensely feeling the adulation and deep need of her audience who steadily confirmed their hunger for her books and her letters. By January 2, 1978, Sarton responded so powerfully to Church's publication of *The Ripened Fields*, fifteen sonnets on her marriage, which reviewers compared to Meredith's *Modern Love* and certainly her best poems to date. She encouraged

Church, too, to write about the sisterhood of women, describing at the same time her deep depression and that "she feels she is walking on quicksand."

At this point in the correspondence, there is a gap of three years and not until November 7, 1983, does Church again write, renewing the correspondence until her death in 1986. There are fourteen letters during these three years, the greatest number and the most intense exchange in the forty years. There seems also to be a subtle shift in these letters from the older Church's steady admiration and encouragement of Sarton to Sarton's own real recognition of Church's talent and final years. In the November 7–November 13 exchange, Church writes Sarton rather wittily about turning 60 and her desire to be known as an old poet. The responding letter from Sarton applies the same term as Sarton wars against the chaos of her desk and recommends the "accepting of heroic helplessness" against the inevitability of old age. Yet in her response, she also realized that her most recent book, *A Reckoning*, was about living not dying. So the words continued between them, and the deeper strand of these is the commitment to poetry as a profession of life force.

During this period, both women discuss moving to retirement homes, the pros and cons of such a move. Church becomes increasingly preoccupied with her unfinished and unpublished work, with its organization, and the future of her files of journals, poems, letters, and manuscripts. In her March 14, 1984, letter she describes aging as a "river sweeping forward," and notes a dream she had about "swimming in a river with her father." As she collects her poems together, possibly for the autobiographical volume of poems she envisions, she notes her own problems of reckoning, alluding to Sarton's book. For Church both her journals and her dream logs were important parts of a dialogue she created for herself, without the plethora of friends to discuss poetry with. When she moves to El Castillo in 1985, she writes she is haunted that her muse—at least one of them—Haniel Long's house is almost directly behind. As she attempts to build a new habitation around herself, bringing some sort of order to this new world, she sends a page from her journal writing to Sarton in the letter of February 2, 1985. "Strange how the past continues an existence of its own, even in the crowded overflow of today," she writes, partly in reference to the changes in Santa Fe. "Parts of our past we never quite outgrow." In an earlier letter, while praising Sarton's work and her productivity, Church revealed a sore truth: she had squandered her muse in part, by publishing so little her last years. But her final book, *Birds of Daybreak,* contained some of her best and most mature poems, poems she admitted to Sarton she had only learned to work on late in life. Sarton responded in her May 9th letter in a way which not only praised this as Church's best work, but illustrates how each woman's writing through time inspired and buoyed the other:

> Dearest of poets, this is an upside down letter. I was going to answer at long last your letter of April 14th yesterday, but got interrupted, and now I am glad I didn't because the poems came in the mail. I read them yesterday and again this morning at five with tears of relief streaming down my cheeks. I have felt so far from poetry, imprisoned by the endless correspondence and no escape ever, but reading you was to feel the source well up with overwhelming force. There is no poem here that did not reach me at the deepest level, and what comes through—long pause while I think— is perhaps more than anything that you are rare in the depth of your roots in that landscape that vertical landscape which goes deep into the past, so must the Delphic oracle have spoken beyond the merely personal with which we are overwhelmed in all the "confessional" self-enclosed poetry I see most of the time. And it is also the grandeur of an old woman and what she has come to know. I really cannot praise this book enough, and you will, I fear, think I am too effusive ... don't.

What sustaining words these were for Church, particularly at this time. Her move to El Castillo was not the valiant one she portrayed but rather a necessity while she knitted together what she all along suspected were the final strands of her life. She responded to Sarton's praise that it was so good to talk to a poet about poetry. And goes on:

> The island of order in all the disorder! Survivor of shipwreck searches the wreckage, constructs and furnishes his new dwelling place out of what the sea has cast up, out of the pieces of driftwood and old bottles. The instinct for order. The bird constructing its nest. We weave our habitations around ourselves. All along in the midst of my indecision and chaos the merging pattern was clear. Like the order in

which poetry emerges. I think of Wallace Stevens, "The Idea of Order at Key West," that all my images should turn to navigation.

But as is key to each woman's side of the letters through the years, something is given for the other by the end. Church responds to Sarton's own attempted stays against the madness of success and the constant interruption she feels so that she often can't work. She writes:

> May, I so wish you didn't have to burden yourself with answering all these letters. But perhaps the awful conflict between the inner voice and the daily necessity is what produces in the end the vein of gold in the hard rock. Poetry will not vanish from you forever—it is the dark of the moon. What haunts me is all that I have left undone. I cherish you for sharing your poet's heart.

In her last letter to Church, July 9, 1986, Sarton calls her a "dear and valiant poet." This description of her friend echoes the imagery Church created in an earlier poem, written in May 1959 and dedicated to May Sarton. The poem, entitled "Lines for a Woman Poet," reads:

> What do I know about your human life?
> Upon your shoulder sits a bird and sings.
> I know that bird. I know that falcon eye,
> those beating wings that drive it toward the sun,
> the whirling plunge of light and the curved beak
> and how it tears the heart to drink the blood,
> the living blood on which its song must feed.
>
> I share being woman with you and I know
> the god's indifference to our mortal pain.
> Daphne who terrified became a tree
> and Leda stretched beneath the dazzling wings
> cried against violation as we cry.
> After the blaze of light the dark comes down
> and we must go, still human and alone
> into the nine months night that forms the child,
>
> into the dark like Cora with her song
> and with her broken flowers still in her hand
> to die like summer back into the earth
> from which all summers spring. We cannot soar
> like birds toward the sun. We must endure

the weight of winter and the darkened moon,
not like Van Gogh who was devoured by light
until his brush bled fire.

Let the fierce phoenix go with his sharp cry
toward the flaming sun, oh mythical bird
that would consume your heart. Lie down, lie down
now among roots and leaves and let your eyes
be dark as the closed child's and let the mole
speak his blind wisdom to your folded hand.
Birth is not had by willing. Let the rose
unfurl, in time like air, what summer knows.

Though this poem was no doubt inspired by the exchange of letters in the early fifties about women and creativity, still the valor
each possessed, struggled for, and encouraged the other in through
time was a sort of interior and intuitive strength. As Sarton's reputation grew through the years, her precious solitude dwindled;
Church gained a measure of solitude into her old age from the
isolation caused by a chemical sensitivity and the loss of her eye-
sight. When she determined to enact a plan she long had held—to
take her own life according to the precepts of the Hemlock Society—she wrote Sarton a last letter with an epitaph which would
later be read at her memorial service. Though many may dispute
the choice as valiant or appropriate, the accrued wisdom Sarton
encouraged her in seems evident in her last farewell to her friend:
"For the sake of poetry," she wrote. As old poets and old friends
who had faced their fears of loss, death, aging, change, and had
forged a sisterhood together as a result, these letters suggest they
companioned each other through a creativity during these years.